T0091798

Rigging for Games

Rigging for Games: A Primer for Technical Artists Using Maya and Python is not just another step-by-step manual of loosely related tutorials. Using characters from the video game *Tin*, it takes you through the real-world creative and technical process of rigging characters for video games and cinematics, allowing readers a complete inside look at a single project.

You'll explore new ways to write scripts and create modular rigs using Maya and Python and automate and speed up the rigging process in your creative pipeline. Finally, you'll learn the most efficient ways of exporting your rigs into the popular game engine Unity. This is the practical, start-to-finish rigging primer you've been waiting for!

- Enhance your skill set by learning how to efficiently rig characters using techniques applicable to both games and cinematics
- Keep up with all the action with behind-the-scenes images and code scripts
- Refine your rigging skills with tutorials and project files available on the companion website

Eyal Assaf is a Technical Artist currently living and working in Toronto, Canada. A graduate from the Ontario College of Art and Design, Eyal has been involved in the animation, gaming and broadcast industries since the mid-90s when digital dinosaurs began to roam the big screens. His wide range of experience led him to positions such as Visual Effects Supervisor on an award-winning animated 3D television show as well as other lead positions in a variety of commercials, broadcast, film, and game projects. He is also an internationally published illustrator in various trade publications and teaches 3D and Design at college level.

Rigging for Games

A Primer for Technical Artists Using Maya and Python

Eyal Assaf

CRC Press
Taylor & Francis Group
Boca Raton London New York

CRC Press is an imprint of the
Taylor & Francis Group, an **informa** business

AN A K PETERS BOOK

CRC Press
Taylor & Francis Group
6000 Broken Sound Parkway NW, Suite 300
Boca Raton, FL 33487–2742

Library of Congress Cataloging-in-Publication Data
Assaf, Eyal.
  Rigging for games : a primer for technical artists using Maya and Python / Eyal Assaf.
    pages cm
  Includes bibliographical references and index.
 1. Rigging (Computer animation) 2. Video games—Design. 3. Computer games—Design. 4. Python (Computer program language) 5. Maya (Computer file) I. Title.
   TR897.77.A87 2016
   006.6'96—dc23
   2015015031

ISBN: 978-0-415-74304-4 (hbk)
ISBN: 978-0-415-74305-1 (pbk)
ISBN: 978-1-315-81391-2 (ebk)

Typeset in Myriad Pro
by Apex CoVantage, LLC

Visit the Taylor & Francis Web site at http://www.taylorandfrancis.com and the CRC Press Web site at http://www.crcpress.com

Contents

Contents

Contents

Contents

Acknowledgments

This story began in San Francisco at the GDC convention back in the spring of 2013. In a moment of serendipity, of being at the right place at the right time, the concept that ultimately became this book was born.

I admit that the road to getting these pages out was not an easy task. It was a challenge, which at times seemed insurmountable. Yet finally seeing the end result that you, Dear Reader, are holding in your hands—I can honestly say it was worth every second of it.

Many have said that writing is a lonely endeavor, and it is a fact I will not refute. Yet I could not have written this book without acknowledging the support and assistance of the following people who were involved in its creation:

First, I want to thank the Focal Press team—Sean Connelly, Lauren Mattos and Haley Swan—who got the ball rolling with this project and helped me navigate the rapids involved in writing these pages. Thank you for your patience and guidance throughout.

Thank you to Rae Morris, my technical editor, who pored over the manuscript and gave timely feedback and suggestions.

To the countless members of the 3D and coding communities, who provided a wealth of knowledge, information and solutions to the constant challenges of producing a video game and insights into the art of good coding practices.

To my college students (current and former) who, through the years, provided me a platform to share my knowledge and who kept asking me the hard questions. I thank you for that opportunity. The great thing about teaching is that in almost every class, I had the occasion to approach a topic that I went over endless times, but often was made to look at it with new set of eyes. Curiosity is a good thing, regardless of what they say about the cat.

Thank you to my fellow professors at George Brown College and Durham College as well as my work colleagues at Arc Productions, who provided advice and were great sounding boards throughout the writing of these pages.

Thanks also to J. P. Amore, Phil Bonner, Kent Martin, Cathy Feraday Miller and Celso Teixeira for sharing their support, technical knowledge and enthusiasm, as well as to Bruno Amezcua, Anthony Harrison, Joseph Kim and David Su for their creative contributions.

A special thank you goes to Ryan Miller, who helped me decipher the intricacies of Unity and shared his wealth of game-making knowledge with me.

To the incredible core team of gals and guys who helped me get this project off the ground and shared endless hours making the world of *Tin* a reality with their creative and technical talents: Erika Fantinic, Josh Kay, Daniel Kim, Galen Manuel, Billy Tremaine, Scott Uminga, Ashley Vanchu and John Yau. Thank you all! I would not have achieved this without you.

To the Assaf and Liao families, who supported and believed in me throughout from near and far. You're the best.

To Yvette, my partner and island of calm, who stood by my side and offered her patience, encouragement, love and unconditional support while these pages slowly came to life.

And finally, to my wonderful, amazing daughter Liran, who was the inspiration behind the writing of this book. The character of *Leaf* and the world of *Tin* would not have been realized if it weren't for you. You inspired me to create and imagine a magical world and to rediscover the joys of daydreaming. This book is for you.

Eyal Assaf, March 2015

"Experience is the only thing that brings knowledge, and the longer you are on earth the more experience you are sure to get."

L. Frank Baum, *The Wonderful Wizard of Oz*

Introduction

Welcome to the wonderful world of 3D rigging. First, allow me to thank you for taking the time to read this book. I hope that the information and examples you will find within these pages will be useful to your own creative productions—be it a video game, a short film (or cinematic epic) or simply creating digital art for the sake art itself.

In this book, you will be introduced to the rigging concepts of a couple of characters from a game I'm developing called *Tin*. There is a very important point I'd like to make: Although I will discuss throughout this book the steps of creating specific rigging setups, the main purpose is to explore the thought process *behind* these rigging workflows, and, where possible, discuss how we can automate those workflows through scripting and coding custom tools. There are many excellent tutorials, videos and books that deal with rigging which cover everything from the most basic rigging foundations to super complex rigging systems. With this book, the goal is not to repeat what are already considered accepted general rigging techniques. Rather, I want to introduce an aspect that new riggers in particular tend to shy away from: the writing of custom scripts that will help optimize the rigging process. The main scripting language this book will focus on is Python.

This book will begin with the first stages of a typical production, starting with the concept idea and following through to the character rig. I want to show how these production elements fit with one another in a holistic manner as opposed to being segregated as standalone processes. Now that more and more indie filmmakers and developers are making their own shorts and games, either alone or with small teams, I find it important to show how all of these components interconnect with each other at some level. It might seem an obvious fact in bigger studios with pre-existing, production-tested pipelines. Yet for the indie filmmaker or developer, sometimes the small production tips and workflows that tie everything together—both creative and technical—can mean the difference between the success and completion of a project or its failure. Somebody once said that God is in the details. I find this to be particularly true in this case—regardless of your belief system. Attention to the small details is what makes the production tick smoothly.

One of the evolving paradigms in the computer graphics (CG) and gaming productions is that the separation between the "art" and "technical" operators are merging and blending into one unit. More and more we see the call for technical artists—those individuals who can easily move between the creative aspects of a production and the technical side.

Rigging is the one of the best examples that showcases the skills of a technical artist. On the one hand, you need the creative skills to maintain the vision of the assets in the production—for example, making changes to the model or textures in order to work flawlessly with the rig while at the same time developing and modifying tools and scripts to optimize the rigging pipeline and making it more streamlined and automated.

Think of this book as a journal that offers a glimpse into the process of creating and rigging characters for an indie game production. I have always found that one of the best ways of learning something is actually doing, while knowing that along the way mistakes will be made. Ultimately, learning from those mistakes and finding solutions is what makes the knowledge gained feel like a great sense of accomplishment.

Who Is This Book Intended For?

Although this book will strive to take the reader through the rigging setup of two of the *Tin* characters and show how the rigging system interacts and integrates with the Unity game engine, it is not a comprehensive how-to manual that covers the basic use of the 3D software. You, Dear Reader, are assumed to be familiar with the following tools and concepts.

3D Software: The main 3D tools used for the examples shown in this book at the time of writing are Autodesk's Maya 2015 and Nevercenter's Silo. A solid understanding of the overall 3D workflow will greatly help you with making the most out of this book. Even though Maya will be the main tool used in these examples, many of the concepts described in these pages are software agnostic, meaning that if you are familiar with another 3D package, you should be able to apply these concepts in your 3D software of choice. For some of the modeling portions, I have used Silo. Although an older program with a somewhat erratic history of updates, I find it extremely easy, intuitive and fast to use, especially when building base meshes. Silo is a great example of a program that does what it's meant to do—and does it very well. Any additional tools used will be mentioned in their relevant chapters.

Game Engine: The game engine used in the examples in the last chapter of this book is Unity 4.x. It's a wonderful, accessible and powerful game engine that is gaining huge popularity by the day. Another advantage is that it has a free version that should be more than enough to build fun and engaging games. A familiarity with the use of Unity is recommended, as well as some programming experience.

Another great game engine that I think should be part of any game developer's arsenal is Scirra's Construct 2. It is a 2D game engine based on HTML5, but it can output to a variety of platforms. One of Construct's biggest strengths is that it allows for very fast prototyping, right out of the box. It is a very intuitive program to use, and best of all, you can create games without coding—although understanding logic concepts greatly helps. Testing the core gameplay mechanics of *Tin* was done with Construct 2.

Scripting: Python will be the scripting language used in most of the examples in the book. In the last few years, Python has become one of the main scripting languages in the 3D, gaming and VFX industries. It is used for scripting custom tools (i.e. Maya, Nuke, Modo, etc.) and can be used to create a common platform between all of these software. We will also discuss Maya's Embedded Language (MEL), which acts as the base command foundation for our Python scripting.

Maya's built-in Script Editor has been beefed up in the last few versions and can provide an adequate platform to write your scripts in. As alternate and free general script editors, you can look at Komodo, jEdit or Notepad++. Finally, for those of you who want a robust and complete IDE (Interactive Development Environment), Eclipse is my coding weapon of choice. Another very popular and robust coding platform is Microsoft's Visual Studio. This IDE offers everything *and* the kitchen sink, but can become an overwhelming experience if you don't take the time to learn its ins and outs. These are personal choices only, so make sure to research the various available IDEs and use the editor that will feel comfortable and flexible for your needs.

This is **NOT** a book on computer programming or how to be a programmer. The code and scripting examples that you will find in this book are simply ways of thinking about how to optimize and automate the creative process of using 3D software. I am not a computer programmer nor do I have a computer science degree. I am just someone who found that, with a little bit of curiosity and passion to learn beyond the basics, I could take full advantage of the 3D software rather than be limited to whatever's offered out of the box. If, after reading through this book, you find that you want to further explore the wonderful world of computer languages and programming—by all means do so. You'll quickly realize that most computer languages are based on the same logic, with syntax being the most obvious difference. Having said that, I always found that, being a technical artist, the learning process is constant and discovering new and streamlined ways of achieving a specific effect or writing a custom tool makes the job of being a 3D artist so engaging and fun.

Writing this book has been a tremendous learning experience for me as well. I found that writing code is a balance between achieving the intended result and doing so in the most effective and elegant manner. Ideally, both of these goals are achieved in perfect harmony and cause the birth of a rainbow-streaming unicorn somewhere in the heavens. Yet sometimes, achieving the intended result leaves a trail of messy code behind, while writing elegant and concise code can make it appear abstract and unreadable to most inexperienced coders. I think the trick here is to find the balance in writing a script that is effective and streamlined, yet legible enough that it allows the reader to follow the logic behind it.

Some of the code you will find in the examples falls somewhere within those lines. Experienced computer programmers will surely find a way to condense four lines of code into one super-efficient command filled with esoteric commands. That is wonderful and it is something which, with experience and practice, we should be able to accomplish. But on the road to achieve that level of efficiency, understanding what it is that we are trying to accomplish and doing so in a more verbose manner helps with the learning process.

The Story Behind *Tin*

The character of Leaf the Tin Girl was inspired by my daughter, Liran. When she was in the fourth grade, her class put together a play based on L. Frank Baum's "The Wizard of Oz". Liran, (or Li as her friends call her) played the role of the Tin Man—well, girl, in her case. I remember sitting in the audience, surrounded by the other kids' parents and grandparents, most holding cameras and video recorders, waiting to immortalize their offspring's thespian abilities on digital media. Along with my camera, I also brought my small pocket sketchbook and a pencil. The play was entertaining in a way that only 10-year-olds can pull it off. As I watched it unfold, retelling the adventures of Dorothy and her friends, I managed to capture Li in a series of quick sketches in her acting role. One of those sketches really struck a chord with me (see figure 0.1). This particular quick doodle has ever since been in the back of my mind, waiting for an opportunity for the idea of *Tin* to be developed into something more.

That opportunity came up a couple of years later, when serendipity struck and the prospect of writing this book came to be. This was to be the perfect opportunity to develop the character of Tin Girl and create a narrative around her. I have always been a big fan of the world of Oz and the wildly imaginative characters in it. In this case, I decided to expand on the existing literary world described by Baum and create an alternate version of it, with my own locales and characters. The video game platform seemed to be the perfect combination of all worlds, allowing the characters to be part of a narrative as well as to interact with the world around them, while—hopefully—providing entertainment to the players.

So without further ado, limber up those fingers and let us dive into the wonderful world of 3D rigging.

FIGURE 0.1 Sketch of Li and friend as Tin Man and Lion in Oz school play

Chapter 1
The Creative Cycle

From Page to Screen

In the beginning was the creative Idea, and the Idea was an interesting one. At least that's what we thought. So we thought about it some more, did some quick sketches in our sketchbook and slowly began seeing the potential of it. We wrote it down, highlighting in point form the good bits. We even Googled it—hoping that nobody else thought about our same exact Idea already. And behold! No one has claimed it. We then wrote a few paragraphs, fleshed out the Idea from an amorphous concept to something a little more substantial. We did some research, some preliminary concept art and decided that the Idea had a definite future and was yearning to be born and be shared amongst the people of the world (or not, but that's a personal choice). A long period of dedication, hard work, sweat and personal sacrifices—along with guzzling vast amounts of caffeine—ensued. It enveloped our every waking hour in order to bring the Idea into a state of Reality. And finally one fine morning, the Idea *did* become a Reality and went forth amongst the other creative Ideas that became Realities. And all was good.

That was the Creative Cycle (yes, capitalized) in a very loose nutshell. For the most part, in the professional world of CG animation—be it for feature films, broadcast or video games—modelers, riggers and animators do not always have the opportunity to be included in the creative process at its conceptual stages. Usually by the time they get involved, the production process is already in full-throttle and they are using their particular areas of expertise to move the project along. Being involved in the conceptual stages of a production can be an extremely rewarding experience and allows the flexing of the creative muscles. At this stage, nothing is impossible and like the old cliché goes—the imagination is the limit.

In the next few pages we will discuss the typical process of bringing the Idea from a concept that exists in our heads to a "tangible" creative expression. I placed *tangible* in quotes since for the most part, the art that we create in the CG animation industry is audio-visual, and not tangible in a physical sense. But then again, at the rate technology is moving, who knows what the morrow will bring.

Although this book, by its nature, will deal mainly with the rigging aspects within a game development cycle, we will cover some of the other aspects of production that typically come before and after the rigging component. In the case of *Tin*, there is also a cinematic component planned that acts as the introduction of the game, and which follows a traditional production cycle similar to those found in films and broadcast productions

Generally, the creative cycle of a typical creative production consists of three main sections. First, we have the **pre-production** phase, which is the solid foundation base of the Idea and where everything is built upon. Next, we have the actual **production** phase, where everything that went into the Idea gets built, painted, engineered, coded, moved and lit. Finally, the **post-production** phase is where all of the various components come together, get spliced, buffed, tested, edited and have the *slick factor*™ applied to them. The Idea is then finally ready for reality prime time (see figure 1.1).

> **NOTE:** To clarify—when video games will be discussed from this point on, it will refer to the general narrative-based games, where characters (organic, alien, or mechanical and even vehicular at times) are the main protagonists and follow some kind of story arc. Game types such as card games, luck games, match-3 games, and other types of games that depend on mechanics such as simple point or score collections, random placement, or that are purely representations of game pieces (i.e. cards, alphanumerical, tokens, etc.) won't necessarily fit within the guidelines we will discuss in the book. This doesn't mean that there are not useful practices and techniques present in these pages that can be applied to it. On the contrary, properly organizing your ideas and processes will always help in achieving your goal. Rather, the main game style discussed will be of a player navigating a character through a game level, exploring and interacting with the game world.

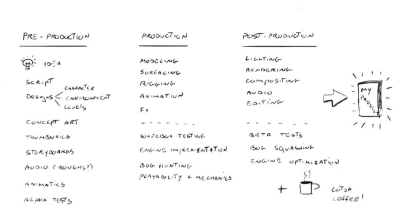

FIGURE 1.1 Hand drawn diagram of the production cycle

Where Do Ideas Come From?

Before we start discussing the details of the pre-production phase and all that it entails, let us go back to the very beginning and try to figure out the answer to the question: "So where do good Ideas come from?"

Unfortunately, there is no magical idea place where you can send your mind to and shop around for Ideas—at least not that I know about. Frankly, I don't think anyone really knows where and how those ideas generate, and asking writers and other creative types about it more often than not will result in an annoyed response.

Now, since we *are* creative individuals, we are going to tackle this inquiry head-on and try to come up with some kind of solution to this rhetorical question. Hint: there are no wrong answers.

Let's start with the typical run-of-the-mill places where good creative Ideas might be hiding. Here is a very short and definitely non-comprehensive list I compiled which I'd like to share with you.

- **Your personal life experiences**—Your unique perspective on life. Look back on some of the events and experiences that shaped your life and see if your fears, your joys or just the way you look at the world around you can trigger the creative process. Sometimes being in the right place at the right time can trigger that "Aha!" moment and get the creative wheels turning.
- **Literature**—A common tactic is finding inspiration in the endless twists and plots found in the written words of literature. The archetypal stories passed on from generation to generation, throughout the ages and cultures. What you might find interesting is that at the end, there are only a handful of narratives that get recycled time and again. Or, according to Joseph Campbell, there is only one main narrative which falls under The Hero's Journey (or the *Monomyth*). Sometimes all you need is a paragraph or a description of a character or event in an existing piece of literature to trigger a brave new world in your mind.
- **Music**—There is something about listening to certain songs or musical compositions that can take your mind on a trip along an aural landscape. Music can affect emotions on a primal level. Sometimes you just have to go with the flow (pun intended) and see what creative doors open with the music.
- **Popular media**—We are surrounded by the media, especially now in the Information Age. It is almost impossible to escape the constant bombardment of visuals and sounds that surround us, especially in metropolitan urban settings. On the one hand, we are more than ever connected to our surroundings, and are offered a continuous stream of inputs to stimulate our minds. Yet on the other hand, it could limit the

creative ability to truly expand and pursue our own creativity. A lot of things end up being derivative of existing media that is out there. Too much media can be detrimental to your creative and imaginative health.

- **Putting your body on auto-pilot**—A great example for this is to go on long hikes in nature, if possible. I found that once the body gets into the rhythm of walking, it takes over and effectively frees the mind to soar. It's a great way to open up your creative senses. As a bonus, you get to get out, breathe some fresh air and not stare at a screen for hours on end.
- **Travel**—Relating to the point above, if you have the chance and opportunity to travel, be it within your own country, or somewhere in the world, do it! Experiencing new places, cultures, traditions, sights, sounds and smells personally is one of the best ways to expand your creative senses. And one of the best ways I found to do so was to get off the beaten track and talk to the locals, hear the stories they have to tell and experience their country or locale from their perspective. And as always, remember that common sense is your best guide.
- **Focused observation**—This point might be the opposite of the previous two in the sense that it means focusing on one very particular object (or situation, condition, setting, etc.) and asking yourself "what if. . .?". An example might be, say, if you're doodling on your sketchbook and you look at your pencil and ask yourself "What if I could use this pencil to draw a door into another part of the city?" It's an absolutely ridiculous notion, but for one second there—as you were thinking that thought—a myriad of possibilities appeared in your mind and opened up endless creative options.

As you can see, a lot of the points in this list are very subjective and necessitate an active use of your senses to get the gears in your mind to start rolling and hopefully generate the elusive Idea.

Yet, what if none of this works? We all have at some point in our lives hit that dreaded creative block, that blank page/canvas/wall where nothing we did got us through and our Idea-generating tools remained very still and silent. How do you get them to start turning again?

Here's a trick I learned when I was in art school years ago during a first-year course in 3D design—back when 3D meant building things with your hands out of tangible material, not virtual pixels and polygons. We had a group project that required us to create a sculpture/installation that told some kind of narrative, made out of found objects. The clincher was that the narrative had to be randomly generated, without pre-conceived structure from the group members, yet finalized into a cohesive story and put together as a physical structure.

The whole purpose of this trick was to get the creative gears in our minds rolling, and now I shall share it with you. For this, you will need a pen or pencil, paper to write on and the most important item: *a dictionary*. Now—a very important detail for this to work—the dictionary must be the one that comes in book form, made out of honest-to-goodness tree pulp which you can handle physically and feel the pages. Not—and I repeat—*not* a dictionary app in your mobile or web-connected device.

Here's what you do: the goal is to pick a handful or random words from the dictionary and write them down. See if there is some kind of connection between them and if they generate some kind of narrative or visual in your mind. For example, here are some words that were randomly picked from the dictionary—as in flip to a random page, put my finger on the page and write down the word underneath it:

Dream, Medication, Hebetic, Dungaree, Prusik, Glue, Rigor.

At first look, a random bunch of words. On a closer look, though, we can see that by combining some of those words together, we can start making connections between them and create a rudimentary narrative.

Take, for example, the words *hebetic* (which means youth, youthful, occurring at puberty) and *dungaree*. These two words already can define the type of character we can start developing, such as a young person wearing work clothes. Male or female, that is something you can decide, but this description already gives you a starting point. Maybe our character is a young woman, who works in a job that requires dungarees—say, a mechanic. Great, we have a protagonist to get us started.

Next, we will look at the word *rigor*. It has multiple meanings including *unyielding, tremors caused by a cold chill, and a situation making life difficult.* Let's use the "making life difficult" meaning, because we all like drama and tie it in with our protagonist. See? The gears in your mind already started turning! An image or situation is already taking place in your mind's eye, waiting to be elaborated upon.

Sometimes, the words you randomly pick will not make sense at all, or fit with the rest of what you have. Worry not, that is completely fine. Another trick we will use to get around this is word association. Let us analyze the word *Prusik*. Not the most common word in the lexicon. A Prusik is a type of knot that loops around a main rope and tightens as weight is placed on it. It is mainly used in rock climbing, mountaineering, caving and other activities that require ropes.

Using word association, we can take the word *Prusik* (which was allegedly named after its inventor, an Austrian mountaineer by the name of Karl Prusik) and follow some logical connections (at least to me).

Prusik → mountain → avalanche → hidden cave

Using the same word-association technique, we can apply it to the words *medication* and *glue*:

Medication → illness → viral → pandemic
Glue → broken → fix

So far, looking at what we have, we can start telling this story:

In a not-so-distant future, where the rigors of life took their toll on the last of the human colonies who survived the pandemic apocalypse, our protagonist—a young female apprentice mechanic who is gifted with the ability to fix old, broken down machinery—is beset by a prophetic dream revealed to her as she leaves the innocence of childhood behind and enters the world of adulthood. In it, the salvation of humanity lies in finding an alien artifact long buried in a cave that was exposed by an avalanche.

There you have it—the making for a story. As the Fates would have it, these random words chosen for this exercise—through cosmic confluence (or some metaphysical happening that is best analyzed while sitting in a solitary chateau, full moon lighting the landscape and the howling of wolves heard in the distance) —created a kind of parallel story to *Tin*. I wonder what I was channeling. Stranger things have been known to happen. . . .

Anyway, I digress. Getting back to our point, for those few minutes that you were reading the above story synopsis, an image formed in your mind and created a living world in your imagination. The gears started spinning, and the dreaded creative block was lifted, opening up countless possibilities. Now that this initial narrative is in place, you can run ahead with it and mold the story further into new directions and experiment with them.

So now there are no more excuses for "I don't have any ideas!" Get those creative gears spinning and start generating Ideas. And like most things in life, the more you practice and hone those skills, the easier and better they will get with time. You can apply this method to any type of creative endeavor, be it a concept for an illustration, a written story, a short film, a video game concept or any other creative undertaking.

The Production Cycle

As we discussed earlier, the production cycle is typically broken down into three main sections. Following them in the suggested order makes common sense, although nothing is ever written down in stone when it comes to following a set order. Depending on the production involved, deadlines, talent and endless other factors, sometimes the steps described will shift, omit or rearrange themselves in order to meet the production requirements.

In this section we will go over what goes on during each step of a typical CG production, and its applications.

Pre-Production

From my experiences, without good pre-production planning, the rest of the production cycle will definitely suffer and there is a good chance it either won't match the original vision or even not get produced at all. It is very easy to get lost in the initial excitement of the creative process, but like in most relationships, once you are past the initial honeymoon phase you have to start working hard to maintain it and keep it going forward.

One of the critical aspects that pre-production helps with is the setting of expectations as it relates to the overall project timeline and complexity. In other words, answering the question, "Is the idea doable?". At this stage, prior to starting with the creative production process, the following questions should be asked:

- Is the idea doable within the time allotted for it? Will I meet the deadlines set?
- Is the idea doable in terms of the technological complexities set? Will features X, Y and Z be able to be implemented within the deadline? If not, is there a plan B or does the production absolutely revolve around those features?
- Do I possess the proper skills to produce the idea? If not, can I put together a team to help with the production?
- Is the idea doable within the budget parameters set? Will that budget be able to compensate for the production expenses (personnel, equipment, etc.)?

Be honest with the replies you provide. The more realistic you are with the answers, the truer the expectations and results will be with the production. One thing in regard to a budget—it does not necessarily mean money only, but also man-hours provided to get the idea produced. You might get a team of friends or colleagues, or sometimes even strangers (through the wonders of the Internet) to volunteer and help out with your production. But remember, volunteer time is very valuable and should be acknowledged. Be conscious of how it is used, and make sure to credit all of those who helped out making your idea a reality.

Step 1: Planning the Story / Game Outline

The first step in the beginning of the production is to get the idea from a state of thought in your head to words or quick sketches on a page and ultimately tell a story with it. For our purposes, we will start with the written word, although some might prefer to start with basic thumbnails instead.

In the case of a cinematic, the story is the foundation upon which your whole production will stand. For example, a full animated feature will include multiple characters, plot twists, climax, conflict resolution and conclusion, while a short film may only focus on one character and a specific event.

On the other hand, the story for a casual game can be shown as a simple sequence of illustrations and defined as "a game where the player has to collect as many magical crystals as possible within a set time limit" or be as epic as a full-blown feature-film trilogy. This is where lines tend to blur sometimes between the two media, and as technology evolves and progresses, that line will blur even further.

Back to the cinematics, it is important that the narrative told be memorable and enjoyable and that it strives to engage the viewers on an emotional level if possible. A word of advice: ***make sure that you absolutely love the story you are about to tell and produce***. If you are hesitant about the story or are not "feeling" it, do not proceed with it. This is especially true if you will be working with additional team members who will be helping you out with the production. If you are not sold on the story, how will you sell the idea of it to others?

You can start by jotting down words and sentences in point form to anchor the sense of the idea down. Once that is done, writing a short synopsis of the idea can really help cement the concept. At this stage, there is no need to go into complex details. Simply paint the idea with broad concepts and establish the basic *who*, *what*, *where*, *when* and *why* of your story.

The next step will be to write a detailed outline of your story, describing in detail the various components of the narrative. I found that at this stage, writing it in prose—in other words, as a short story—works the best. Don't edit—just write and get it out on the page. Once the initial draft outline is written, go over it, review what you have written and start the editing process. Begin to streamline the prose and keep it short and to the point. Also, depending on the type of story you want to tell, the length and complexity of your production will, obviously, be reflected in what is written in your final story outline. Choose your words wisely. Focus on the pacing of the story, the main actions of your characters, and the evolution of the overall story. Remember that you're not writing a literary piece of work but rather getting the narrative down to be used as a stepping stone to the next stage: the script. Once the edits are done and you are happy with the final version of your outline, you can move on to the next section.

Here is the base outline of the *Tin* cinematic:

This story takes place in an alternate version of the Land of Oz. The heroine of this tale is Leaf, a Tin Girl. Her father, a Tin Man who worked as a forest ranger, left to fight in the Great Elemental War when she was a young Tin toddler, and she hasn't seen him since. The only memento she has of her father is a faded photograph showing him holding her in his arms, as well as a necklace with a pendant covered in odd designs.

Leaf—like her father before her—is now a forest ranger and lives in a small hut in a clearing with Meep, her hyperactive mechanical pet bird, whom she built from spare parts.

Being a skilled tree mechanic is one of the basic training requirements of a forest ranger. Leaf maintains the clockwork trees in the forest and makes sure they are properly taken care of by oiling their roots, winding their springs, and tightening any loose bolts that hold the branches together.

Our adventure starts one fall day, as Leaf—during her rounds—notices Meep trying to catch an odd-looking butterfly-like creature. The butterfly nimbly evades Meep's attempts and begins to lead the bird through a dense patch of wild forest. Leaf runs after Meep, trying to catch him. As she follows deeper and deeper, she stumbles through the woods and eventually finds herself in front of an enormous, rusty and crumbling clockwork tree.

Meanwhile, Meep, oblivious to the surroundings, still tries to catch the butterfly and gets stuck in a tree hollow. Leaf rescues Meep and finds a small box lodged in the hollow.

As she opens it, she finds what looks like small wedge and half of a mechanical heart, with cogs and gears rusted together. She grabs the wedge, and as she examines it, she realizes it has the same markings as the pendant on her necklace. As she brings both side by side to compare the markings, the wedge suddenly flies out of her hand and snaps together with the pendant. It's a key!

As Leaf looks for clues as to where the key would fit, Meep—still set on capturing the butterfly—notices it fluttering against a rusty panel on the side of the tree trunk. He zips towards the butterfly but misses his nimble target and hits the tree trunk with a solid thunk! The impact loosens the rusty panel, causing it to fall to the ground. Leaf rushes toward Meep to see if he caused himself any damage, and after checking to see nothing got broken, notices the space that was exposed by the falling panel. She takes a closer look at the opening left behind the panel, and discovers a lever hidden in the recesses of the tree. Curious about her find, she pulls on the lever. Suddenly, loud rumbling sounds begin to emanate from underground, and the massive tree begins to shake and shift. Some of the roots move apart and reveal an opening with stairs leading into the depths of the earth.

The butterfly flies into the opening and stops just inside the doorway, gently flapping its wings, as if beckoning them forth. Leaf realizes the butterfly is trying to lead them somewhere, and follows it under the roots of the tree, with Meep in tow.

Hiding among the thick foliage a distance away, a dark shape is watching their every move, and silently floats away as they enter the opening.

// END CINEMATIC

// START OF GAME

Moving into the game side, this stage will include the conceptualization of the various game levels or worlds. Establishing goals and achievements that the player will have to meet in order to progress further in the game will be identified at this stage and worked through. Due to the immense variation of game styles available, defining a game genre is also a critical step at this level. For example, developing a side-scrolling platformer will necessitate a very different approach than a 3D real-time strategy game or a casual 2D match-3 game.

This leads us to the Game Design Document, which we will discuss in the next step.

Step 2: The Script / Game Design Document

Think of the script as the bridge between the words describing the story and the visual direction the animated feature will take. The main purpose of the script at this point is to describe the action in the outline as viewed through the lens of the camera. Show the audience, don't tell them. Camera moves, character actions, transitions and any other descriptive elements are written down in the script, all to facilitate the visualization of the scene as it begins to take shape within the stage of the 3D world you will be creating. Another aspect of the script that is no less important is describing what the audience will hear. Audio oftentimes gets put aside or relegated to "later . . . ". It's important to remember that if there is going to be dialogue in your production, to get the audio component alongside the visual right at the beginning.

As an aside, there are many great resources regarding proper script writing and the accepted traditional formats. We will discuss the main elements of writing a script in this book, but will not go into the depths of script writing. If you wish to read more about the writing process, a good starting point is Jeffrey Scott's *How to Write for Animation*.

The typical script format allows the reader to clearly follow the action taking place in the narrative, the character's dialogue and the transitions between the scenes.

For games, the game design document is what drives the overall direction and feel of the game. In it, all of gameplay mechanics, goals, narrative (if any) and other relevant game elements exist and act as a map to the whole development team in all of their capacities. If there is a strong narrative arc in the game itself, for example like in the excellent *Mass Effect* series from Bioware, a proper script as described above will be in place and be dynamically called on, depending on the player's actions. Games are typically a lot more involved than a cinematic production due to their interactive nature and the multiple variations that can be achieved through the gameplay.

Step 3: Concept Art

The story is finally beginning to coalesce and take shape. The plot is set, the characters are ready to act out their roles and the camera is ready to follow them throughout their twists and turns. Alternatively, your game character is ready to explore/interact/shoot its way through a game level. But wait . . . who are your characters? Where exactly does the story take place? When describing a narrative through words, the reader uses their imagination to interpret and turn your vision into their own conceptual imagery. That would work if you were writing a literary piece and stopped the creative process right there. But since the end result is an interactive story—in this case in the form of a video game— the road ahead of us is still open and waiting for further input from us.

This is where creating concept art comes into play. We finally have a chance to doodle or draw—depending on our abilities—the main characters and settings of our narrative. As the creators, our vision is what leads the creative process and moves it forward. Now, we might not be the most artistically talented individuals, and drawing stick figures is maybe the most we can manage at this stage. That's ok. Not to worry. If that is the case, this might be the time to expand our team and/or hire outside talent to help us bring our vision to the page.

This is also where you will have to exchange your writer's hat and become the art director. The ways you present your story (remember a few pages ago—you must absolutely believe in it and love it since you will have to share that vision with others) will offer the proper direction to the concept artists working with you. This particular step is also a great opportunity for a creative melding of minds! Your vision of the story will act as the main guidelines, but with the talent of the concept artists, you might discover new interpretations that will enrich your narrative and characterization further.

Concept art is not very different, regardless of whether you decide to make a game or a cinematic work. The parallels between the two mediums are pretty much identical, and the skills needed to create the concepts are one and the same. We will look at concept art and how it relates to the modeling process in more detail in Chapter 2.

Step 4: Storyboards

The next step in the pre-production is to combine the visual elements from the concept art and match them with the script direction to create visual flow. Great examples of storyboards are comic books and graphic novels. They are the perfect example of visual storytelling, combining the narrative aspect with visuals that ground the reader into the world created by the author and artists.

Storyboarding is another aspect where the more you do, the better it will be for the end result of the production. Depending on the skill of the storyboard artist, the quality of the boards will range from a few basic doodles to refined works of art. Keep in mind, though, that at this stage you are exploring the narrative visually, and that it is a process that will require multiple revisions. You are also—sadly—limited by your resources, timelines and deadlines. A suggestion that can help with the overall storyboarding and production process is to start small and loose and draw quick thumbnails. Initially, each thumbnail should not take more than a few seconds to sketch, just to get a general feel of how the narrative progresses. Don't be afraid to change, edit, discard and restart your thumbnails. In figure 1.2 you can see some of the very early thumbnails used for the *Tin* cinematic. Experiment with drawing the action from different angles, points of view and framings. You might find that translating the written word to images has its own challenges, surprises and sometimes failures. A brief sentence could involve drawing multiple complex elements that might actually distract from the flow of the story. On the other hand, the storyboard artist might sketch visual details that will enhance and embellish the story further than the original outline or script intended. This stage is the perfect time to realize what the necessary elements that will support the core of the story told are, and which details can add to or detract from it. It is also much cheaper—not only financially, but also time-wise—to figure out where the potential visual and narration pitfalls are during the storyboarding stage, rather than during production where assets, rigs and animations have already been created.

Here is a short list of the details you should be thinking about when you draw the thumbnails and eventual storyboards:

1. Staging and framing of the action as it will be seen on the screen
2. Posing of the characters
3. Expressions and visual cues of the characters
4. Story environments and their relation to the narrative flow and composition
5. Continuity
6. Camera transitions

FIGURE 1.2 Thumbnails for *Tin* cinematic

Once you're happy with the direction and clarity of the thumbnails, you can
then create more detailed and refined boards. If you are working solo, then
you might not need to redo this stage, since you will understand what is going

on. But, if you are working as part of a team, then make sure that the boards clearly convey how the story will unfold. There is an art to storyboarding, and there are many resources out there to help you hone this craft should you wish to explore it further.

Storyboarding may or may not be used in the pre-production phase of a video game, but again, that depends on the game genre. A story-based game with cinematic sequences will use them, while a simple casual game won't necessarily. Even so, storyboards are a very effective way of conveying ideas in a visual manner and can be a great asset during any type of creative production, regardless of the final output medium. And, with today's technologies, game engines can begin to replace and take over some of the features of creating cinematics in-engine as opposed to bringing in pre-rendered video sequences.

Planning the Storyboard Scenes

As the storyboards start taking shape, it is a good time to step back and figure out how to break down the story into organized sequences. If you look at most literary works, the story is typically broken into acts. These in turn are divided into chapters, each chapter into paragraphs, each paragraph into sentences, and sentences into words. Similar breakdowns exist in animation productions and in narrative-driven games. In the cinematic for *Tin*, there are five scene segments (see figure 1.3). Scenes usually define a self-contained story action that takes place in a set environment. The first scene acts as the lead-in to the story, establishing the setting and introducing our main characters. The second scene is the chase scene in the dark forest. The third scene is Leaf's fall and tumble down the pipes. The fourth scene in the story is Leaf's (temporarily) busted arm, fix-up and realization that she is in an unexplored part of the forest. The fifth and final scene in the cinematic is Leaf's discovery of the Great Tree and the start of her "game" adventure.

Each scene in turn, is made up of a sequence of *shots*. Think of a shot as a continuous action segment bound by a cinematic cut. In other words, when the camera changes position from one point of view to another, that change would be identified as a shot. Keep in mind, though, that the camera does not necessarily have to be a static camera, and a shot can include dynamic motions like trucks, pans, tilts and cranes. The next shot happens when a cut, a fade or some other type of camera transition takes place. Here is an example of a shot breakdown for the first scene in *Tin* (see figure 1.4). In the first shot, the camera trucks from left to right, establishing the environment, and slows to a stop when it reaches the stump. Cut to a static close-up shot of the stump where we see the butterfly gently flapping its wings. Suddenly the butterfly flies off-screen and Meep's beak snaps a fraction of a second later in the same spot the butterfly stood. Cut

Scene I

Scene II

Scene III

Scene IV

Scene V

FIGURE 1.3 Cinematic scene breakdown

to a medium-wide shot of Meep tumbling head over heels and crashing into the ground, looking a bit dazed.

Within the shots, the action is broken into individual *action beats*. These beats define unique segments within the action arc. For example, imagine this: a medium shot framing a bench in an urban park. Sitting on one side of it, we see a wrinkled, grey-haired, older gentleman reading a newspaper. After a few seconds, he puts the newspaper down beside him on the bench, gets up, stretches his back, looks around to see if there's anyone around and then does a bunch of backflips along the park path. Didn't expect that, did you?!

The beats describing that sequence will be each one of the individual actions, namely reading the paper, putting it down, getting up and stretching, looking around and finally doing the backflips. Planning for those story beats will also give you a sense of how long each action should take and help with the pacing of the story. They will also help during the animation sequences to identify the major key poses, thus providing an opportunity to review for continuity and flow of the overall action.

Color Scripts
Another set of visual guides that will be worth their weight in production gold are color scripts. As opposed to the written scripts that we have discussed so far, color scripts are similar to thumbnail frames, but rather than visually

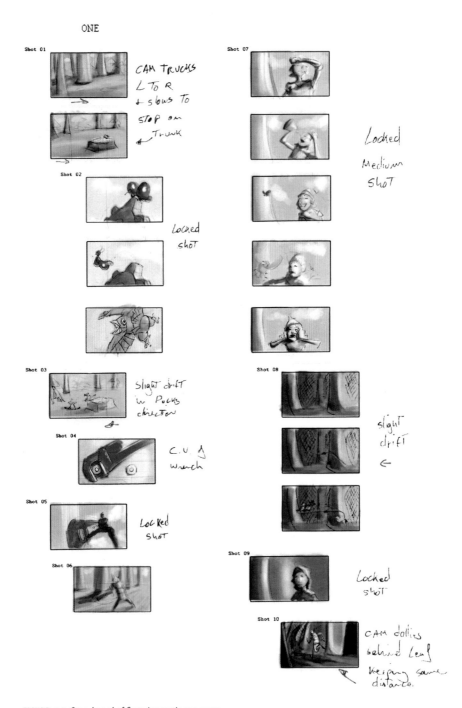

ONE

Shot 01
CAM TRUCKS
L TO R
+ slows to
stop on
Trunk

Shot 02
Locked
shot

Shot 03
Slight drift
in Polks
direction

Shot 04
C.U. of
Wrench

Shot 05
Locked
shot

Shot 06

Shot 07
Locked
Medium
shot

Shot 08
slight
drift

Shot 09
Locked
shot

Shot 10
CAM dollies
behind Leaf
keeping same
distance.

FIGURE 1.4 Storyboard of first cinematic sequence

showing the narrative, they show the overall color and lighting values of your animation. Typically, each color script frame—or tab—should define the areas of light and shadow, the direction of the main light source and overall tonal continuity. Depending on the direction, you might need to create between one and a few tabs to represent the tonal changes. In figure 1.5 you can see the color script used for the *Tin* cinematic. Color is also a great way to affect mood, and, looking at the color script in the example, you can get a general feel for the way the action evolves and the emotions it invokes.

The color script will also greatly help during the lighting, rendering and compositing stage since it does away with the guesswork in terms of managing light values: a must in any successful production!

TiN GiRL PROJECT - scene colour swatches

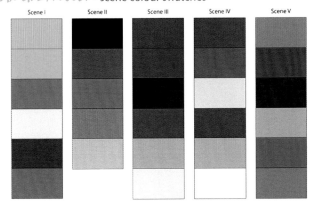

Scene V

Scene IV

Scene I

Scene II

Scene III

FIGURE 1.5 Color script example

Step 5: Asset Lists

One of the key documents in a production is the asset list (see figure 1.6). Think of it as shopping list of ingredients for your project. The asset list will list all of the models that will need to be created, from the main hero characters to the lowliest pebble rendered on the side of a virtual road.

ASSET NAME	Date	Concept	Model	Textured	Rigged	Lighting	Animation	Comped
CHARACTERS								
Leaf								
Meep								
Great Tree								
Slinker								
Butterfly								
ENVIRONMENTS								
Intro clearing								
Dark forest								
Chute								
Great Tree clearing								
Entrance under GT								
PROPS								
Monkey wrench								
Box								
Key								
Mechanical heart								
MultiTool								
Trees								
Stumps								
Branches								
Rocks								
Sky								
Clouds								
Dirt								
Grass								
Flowers								
Cogs								
Gears								
Greebles & misc								

FIGURE 1.6 Example of an asset list

The asset list will help break down each game level, scene and shot into its individual components and allow for a more realistic breakdown of the factors needed to create them. It works almost as a reality check to the concept art. It's very easy to draw little details and visual suggestions in the concept stage, but, ultimately, the content of each drawing will have to be created to match the vision of the project. By listing those details and keeping track of all the assets created, you can be certain that each frame in your production will be properly populated.

Step 6: Asset Management and Organization

It's important to be methodical with how you plan your production. Establish a set of naming conventions early on for your project files, as well as naming conventions for the various digital assets created in the production. If you are working with a team, confirm that everyone is following these conventions.

It will greatly help keep everybody organized and reduce the chance of confusion. Every production will have its own unique methods of organization and asset management. Remember, there are no standards in doing "proper" naming conventions. Find a system that works for you and your specific project, and follow it through until the production wraps up. Also, some scripts and automatic functions are name dependent, and not following an established convention can lead to errors in the script execution.

When naming the files and assets, make sure that they are descriptive enough to identify them but are not too long of a description as to make them unmanageable. For example:

>   *productionName_scene001_shot004_animatic_version015.ma*—too long
>   *scene001_shot004_ver015_animatic.ma*—still too wordy
>   *sc001_sh004_015_ani.ma*—ideal naming convention

The same goes when naming objects within the 2D and 3D files. For example, while *polyCube54* tells us nothing about the nature of the object—other than it starting as a polygonal cube, the same asset renamed *BND_L_pinky01_JNT* gives us a much more detailed description of its purpose. Make a list of custom naming conventions and apply them across your production's assets. For example:

>   Left = L
>   Right = R
>   Joint = JNT
>   Material = MAT
>   Texture = TEX

And so on . . .

In terms of file management, a very basic way of structuring your project is to create a project file folder on your system (or server), broken down into production-specific sub-folders. A section can be dedicated to the scene and shot breakdown, another to the various modeling assets, and further into texture folders. The combinations are practically limitless, so plan ahead before committing. Once the structure is organized and set up, place your files and assets accordingly in their relevant folders. If you are working with a team, everyone involved should have a copy of that structure on their work systems. You can then decide when and how often the main folder structure gets updated and the files synced. Depending on your technical abilities, you can automate the folder-creation process via scripts, saving a lot of tedious and manual repetition—and the dreaded human error factor.

In larger productions, asset management tools are part of the pipeline setup. There are many open-source and commercial solutions, each with their benefits and drawbacks. For the most part, these asset project managers will allow you to delegate, track, plan and review the various production elements. One of the advantages they offer—especially since they are set up on a central server—is the ability to save versions of your files. The little production gremlins—which will invariably show up at some point during the production—will do their best to wreak havoc in your files, and having access to old revisions and backups will prove to be a lifesaver. And speaking of . . . save, and save often! And backup your files in multiple locations.

Step 7: Animatic / First Playable Prototype

The animatic term is more relevant to the cinematic productions. In this stage, a rough version of the animation is created, typically with low-resolution proxy objects acting as stand-ins to the final objects. The main goal of the animatic is to lock down the camera's movements, if any, and finalize the timing of each of the shots. An audio track, be it rough or final, is also usually a part of the animatic process. By adding the audio component, it helps tweak even further what the final version of the cinematic will be.

A very important point to remember: make sure that the **scale and dimensions** of the low-resolution proxy objects **are the same** as the final high-resolution ones. If they're not, all the camera work you do during the animatic stage is worthless, since it won't use the same frame of reference. It seems an obvious thing, but you'd be surprised how often this honest mistake happens.

When testing the video game mechanics, a first playable prototype is set up by using primitive proxy objects representing the environment, characters and effects of the game. This step offers the game designers and programmers the opportunity to focus on pure gameplay and test out game features rather than being distracted by the pretty graphics (which may not be even created at this stage).

These steps cover most of what happens in the pre-production process. Of course, every project will have its own specific requirements, but in general, most of the points raised above will—in some form or another—be present in the pre-production stages.

Production

Usually, game and cinematic productions involving a 3D pipeline will share an almost identical workflow in the first stages of production. Where they might differ is typically the level of complexity allowed as defined by the game engine. This usually includes the polygon count on the meshes, the number of joints, types of deformers allowed and various other specific technical limitations. In a cinematic, these limitations rarely exist since the final medium is a sequential set of images edited as a movie clip, as opposed to an interactive medium where current processing power sets the limits. The divergence starts after the animation process, where in a feature or broadcast production, the 3D scenes are lit, rendered, composited and edited whereas in a game production they are sent to the game engine which takes care of these aspects.

Below is the list of the common stages for both game and cinematic pipelines.

Modeling

The first 3D production phase that is ready to start once pre-production is underway and concepts are drawn is to model the characters, props and sets in 3D. There are many ways to achieve this, from using standard 3D modeling tools, to sculpting high-resolution meshes with programs like ZBrush, Mudbox and 3D-Coat, to 3D scanning physical objects and converting them into 3D meshes. The skills of the modelers are critical since they create literally the foundation upon which the other stages of the 3D production will be built upon. A good mesh—properly built and optimized for animation—will help streamline and move the production pipeline forward. On the other hand, a poorly modeled object will open a veritable can of worms and necessitate fixes and tweaks, thus slowing down the overall process. Pay attention to your production meshes from the get go!

Surfacing

Once the 3D mesh is built, it needs to be presentable and all dressed up. This is where surfacing comes into play. Surfacing includes all of the aspects of dealing with the "skin" of the 3D mesh. Things like setting the UV layouts, painting the textures and creating the surface shaders that will emulate the material quality of the 3D mesh are all part of the surfacing process. Some of the new tools that have made their way into the 3D pipeline in recent years have made this process a lot of fun. For example, Substance Designer and Filter Forge for the creation of procedural 3D and 2D textures, Mari and Substance Painter for painting directly on the 3D mesh and a multitude of free and commercial plugins to help with the UV layout process. And of course, we can't forget the venerable Photoshop in all of this.

The list of surfacing tools keeps growing day by day, and every new tool and/ or feature can impact the pipeline based on how they approach this stage. Make sure that, prior to the start of the production, you establish a foolproof workflow and stick to it throughout the length of your production. It's tempting at times to hear about a brand new feature that promises to make the work you're currently doing a snap, but being a first-adopter and trying to fit it within your established workflow without heavy testing can actually slow down the process rather than speed it up.

Rigging

This is probably the most technical aspect of the 3D pipeline overall. Rigging, by definition, is the setup of controls over 3D elements in order to facilitate their integration within the 3D pipeline. It's often considered the stepping stone to the animation process. As a side note, rigging is not limited solely to character controls but also to lights, VFX and any other 3D element that animators will need to interact with.

Rigging for games and for cinematics also differ in their approach—at least at the time of writing this book. Cinematic rigs can afford higher levels of complexity since there are no set limitations on how many deformers and controls one can use. This is not the case with game rigs, since the game engines do limit the amount of deformers that can be used. Another issue that sometimes arises is that certain types of features in 3D packages do not carry over well—or at all—to the game engines and can cause problems down the road.

Common rig setups include single control/bind rigs that provide an all-in-one solution. They are usually simpler to create since they focus only on one rig, but can be limiting in some instances. Another setup, which we will explore in this book, involves the creation of a bind rig that is connected to the mesh, and a separate control rig that offers the various animation controls which are then transferred onto the bind rig.

Animation

This is the stage where the characters and occasional props change from static meshes to articulated, interactive elements. In feature animation, each shot is carefully storyboarded and the animators bring the narrative to life according to the script. In the video game side of things, each character has a defined number of actions, and these are then created as cycles which in turn are brought into the game engine for further interaction with external controllers such as keyboards, joysticks, touch devices and others. Another typical difference is that game character animation usually stays "on the coin", meaning they are animated on the spot and then moved across the game world through user interaction, while in feature animation the characters often move in 3D space during their shots.

As mentioned above, this is where cinematics and game split apart and go their mostly separate ways. With games, there is an integral connection with the programming side of things which affects how the various elements interact with the game engine and game world. In a way, cinematics remain mostly within the realm of the art side, while games balance between the art and technical.

Post-Production

The final stage in the production cycle involves the combination of all of the prior production elements into a cohesive whole. For example, in a cinematic production, that would include lighting the animated shots, rendering them and compositing the final renders together. Any special effects would be added at this stage as well, using the talents of VFX artists. Once everything is set, it is then edited with a refined audio track, color corrected and neatly packaged for audio-visual consumption. Renderers like Mental Ray, V-Ray, Renderman, Arnold and others take care of the rendering heavy-lifting. Each of these renderers has their own strengths and advantages (as well as associated costs).

For the compositing of rendered images and the creation of spectacular visual effects, tools such as Nuke, After Effects, Fusion and others are often used to combine the multiple rendered layers and create the incredible visuals we see these days in films, broadcast and game cinematics.

> **NOTE:** The cinematic production cycle we're currently discussing is purely 3D, without any live-action elements. Introducing live action entails a whole additional set of specific skills, which are beyond the scope of this book.

In the gaming world, post-production would include the refinement of the visuals and special effects; testing, testing and more testing of game mechanics; game balancing and hopefully the delivery of a bug-free game to the eagerly awaiting gamer hordes. Once the game is published, the maintenance stage begins, which commonly consists of fixing various coding bugs as they crop up, creating patches, and other common modern video game–related issues.

There is no set toolset for game creation, especially on the programming side, since the options are numerous and limited only by the coding skills of the developers. There are many existing game engines that can help with the burden of getting a game going without having to write them up from scratch. Some of the popular 2D and 3D game engines include Unity, Unreal 4, CryEngine, Construct 2 and GameMaker: Studio among others. On the same token, many programmers will create their own custom game engines to fit the requirements of the game being developed.

So there you have it—the frame of a somewhat typical production cycle. Now we all know that there is no such thing as a "typical" production, but for argument's sake, let's assume it to be so. There are many great resources out there that discuss this process in much more depth, but I hope that these last few pages gave you, Dear Reader, a glimpse into what goes into a game and cinematic production.

Chapter 2
Concept Art and Modeling

Concept Art

For the *Tin* game, the concept began with Leaf, the main character, and the narrative grew around her. The character of Tin Girl was already clearly established in my mind, but needed a bit of a visual push to get it to its final production look. You can see the evolution of the character from my original quick sketch compared to a working concept used for the 3D modeling process (see figures 2.1–2.2.).

Environments, props and anything else that will populate the game or cinematic worlds should also get the concept treatment. The reason is to make sure that all the visual elements that bring your production to life actually belong stylistically to the same universe. Putting characters from *The Simpsons* in the background settings of *Full Metal Alchemist* would not quite work visually. This is especially true if you are bringing multiple artists to help with the concept art. Ultimately, a style guide will have to be set and followed to keep all of the visual assets constant. In some productions, that guide is called the *Production Bible* and has in it all of the elements that deal with the production at hand. The *Production Bible* is not a static thing, in the sense that it continuously evolves and grows in order to fit the requirements of the production itself. Having said that, once elements in the production have been approved and signed off, modifying them for any reason requires approval from the decision makers, while taking into consideration how those changes will affect the rest of the production schedule.

A good tactic for starting your concept art is just to draw, draw, draw! Produce as many sketches as you can, without spending more than a few minutes on each. At this point, you're not aiming for perfection but rather—like we talked earlier about the idea generation—getting your creative gears rolling and getting stuff out on paper (see figures 2.3–2.5). I will emphasize paper because, personally, I find it faster and more intuitive to get doodling rather than sketching directly with the computer. Now, this is changing with all of the improved tablets and painting software available in the digital medium, but, ultimately, you are still limited by technology (menus, saving, key or finger combos, etc.). With a pencil and paper, those limitations are gone and

Concept Art and Modeling

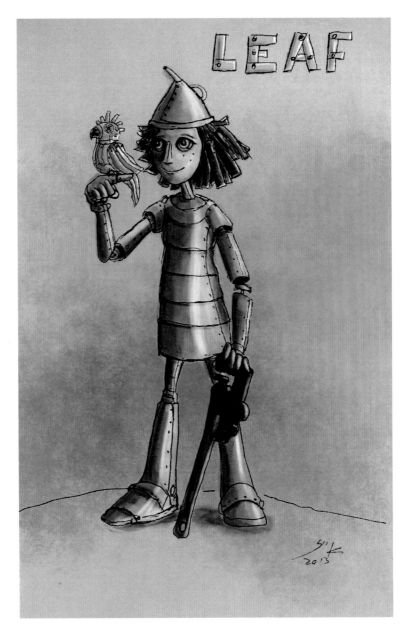

FIGURE 2.1 First concept of Leaf

you can scribble to your heart's content. And if you don't like it, move on to the next doodle or next sheet of paper. On a plus side, 2048 levels of digital pressure do not compare at all to the feeling of holding pencil to paper and seeing the line quality change as you draw it.

26

FIGURE 2.2 **Final concept of Leaf**

FIGURE 2.3 Sketches and thumbnails of Leaf

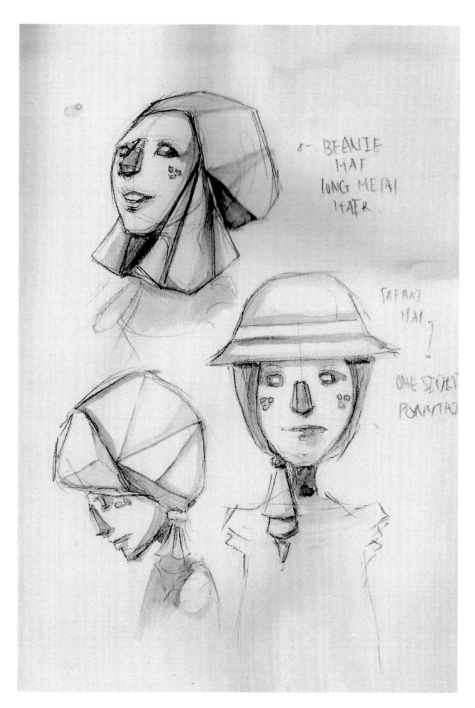

FIGURE 2.4 **Sketches and thumbnails of Leaf**

FIGURE 2.5 Sketches and thumbnails of Leaf

This reminds me of an old joke on how NASA spent millions of dollars developing a pen that could write in zero gravity, underwater and under other adverse conditions. The [fill in your favorite competing space agency] saw what the Americans were doing, put their heads together and came up with the brilliant idea of using a pencil to greater success.

Do not discredit the humble pencil!

Hopefully, by now you'll have tens, if not hundreds, of little doodles and sketches of your characters, environments and props (see figures 2.6–2.8). If you find something that immediately talks to you and that you love, great! If not, start doing the Frankenstein and take parts you like from one sketch and combine it with parts you like from another one. Don't hesitate to experiment with it. Sometimes the best results come from asking "what if. . ." and trying it out.

Work and rework your concept art so that every aspect of the story world you've created matches—or even surpasses—the vision you had when the idea started its evolution. Let the idea grow and take a life of its own. Allow it to fill up all the small nooks and crannies with details, shapes, color and sound. I find that as the concepts get drawn, an added dimension of vibrancy

FIGURE 2.6 Sketches and thumbnails of Leaf

FIGURE 2.7 **Sketches of trees**

gets added to the story, and that is one of the most gratifying experiences of production.

NOTE: You can find many more sketches, concept art and updates for the game *Tin* on www.thetingirl.com

References

I cannot emphasize how important it is to have real-world examples to draw from—literally—in order to get your ideas properly and on the page or screen. Working from the top of your head is a good start, but without having a real-life reference to anchor it in, it will always lack something fundamental. I admit that there are some very talented artists who can

FIGURE 2.8 **Sketches of trees**

come up with concepts without looking at anything and simply draw it perfectly, but they are few and very, very far between. For the rest of us, having a collection of references to work from is an essential part of the pre-production process.

Let us do a little experiment. Put the book away for a minute, take a piece of paper and pen, and draw a lamppost on it. Don't think too much about it, just sketch out whatever comes to your mind. Once you're done, keep on reading.

Now, I am sure you would have no problems getting the general *idea* of a lamppost. You would probably have a long column, from which an extension at its topmost part extends outwards, with some kind of light at the end. That's the idea of a lamppost. It's not wrong, but it's not quite right either.

Is the main column made out of metal, concrete, wood or some other material? How does it attach to the ground surface? How many bolts or brackets hold it in place? Are there any panels on that main column? Is the light attached at the top of the column, or does it extend outward? How many lanterns are there? Is it ornate, or is its design purely functional? Is it new, rusted or chipped? Is it electric, gas or solar powered? Is it designed for highways, small streets or private homes? How tall is it compared to an average human?

Without references to base it on, the lamppost you originally drew would be recognized as one, but should you want to use it in a production setting, would it actually look "right"?

Let's say you want to design and model a massive interstellar starship, capable of traversing the depths of space and travel between the stars. As far as we know, no such thing exists (yet!). But, using a bit of common sense, creativity and references, we can come up with a pretty good approximation of it. Last I checked, the closest thing we have to an interstellar starship on earth are military aircraft carriers, cruise ships or battleships (see figure 2.9). These are massive constructs, full of plates, angles, greebles[1] and all assorted odds and ends. Using these existing ships as a starting point, you can then begin to envision your own imaginary interstellar starship. By grounding it in reality, no matter how fantastic an object is, your audience will have an easier time relating to it.

FIGURE 2.9 **Image of USS Texas battleship (public domain)**

Start collecting references about anything you think you might need for your production. For example, once you know the time of day, season and type of weather for each of the scenes, do some research and grab a few photographs that show roughly what you had in mind. Doing it the traditional way meant cutting out pictures from magazines and newspapers, or going to the reference library and asking the librarian to photocopy images from books for us. Sadly, too many books were hurt during this process, because a few bad apples actually cut the images for themselves, butchering the book and wrecking it for the rest of us. Oh, the humanity!

Online resources like Google, Flickr, Bing, Pinterest, Tumblr and some of the other image-search engines are great reference aggregators, literally at your fingertips. Type away, press enter and a cornucopia of images magically appears in front of you to choose from.

Be organized about collecting your references. You never know when you might need them again. If you have hard copies of references, use descriptive file folders to separate them in logical divisions. Digitally, the job is much easier, and with the almost infinite storage space available these days, your references can easily contain thousands of images. A good method that I found works for me is to create file directories broken down into broad general categories, and then further sub-categories specific to your needs.

Character Sheets

By now, the direction of your project should be well under way and a clear idea as to who your main characters are will be well cemented. During the concept art stage, brainstorming the various looks and styles of the short were explored, and hopefully a cohesive look was established. The character sheets further refine those art concepts and provide detailed information on each of the main actors in the production.

Typically, drawings of the characters in various views will be provided, including detailed drawings of facial expressions (see figure 2.10) and emotions the character will assume during the animation. A sequence of various body poses fitting the character's personality will also be drawn. In general, the more you plan on paper, the smoother the 3D production will go. Think about all of the characteristics of your character, what they wear, which accessories they use, their emotional demeanors and attitudes and the body language they convey straight off the page. You might have a technical character sheet used to establish dimensions and guidelines for the modelers to use as reference for the 3D builds, and another set showing the characters in various poses and expressions geared towards the animators (see figures 2.11–2.12).

FIGURE 2.10 **Facial expressions of Leaf**

FIGURE 2.11 Leaf body sketch

FIGURE 2.12 **Leaf body sketch**

As part of creating the character sheets, you might also want to create a scale sheet where you place all of the characters in your production side by side and show the height and size relation between them. Typically, your main character will be the standard from which all other characters and creatures refer (see figure 2.13).

37

FIGURE 2.13 **Character scale sheet**

Add as many detailed explanations and sketches as you need to detail the unique aspects of your character. For example, for the production of the game *Tin*, Meep—being a mechanical bird construct—is made up of multiple moving parts. By sketching the workings of the parts on paper, literally engineering them and figuring out how they will move in relation to one another, greatly helped with the modeling and rigging processes (see figure 2.14).

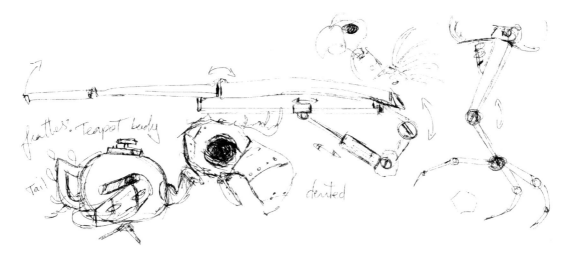

FIGURE 2.14 **Meep planning sketch**

3D Modeling

3D modeling, like drawing, is a very subjective skill. It is, after all, a form of digital sculpting, and every modeler will have their own look and style. We won't discuss here how to model in 3D—there are many very good references out there that can help you cover this aspect of the production. Rather, I will share a few tips with you to ensure that the models produced—either by yourself or from a modeler working with you—are properly set for rigging. We will focus on creature modeling—humanoid and otherwise. These tips apply to all meshes, regardless of the 3D package used to create them. As mentioned earlier, a poorly modeled mesh can sabotage a good rig and cause unnecessary headaches.

Once you have collected your references and concept art, here is a list of key points that will keep your model in tip-top shape

Output Medium

The output medium will establish the kind of model budget you will have available to you. If it's a mesh geared toward a video game, the polygon count will be substantially lower than one geared toward cinematic. As the game technologies improve and computing power increases, this differentiation will decrease, but at the moment, it's still a point to take under consideration.

Another facet of the output medium is the distance of the mesh to the camera. For example, a game character in a platformer game will have, for the most part, a set size in relation to the game level. In this case, model enough detail so that character will look good at that size. Anything beyond will be overkill and a waste of resources. On the same token, in a first-person shooter game, where you see mainly your character's hands (with or without a weapon), the mesh detail on the hands will have to be relatively high since they are closer to the game "camera" and take up more screen real estate. Other game types, such as over-the-shoulder– or isometric-style games with zoom in and out capabilities, will also need a somewhat more detailed mesh. "Adapt the mesh to the medium" is a good motto to go by. It boils down also to efficiency. Any extra resources spent on things you will not see are effectively wasted and could have been used toward something more relevant to the project.

In the case of cinematic models, the meshes will generally be of a much higher resolution. This is necessary in order to provide the ability to do close-up shots and show detailed deformations in areas like the face. Again, depending on the production and schedule, multiple variants of the same character might be built, depending on where in the shot they stand and their relative distance from the camera.

Level of Detail and Topology

Areas on the mesh with a high level of deformation will obviously have a much denser polygon count, compared to more rigid areas. Modeling the face of a cinematic character, for example, will need a lot of properly placed polygons in order to allow for correct deformations—for instance, the mouth and eyes area, since the amount of subtle movement required to animate properly is quite high (see figure 2.15). On the other hand, an area like the shin can be taken care of with a lower number of polygons, enough to convey the shape and volume of that section of the mesh.

FIGURE 2.15 Leaf cinematic model and game model side by side

The topology of the mesh of your creature is very important, especially if it's going to be articulated, rigged and animated. Properly placing edge loops on the model can mean the difference between a flexible, flowing and working rig and an unusable one. Think of the edge loops as the natural line that musculature follows to define a shape, and model your characters accordingly. In a humanoid character, the areas you should pay attention to have proper edge loops are:

- The face, especially around the eyes and mouth
- The shoulders and armpits, to ensure proper deformation when moving the arms up and down, and forward and back
- The hips and crotch area (if wearing pants or skin-tight superhero outfits) to allow for a wide range of motion for the legs such as kicking, jumping, etc.
- The fingers—if they are articulated and shown as close ups

If you feel it's needed, add extra edge loops to ensure you'll get proper deformation. With game models that have a poly count budget, it's more of a juggling matter to guarantee that areas of high deformation get the detail, while more rigid areas can do with less.

Square Is Good—Polygon Types to Use and Avoid

As a rule of thumb, modeling in quads is the way to go. Quadrangles—four-sided polygon faces—give the best results in terms of mesh consistency and provide clean subdivided meshes. It's easier also to predict the topology of a mesh with quads than with triangles.

There will be times, though, when you won't have a choice but to use triangles. Those are fine too, but try to limit their use. If you can place them in hidden parts of the mesh, i.e., behind the character's ears, or in areas where deformation is minimal, that would be best.

NOTE: Meshes are usually tessellated into triangles during render time or when brought into a game engine.

The type of polygon you want to avoid is the n-gon (polygons made up of more than four sides). Those will wreak havoc with your meshes and will pose problems with textures and during subdivisions (see figure 2.16). Also, programs like ZBrush and Mudbox don't like meshes with n-gons at all. Properly divided meshes containing quad faces are perfect for them. Otherwise you might get some strange deformations and even holes in the mesh.

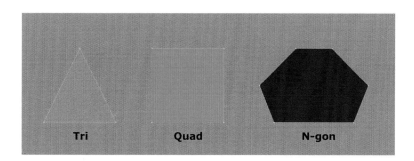

Tri   **Quad**   **N-gon**

FIGURE 2.16 **Tris, quads and n-gons**

One common occurrence with quads and *no-no* n-gons is creating non-planar faces. This happens when one or more of the vertices do not lie on the same plane as the others. This will result in visual glitches or odd deformations. This cannot happen with triangles, ergo the tessellations mentioned above.

We've mentioned subdivisions a couple of times already. It's a set of algorithms that divide each polygonal face by four and smooth it out. There are two types of subdivisions:

1. **"Physical" mesh subdivision**—This type adds polygon faces to the mesh, making it denser, thus increasing the poly count. For example, in Maya you would find that in the Polygon menu set under **Mesh > Smooth**. With history enabled, you can increase and decrease the levels of divisions.

Different modeling programs offer that same ability, albeit under different names and with different features.

2. **Render-time subdivision**—This form of subdivision keeps the mesh at a lower resolution but creates the subdivision smoothing at render time. Mind you, only certain rendering engines provide this ability, i.e., Mental Ray. Maya's default software renderer will not subdivide at render time.

Another type of geometry glitch you want to avoid is non-manifold geometry. Maya defines non-manifold geometry as "polygons that have a configuration that cannot be unfolded into a continuous flat piece". A very common scenario of non-manifold geometry happens when the same face is extruded by mistake twice on the same spot, without transforming the first extrusion. Without subdividing the mesh, it's almost impossible to notice that there is something wrong with the geometry, but down the road, that will cause a lot of problems with texturing and smoothing. Another example is when two objects share a vertex without sharing an edge (see figure 2.17). Look at your 3D software's documentation for more details on this.

Maya offers a way to identify and clean up the mesh. Select your 3D model and run **Mesh > Cleanup**. There are quite a few options there that should help out with the mesh cleanup. Hopefully that will find any potential trouble spots on your mesh and get it all ready and proper for production.

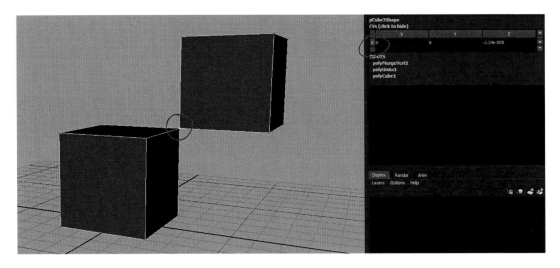

FIGURE 2.17 **Non-manifold geometry example in which two objects share the same vertex**

Alternatives to Mesh Density

In situations where a polygon budget is required (I'm looking at you, video games), other methods can provide a good alternative to details created through mesh density. These methods include the use of non-illuminated texture maps that provide height information and give the illusion of additional mesh detail.

First, we have the venerable **bump map**, introduced by James Blinn in 1978. This is a grey-scale map that perturbs the surface normals of the mesh and gives the illusion of additional irregular detail on the mesh face. Lighter pixels in the grey-scale map will give the illusion that the surface is pulled up while darker ones will seem as if they're pushed down.

Normal maps work similarly to bump maps, except that instead of using a grey-scale texture map, they use an RGB one, with each color controlling a rough direction (Red/X—left to right, Green/Y—up and down, Blue/Z—depth, similar to bump). They are very effective when using dynamic lighting, and commonly used in video games. Normal maps can be extracted from high-detailed sculpts and offer creative ways of making lower-resolution meshes look very detailed (see figure 2.18).

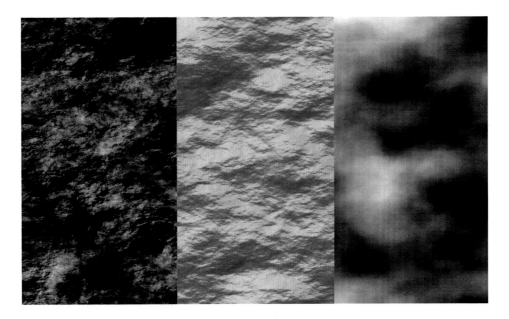

FIGURE 2.18 Color map, normal map and bump map

The other type of texture map that is used to add more detail is the **displacement map**. It's a grey-scale texture map that, as opposed to the bump and normal maps—which do not change the silhouette of the mesh—actually *deforms* the geometry. In order for the displacement map to work effectively, the geometry needs to have a relatively dense poly count, making it counter-intuitive to use in game engines. With proper planning, and considering again the level of detail and distance of the 3D mesh to the camera, a lot of details can be created as texture maps, thus keeping the geometry relatively light. This is especially true in the case of video games.

Additional techniques such as baking ambient occlusion maps on the mesh will create areas of light and shadow that can emulate modeled detail and, again, create the illusion that the mesh is more detailed than it really is. In the end, it's all about the cheats and workarounds that give the illusion of detailed artwork without taxing the system.

Sculpting Pitfalls

3D sculpting tools like ZBrush, Mudbox, 3D-Coat, Modo and others have revolutionized the way 3D models are created and propelled the quality of the meshes we see now in animated features and video games to incredible heights. Gone are the days of painfully manipulating NURBS surfaces, making all the models look as if they came from the same mold. With all due respect to NURBS and their very useful applications—we've come a long way since the 1990s way of building 3D geometry. With this current crop of modeling and sculpting software, the gaps created by the uncanny valley are constantly being eroded. I expect that soon technology will provide us with tools that will allow us to create models that look exactly like copies of living creatures (see figure 2.19).

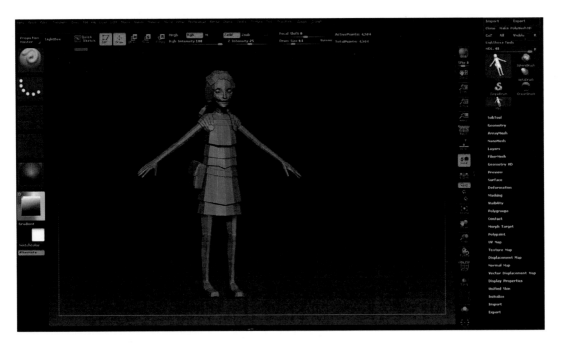

FIGURE 2.19 **Sculpting geometry with ZBrush**

Sculpting workflows these days give the modelers total freedom in defining 3D shapes and adding extremely fine details with the use of custom brushes. Additional features like voxel modeling—which are not limited to the stretchy behavior of polygons as they are shaped, make the process even more fluid and intuitive.

So where's the problem, you might ask yourself? Well, using these fantastic tools to create 3D models usually leave a messy and dense underlying mesh that is not fit to be animated. In fact, it ranks high among every rigger's nightmare to rig such a mesh. The same, by the way, goes for 3D scanned objects.

To fix this, the bright minds working in the 3D industry developed additional tools that help retopologize existing meshes. You can use your very beautiful yet dense and unmanageable sculpted mesh as the underlying base, and start rebuilding it face by face by following the tips and techniques we discussed above. Retopology tools allow you to place new geometry while keeping the contours of the base mesh in place, and act as magnets, in a way.

The end result is an optimized and well-built model that has the shape, volume and form of the sculpted mesh, but is ready to be rigged and animated. As mentioned above, the fine details from the sculpted mesh can now be applied on the animation-ready rig through the use of normal maps, and can "fake" more detail that there really is. With a proper workflow, you can create amazing looking models that are ready to be animated and that still maintain a relatively low polygon count.

UV Maps

We can't talk about modeling without mentioning UV maps (see figure 2.20). UVs are a 2D texture coordinate system that represents 3D geometry. Every vertex on the mesh has a matching point in the UV texture space and allows for specific placement of texture maps on the model. The U and V are the two axes in the texture space—U for the horizontal coordinates and V for the vertical ones.

3D primitive objects such as spheres, cubes, cylinders, etc. typically have a basic UV map generated by default. Most times, though, this UV map is too generic and does not provide the proper layout to place custom textures. Further manipulation and manual placement of the UVs by the modeler or surfacing artist is recommended in most cases. A common technique is the unwrapping of the UVs, where edges are marked on the model and are used as cut lines to "unwrap" the UVs. Think of an orange, where you'd cut the top and bottom parts of it, and then make a single cut in the mid-section and peel it from there.

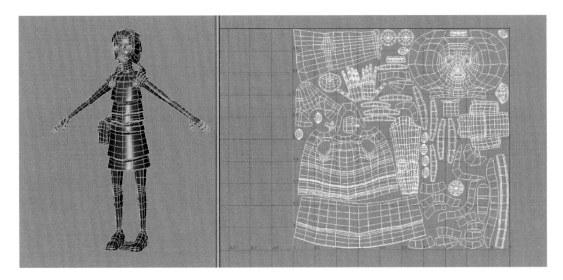

FIGURE 2.20 **UV map of Leaf**

There are many tools available that will facilitate the creation of custom UVs. Maya's new **Unfold** tool, in combination with the UV scripts found in the freely available bonus tools make unwrapping the mesh a very intuitive and fast process. Another excellent 3D package with great UV unwrapping tools is Modo.

> **NOTE:** You can download the bonus tools from Maya's Help menu (**Help > Resources and Tools > Download Bonus Tools).**

When working on game models, there is also a texture budget, unfortunately, that limits the amount of texture space that can be used. That's where creative unwrapping comes into play. The goal is to optimize the UV texture space as much as possible and put the maximum amount of UVs in that 0,1 area. A common practice would be to texture one or more objects with one texture map. This limitation does not usually occur with cinematic models. The key is to have the main texture elements that will have the most detail take up the majority of the UV space, while secondary elements can be shrunk and arranged so they don't take up as much of that space.

UVs are also important to the setup of hair and fur effects. A proper UV layout will help with getting predictable results on your mesh. In short, good, properly laid out UV maps will go a long way to help your 3D pipeline work smoothly. Do take the time to get this stage done right and well.

NOTE: A useful little trick with UV maps that can help with rigging is that once the UVs are established, you can select the shell, which will isolate those faces from the rest of the mesh. You can then paint weights or create blendshapes much more easily than if you had to work with the full model.

File Referencing

Depending on the pipeline you are using in your production, file referencing might well be an integral part of it. It does take some pre-planning to adapt to this workflow, but the advantages are well worth the effort.

File referencing allows the linking of external files with all of their content into a main, *parent* scene file. In other words, you can work on an asset and save it as its own file. You would then create a new parent scene file and reference that asset into it. You can then further manipulate the referenced asset and create certain changes to it (via reference edits).

The advantages of file referencing are:

1. **File size**—The *parent* scene file remains small in terms of size, since it's only creating a link to the referenced file (*child* scene file) rather than importing it into the scene. This helps keep the loading times of the files short. A tip would be to save the files as ASCII files (.ma) rather than binary files, since this format allows you to manually edit the data inside the scene files.
2. **Change once, update all**—Just like nodes in the Node Editor, any changes made in the referenced, child file propagates throughout all of the instances where they are referenced. In all cases, the data in the referenced file remains separate from the parent file. This workflow allows you, for example, to use early versions of the 3D mesh model and reference them inside a separate rig file. As the rig begins to be built, the mesh—separately—continues to be refined, updated, UVed, and textured separately. Thus, every time the rig file is opened, an updated mesh is loaded into it. This also allows for a dynamic dialogue between the rigger and the modeler to resolve conflicts in a non-destructive manner.

In a cinematic production, using a file referencing system will make a lot of sense, since for the most part, the referencing lives in a closed system defined by the 3D software. In a video game environment, though, it is possible, but extra care needs to be taken since the mesh, rig and animation will have to be exported into the game engine and that might cause issues if not properly accounted for. We will further discuss how to apply file referencing for 3D models and exporting them into a game engine in Chapter 8.

To improve and optimize the file referencing pipeline, you'll find below a list of tips that will help with the process.

- **Clean meshes**—Once the model is done, make sure to name all of the geometry properly, freeze transformations and delete any history attached to it. Any animation keys on the mesh should be removed. As well, remove any additional elements that are not necessary to the final mesh functionality, i.e., test shaders, display and render layers, lights and cameras, sets, image planes, etc.
- **Organized outliner**—Group your meshes under a defined group. Remember that the parenting hierarchy cannot be changed in the parent reference file. If you will be binding the geometry in a rig file, keep all the mesh elements separate. Planning and organizing the outliner with that in mind will help with any unexpected surprises.
- **Proper UV layout**—As we mentioned earlier, organize and optimize your UV maps on the mesh to prevent any complications down the pipeline.
- **Reference name**—For example, let's say you're creating a lovely cube character called Bob. The workflow would be to create a top group node called **MDL** and place the geometry underneath it. When you save out the file, save it as **bob.ma**. When you reference **bob.ma** into your parent scene file (if you keep the default settings), the namespace will be **bob:MDL**. Keep the filenames short and descriptive.
  Speaking of namespaces, make sure to name your objects in a logical and descriptive manner. In order to maintain a proper naming convention throughout, regardless of the reference version you use, here are two techniques you can apply to help you with that:

1. **Consistent namespace**—Let's say you have a file called **check_cube_seams_05.ma** which you want to reference. By default, that is going to be its namespace, which can be awkward to work with. You can change it in the Reference Editor (**File > Reference Editor**), beside the *Namespace*: field to **bob**, and from now on, any link to that referenced file, regardless of its name, will be called **bob** (see figures 2.21–2.23).

2. **No namespace**—You can do away with the namespaces completely, and let the objects in your scene go directly to the scene root. To do so, open the Create Reference options (**File > Create Reference. . . > □**) and scroll down to the Reference Options sub-menu. Select the bottom radio button options ("Merge into selected namespace and rename incoming objects that match"), and your referenced object will now have the default root namespace of the scene (see figure 2.24).

Once the file is referenced into a parent scene file, any manipulation and edits done on the reference file will be saved under a reference node. It's important to understand what is saved under those nodes in order to maximize the effectiveness of the reference file. Any changes made in the parent scene file are not sent back to the child/referenced file, *unless* specifically saved as such. You can do that by selecting the reference from the Outliner and right-

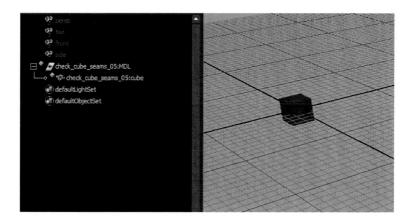

FIGURE 2.21 Naming conventions when using reference files

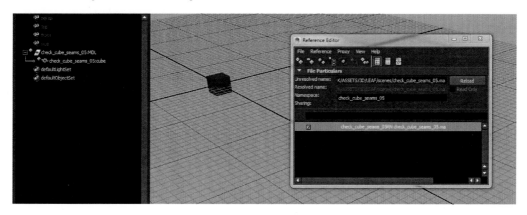

FIGURE 2.22 Naming conventions when using reference files

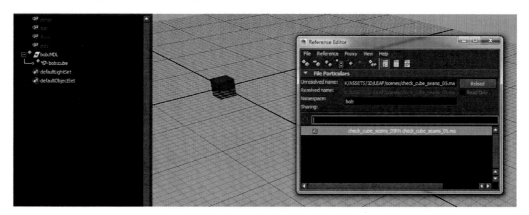

FIGURE 2.23 Naming conventions when using reference files

FIGURE 2.24 Set referenced objects to inherit the root name of the scene

clicking on **Reference > Save Edit**. In other words, applying a transformation to a referenced child scene within a parent scene—say scaling and rotating the mesh—will keep that info within the parent scene and not update the child scene. You can view the reference edits on the mesh through **Reference > List Edits. . .** as well as export them as external files (and import them back from such).

There is in-depth documentation discussing this and other aspects of file references in the Maya help menu, including limitations and workarounds.

From my experiences, I found that loading a double-reference file into a parent scene, i.e., ***model_file.ma >> rig_file.ma >> animation_file.ma*** may cause a break in the reference and result in odd behavior. The Maya documentation also states that saving reference edits cannot go past grandchild nodes, so keep that in mind when planning your reference pipeline. As always, the rule of thumb in a 3D production is test, test, test before pushing it forward down the pipeline.

Hopefully these tips will provide you a good and solid base for your models and get you ready to implement your modeling assets into the next stage— rigging!

Note

1 A small detail, usually made up of primitive shapes (cylinders, rectangles, spheres) that add visual complexity to an object, making it look more interesting.

Chapter 3
Rigging Concepts

An Overview of Rigging

Rigging, alongside procedural VFX such as particles and dynamics, are probably the most complex and challenging areas in the 3D pipeline. In addition to the creative aspect of it, they offer for the most part technical challenges that are not found to the same extent in the other production departments. Riggers usually embody a combination of artistic skill and technical know-how. They oftentimes have to create their own custom tools to automate and simplify the rigging process as well as dig into the guts of the 3D software to get some obscure function or particular feature tweak to work properly. Rigging using only the default available tools is doable, but it will take some time to set up properly. Eventually it will work out, but in terms of the functionality of the rig, certain elements will be limited in their scope. This is mainly due to the constraints and limitations of what the 3D software offers out of the box. There are only so many tools and options that can be made available by default. Now imagine repeating that process over and over to meet your production requirements. The time taken to do so properly and the potential for human error increase exponentially. And, honestly, the dull repetitiveness of re-rigging yet another character in a cast of hundreds can drive anyone bonkers. This is where a good, solid understanding of the rigging options available comes into play, as well as being aware of the process of automating the rigging pipeline as efficiently as possible. Of course, not everything can be automated, but if you can create custom tools to help the process along and save some time to focus more on the creative aspects, then the production flow becomes more enjoyable and less tedious.

We will explore and attempt to unravel the intricacies of the rigging process throughout the book, and hopefully offer a new perspective to this sometimes misunderstood skill.

The Basics

Before jumping into specific details, let's review a few basic core concepts first. As mentioned in the book's introduction, the software of choice for this project is Autodesk's Maya 2015. We will discuss Maya's structure in order to explain these notions. For the most part, the general structure can be applied to other 3D packages with some slight modifications.

Nodes and Connections

Maya's architectural foundation is based on individual nodes connected and communicating with one another. For example, let's create a default polygon cube, and apply a **Bevel** and **Smooth** operators to it (see figure 3.1). To understand what went into making this unassuming little box, let's open the **Hypergraph**. If you look under the **Window** menu, you'll see **Hypergraph: Hierarchy** and **Hypergraph: Connections**. It's important to make the distinction between these two views.

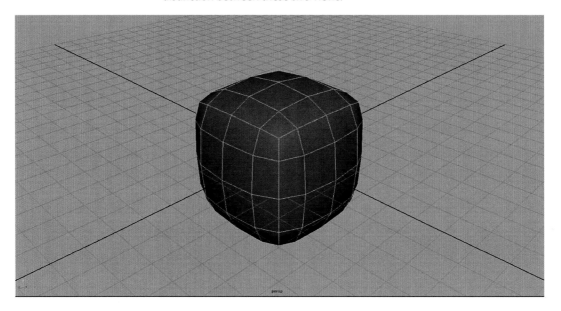

FIGURE 3.1 **Smoothed and beveled poly cube**

Hypergraph: Hierarchy (see figure 3.2)—this view shows the **DAG** (directed acyclic graph) nodes. These nodes are a specialized type of *dependency graph* nodes (explained below). The main use of DAG nodes is to show the Transform and Shape nodes of an object. The Shape nodes represent the data that defines an object. The Transform nodes are the enablers that allow the Shape nodes to be positioned, rotated, scaled, etc. in the 3D environment. DAG nodes connect to one another via a *linear* hierarchical structure. This would be similar to a fractal or a tree structure, where one top node can have multiple branches, and in turn, each branch can have additional branches of their own, and on and on. In our example, since the default view only shows the Transform node, we see the cube node by its lonely self. Think of DAG nodes this way: any node that you select in the viewport when you're in Object Mode and that you can manipulate is a DAG node. To see the relationship between the Transform and Shape nodes, select **Options > Display >**

Shape Nodes in the Hypergraph, and you will then see the Shape DAG node connected to the Transform node.

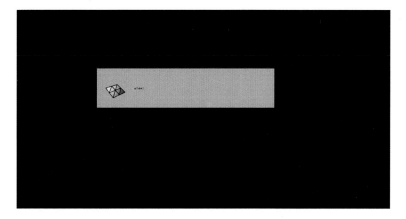

FIGURE 3.2 **Hypergraph: Hierarchy of cube. DAG (direct acyclic graph) node**

Hypergraph: Connections (see figure 3.3)—This view of the Hypergraph shows the *DG* (dependency graph) nodes. These are the building blocks of Maya and represent the connections, attributes and overall makeup of all of the elements within Maya. The main difference is that, as opposed to unidirectional DAG nodes, DG nodes can be looped on themselves—or

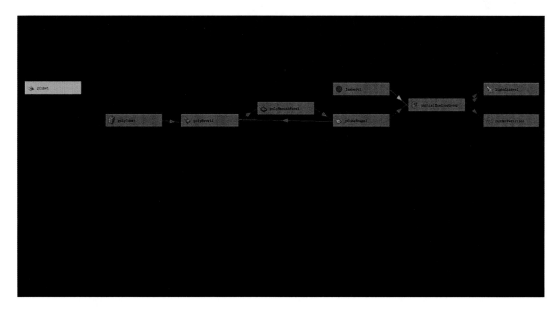

FIGURE 3.3 **Hypergraph: Connections of cube. DG (dependency graph) nodes**

cycled. It is not a good idea to do so, since it can cause a state of an infinite loop—but the option is available, albeit with Maya throwing in a warning of following up with such an action. With the cube object selected, we can see the various DG nodes that went into creating our smoothed and beveled cube. Notice also how *pCubeShape1* creates a cycle back to the *polyBevel1* node as well as continuing forward into the *initialShadingGroup* node.

If you understand the concept of those two types of connection nodes, dealing with Maya becomes a little bit easier. It's like a logic puzzle, and figuring out what goes where and understanding the effects the nodes have on each other depends on how they are connected.

There are a few ways to see, edit and manipulate the DAG and DG nodes in Maya. The first, as we saw, is the Hypergraph and its two views—one each for DAG and DG nodes. Another way to show the DAG nodes is the Outliner (**Window > Outliner**). The Outliner shows a hierarchical list of all the objects in the scene, similar to what you would see in an OS file manager. It will not show DG node connections, only parent/child nodes.

A neat little trick that surprisingly a lot of Maya users still don't know about or simply don't use is the ability to split the Outliner into two. If you place your cursor at the bottom of the Outliner window, you'll see a dotted line (see figure 3.4). You can drag that line up and now have two Outliners instead of one. It makes it easier to manipulate objects around without worrying about dragging/scrolling around the Outliner view.

For viewing DG nodes, the Hypershade has been a staple since the first days of Maya, when CG dinosaurs roamed the cinema screens. A new and welcome addition since Maya 2013 has been the node editor (**Window > Node Editor**) (see figure 3.5). It has similar features as the Hypershade, and adds the functionality of the connection editor and hypergraph. In my opinion, it's more neatly organized and put together than the other editors separately.

> **NOTE:** A major component of working with DG nodes is the fact that **Construction History** is enabled (it's on by default, although you can turn it off). Almost every action creates a node in the construction history of the object you're working on. At times, the object's history can become complex and unruly and begins affecting Maya's performance.
>
> A way to remove the history is by selecting **Edit > Delete by Type > History**. This will clear up all the input nodes connected to the object up to that point. Mind you, if you have animation on an object or are using blendshapes, deleting history might not be such a great idea. Another option, if you only want to keep the deformer connections intact, is to **Edit > Delete by Type > Non-Deformer History**.

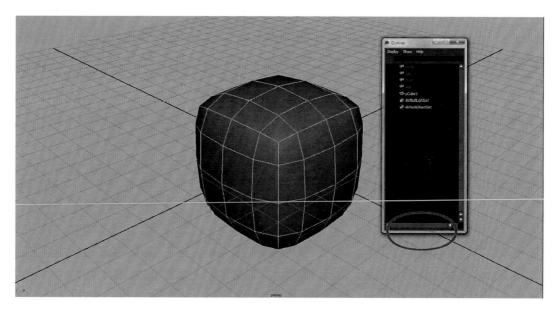

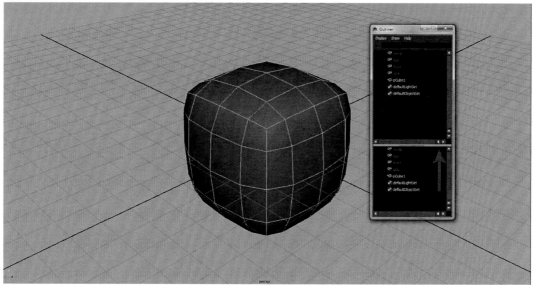

FIGURE 3.4 Split Outliner (2 images)

Parenting

Scene hierarchy—or more commonly known as *parenting*—is the grouping of child nodes under a parent node. It is considered to be one of the primary and basic functions of 3D object manipulation, and I will safely assume that you,

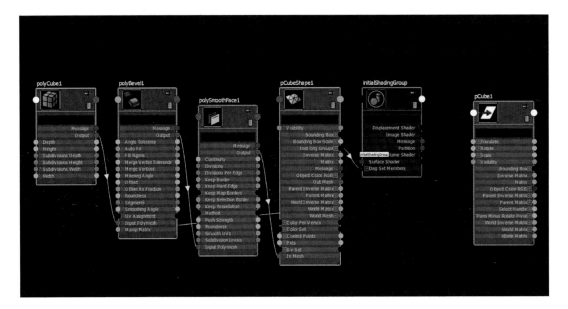

FIGURE 3.5 **Node editor**

Dear Reader, are familiar with its uses. Nevertheless, I will dedicate a few lines to this action, since it is one of the foundations of good rigging.

As mentioned above, the parenting structure can be compared to a tree or a fractal. It follows a top-down arrangement whereas a parent node can have multiple child nodes, but not vice versa (child with multiple parent nodes). There is an exception that we will discuss shortly, but as a rule, 3D scene hierarchies constitute a single-parent family.

The idea behind parenting is that any transformations applied to the parent node will affect the child node(s), but the child nodes are still independent to transform on their own. Here's an example. Let's say you're taking the train to travel to another city. Until you actually board the train, your movements are relative to the world beneath your feet. Once you're in the train, and the train begins to move and make its way to its destination, you still have the ability to move around inside it. Your point of reference, though, has changed and it is now relative to the train and not the world anymore.

If we apply the same principle to the objects in our scene, we'll get a similar result. By default, any object that is created in Maya is a child of the 3D world space and transforms relative to the scene's origin. As soon as that object gets parented to another object, its coordinate reference changes relative to that of its parent node. In this example, the yellow sphere is parented to the blue cube. The cube has moved 4 units in the Z-axis. If we move the yellow sphere

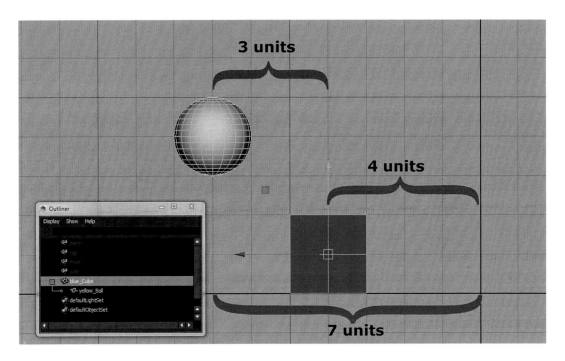

FIGURE 3.6 Translating a child sphere in relation to the parent cube

an additional 3 units in the Z-axis (see figure 3.6), you can see that although it is 7 units from the origin, it still shows only 3 units in the translate Z channel, as it is relative to the position of the blue cube.

There are a few ways to parent objects to each other. The selection order is important. In parenting, the child nodes get selected first and the parent is always the last selected object. The first way is to select the child objects and in the outliner or hypergraph, middle mouse button (MMB)–drag and drop them onto the parent node. Another way is to select the child nodes first, followed by the parent node, and press "p" on your keyboard —which is the default shortcut to **Edit > Parent**.

When nodes are parented to each other, you'll notice that it's the top Transform node that gets parented, not the Shape node! Here's a quick example: Let's make a three-ringed rotation control widget. Go to **Create > NURBS Primitives > Circle >** □ and create 3 circles, making sure that each one has a different axis, starting with X. (see figure 3.7). Name them **circleX**, **circleY** and **circleZ**. Open up the Hypergraph: Hierarchy and make sure that the Shapes nodes option is enabled (**Options > Display > Shape Nodes**). You will see the three Transform nodes for each of the circles you've created, and, connected to each, its associated Shape node. Next, parent **circleZ** to **circleY**, and **circleY** to **circleX** (see figure 3.8). Now you can clearly see how

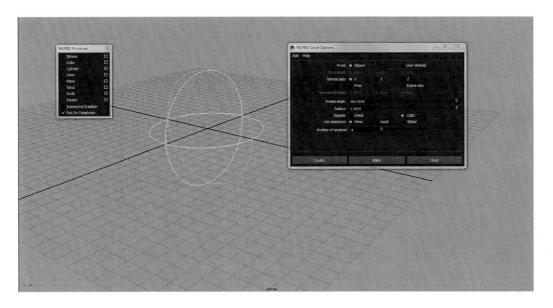

FIGURE 3.7 **Ringed rotation control**

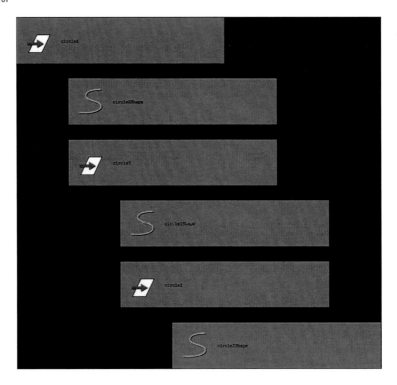

FIGURE 3.8 **Parenting of circles**

the parenting of the Transform nodes is represented. Simple, right? If you now select **circleX**, its child nodes will get selected, and any transformations you subject it to will propagate down the chain and affect the child nodes similarly.

So here's a question: Can a Transform node have multiple child Shape nodes attached to it? Why, what a great question! The answer is a definite yes . . . but it will require some finger flexing first. Let's use our circles again for this example. Unparent them from each other first (shift-P is the Unparent shortcut, or MMB-drag and drop out of the parent node). Now, if you try to simply drag and drop the Shape node on the Transform node, nothing happens. We can safely rule out that method.

We will use a simple MEL command to do so. In the MEL command line, type the following, and then press Enter:

```
parent -shape -relative circleYShape circleZShape circleX;
```

Voila! Three Shape nodes under one Transform. You can delete the leftover Transform nodes. It's a simple trick but it can help create complex control shapes easily. We will cover MEL commands in depth later on.

In regard to a child node having multiple parents, there is one exception. When duplicating an object in Maya, the default is to make a copy of the object. If you open the Duplicate Special options (**Edit > Duplicate Special >** □), you'll see under *Geometry type* the option to make the duplicated object an instance rather than a copy. Instances act like a visual pointer to the original object. A huge advantage is that they take up far less memory to compute compared to a copied object. The difference between instanced and copied objects is that any component modifications you make on an instanced object affect all other instances in the scene. Instances do have unique Transform nodes, so you can translate, rotate and scale them independently from the rest. As a test, instance a handful of polyCubes into your scene.

Looking at the Hypergraph with the Shapes option enabled, you'll notice that each Transform node from the cubes you've created points back to a single Shape node sitting under the original pCube1 you've duplicated (see figure 3. 9).

Constraints

Constraint nodes are another very important part of the rigging toolset that we have available. Their main role is to constrain a specific Transform node to one or more objects. These include the standard translate (Point constrain), rotate (Orient constrain) and scale (Scale constrain) as well as more specialized types of constrain actions that will be discussed

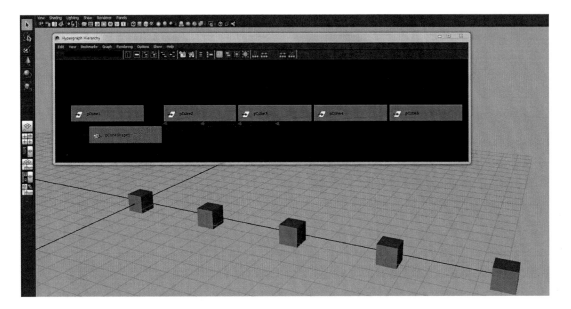

FIGURE 3.9 Instanced copies of cubes

further on in the book. They are found in the Constraint menu of Maya (see figure 3.10).

Some of the advantages of constraints include the following:

- **Dedicated Transform Nodes**—As opposed to parenting, constraints keep the Transform nodes separated, as opposed to in a hierarchy. The link between them is through a newly created Constraint node. The advantage constraints offer over parenting is a greater level of independence. The constrained nodes do not have to follow the hierarchical transforms that a parent node imposes on the child node.
- **Channel Selection**—Constraints offer the option of picking and choosing which Transform channels to constrain, unlike parenting—which "blankets" all the Transform channels of the child nodes. For example, you can select to Point Constrain only the translation in X of an object, and leave Y and Z unconstrained.
- **Multiple Constrainers and Influences**—Constraints can allow multiple objects to act as constrainers (*target* objects), each with a unique level of influence—known as *weights*—on the constrained object. In a parental hierarchy, a child node can have only one parent (except for when it's an instanced object). With constraints, there are no such limits.
- **Offsets**—You have the option to keep the initial transform values of the constrained object in the 3D world using *Maintain Offset* prior to being

FIGURE 3.10 Constraint menu

overridden by the constraint, or have it immediately aligned to the target object.

When setting an object to be constrained, the selection process is important as well. In this case, the target objects (the constrainers) are selected first, and the last object in the selection is the constrained object. It's the opposite of the parenting selection.

The importance and effectiveness of constraints will be explored in greater detail once the rigging procedures start taking shape over the next few chapters.

Direct Connections

Maya offers us a variety of options to make DG node connections between each other. The most common ones have been using the Connection Editor and the Hypershade. From now on, we will use mainly the Node Editor for our purposes.

> **NOTE:** Remember to close down the Node Editor when you are playing back animations on the timeline, or when you load files. It will slow down the system since it will try to refresh each of the actions by default. Load only the nodes you need.

As mentioned earlier, the Node Editor offers a more streamlined way of doing node connections, incorporating aspects of the Hypershade, Hypergraph, and Connection Editor. There are still a few areas where it might be lacking finesse, but using it in combination with the existing editors can provide a very productive workflow.

Let's analyze the structure of a typical node. The purpose of the node is to run a specific *compute* function unique to that node, process it, and push the result to the Output attributes. DG nodes have two connecting sides; an Input (left) and an Output (right) (see figure 3.11). On the Input side, only *one* connection can be piped into an attribute at a time (see figure 3.12). On the Output side, each output attribute can be connected to multiple Inputs (see figure 3.13). These attributes hold an explicit bit of data, tied to a descriptive name and a data type. The Input data bits get processed by the internal workings of the node's main *compute* function, depending on user or external node inputs, and the end result can then be exported through one of the Output nodes. The inner workings of the individual nodes are classified under "magic stuff". Ok, so "magic stuff" is maybe a bit of a stretch, but hopefully the theory of how nodes work is now clear.

The Input attributes of the DG nodes can be manipulated by opening the Attribute Editor (AE). The AE will show which attributes can be manually modified via data entry or manipulating sliders, dropdown menus, checkboxes, etc. It will also offer the option to connect additional Input nodes by either clicking on the small checker icon or dragging and dropping other nodes on top of the attribute name. RMB-clicking on some of these attributes will offer further options for setting keys, adding custom expressions, locking the attribute and more.

Each node specializes solely in executing the *compute* function that it was created for. They exist in isolation from the other nodes, simply waiting for an Input attribute to command them to run their *compute* process. A good way to imagine the workings of nodes is to think of a Rube Goldberg puzzle.

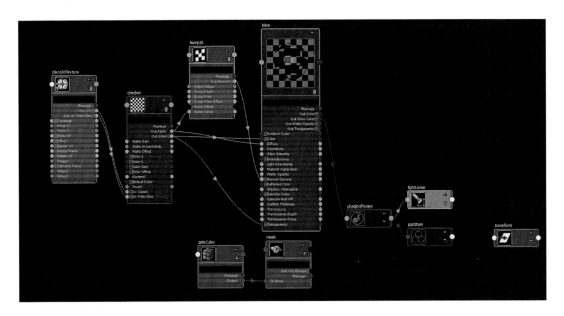

FIGURE 3.11 Node editor

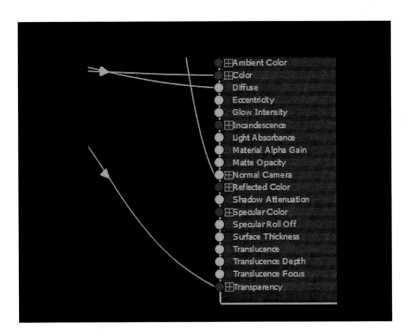

FIGURE 3.12 Node inputs. Only one input per channel

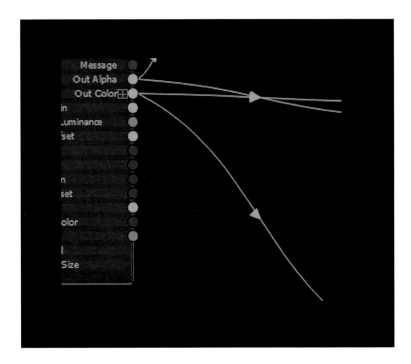

FIGURE 3.13 Node ouputs. Can be connected to multiple separate inputs

Separately, each element of the puzzle doesn't do much. They become active only when something triggers them to execute their specialized function, setting off a chain reaction which typically culminates in a boot kicking someone in the behind. Not that it would ever happen with Maya!

Knowing and understanding the purpose of the different nodes offered in Maya will definitely help harness the power of this great tool. Take a look at the **Window > Create Node** window, and see all the nodes that are available for you to play with. Think of this as a visual way to program—without coding (yet).

> **NOTE:** For more advanced matrix node manipulation, make sure that **matrixNodes.mll** is loaded in your Plug-in Manager (**Window > Settings/ Preferences > Plug-in Manager**).

Connections can be as simple as making a direct link between one object's attribute to another and progress from there in complexity through driven keys, expressions, custom scripts and plug-ins. We will discuss them in greater detail in Chapter 5.

Deformers

According to Maya's very in-depth help (which I highly recommend you refer to often), deformers are "tools that allow the user to manipulate (when modeling) or drive (when animating) low-level components of a target geometry". In other words, they are a set of tools that can alter the shape of our meshes, as well as give us control over their transformations in 3D space. Perfect for our cause!

On a basic level, deformers offer the user the ability to indirectly change the shape of the mesh without going into component mode and manipulate control vertices, faces and edges. You can stack deformers one on top of another to get various creative combinations. Remember, the order in which the deformers are applied will affect the end result. For example, I created a quick approximation of a screw (see figure 3.14) using the non-linear Twist and Flare deformers (sounds like a rock and roll dance from the 50s). You can see the cylinder pre-deformation (L) and post-deformation (R).

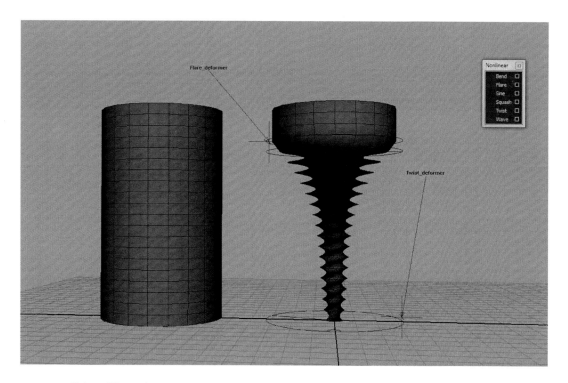

FIGURE 3.14 **Twist and flare tool**

As mentioned above, the sequence order of the deformers that have been applied on the mesh will affect the end result. Here's another example where two deformers were applied on the cylinder (see figure 3.15). The left (blue) deformed cylinder has a Bend deformer applied first, followed by a Squash deformer. The right (orange) deformed cylinder has them in the opposite order : Squash deformer followed by Bend deformer. Notice the shape difference of each.

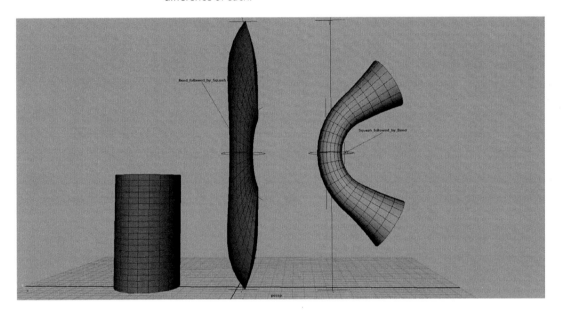

FIGURE 3.15 Deformation order on copies of the same object

The good thing is that you are not stuck with the deformation order stack. Maya allows you to re-order the deformations to get the effect you want. Here's how:

1. Select the object with the deformers
2. RMB-click the object and select **Inputs > All Inputs**
3. The "List of input operations for <object>" window will appear
4. MMB-drag the deform operator up or down the stack to reposition its order

It's a helpful procedure and can help debug some of the potential issues we might encounter while setting up our rigs. Troubleshooting is one of the key skills of a rigger/TD, and this method can help solve some of the problems down the line.

Here is a short description of some of the common deformer types that we will be using during the rigging process:

- **Blendshapes**—a very useful deformer that allows changing the geometry of an object into that of another object. There are certain limitations with this, but nonetheless it's one of the most commonly used deformers, especially with facial rigging.
- **Cluster**—the best way to control groups of vertices, CVs and lattice points. It's a very useful tool for modeling, but also for manipulating curves used in IKs and other types of dynamic deformations.
- **Lattice**—the lattice deformer acts as a cage around the object, with a user-set amount of CVs. By manipulating these CVs, the underlying mesh will change its shape accordingly. Used in combination with Clusters, you can create detailed rigging setups that can emulate organic-looking changes to the mesh, such as a snake swallowing an elephant.
- **Wire Tool**—this deformer allows the change of the mesh topology via NURBS curves. They are great to use with shaping eyebrow and lip deformations in a facial rig.
- **Nonlinear**—this group of deformers help provide basic shape distortion to the mesh and includes Bend, Flare, Sine, Squash, Twist and Wave deformers.

There are a few more deformers, each with a unique function, but the ones mentioned above are used the most often. These deformers directly affect the geometry but not to the extent that our next type of specialized deformer does. And now, introducing. . .

Joints

Setting up joints is an art by and of itself, and we will discuss them further once we start rigging the components in our production. For now, let's review some of the basics behind Maya's joint deformers in order to understand how they work.

Joints are by far the most common type of deformers used to rig and manipulate geometry in 3D programs. Geometry can be connected to joints via parenting, constraining and skinning and can be deformed in a myriad of ways depending on the parameters set during the binding process. They can be placed singularly or connected in hierarchical chains to one or more joints. Maya represents those connections between joints as bones. By default, bones are visually represented as 4-sided pyramids with their tips pointing at the next joint in the chain. Also, as you probably surmised, neither the joints nor their connected bones render.

To access the joint menu, change to the Animation module, and take a look at the **Skeleton** menu. You might want to tear off the menu for easier access by clicking on the dotted tear-off line. The first option is the Joint Tool (**Skeleton > Joint Tool>□**) (see figure 3.16).

FIGURE 3.16 Default skeleton menu

A few things were changed and added since the Maya 2014 version. If you are using an older version of Maya, there are still the tried and true ways of achieving the results we want. With this release though, the folks at Autodesk have added a few little touches that ease the rigging process and speed up some of the workflow involved. The most notable is the new **Symmetry** option, under the Joint Setting's roll-out (see figures 3.17 and 3.18).

When enabled, this feature will create the original (source) joint, as well as a copy (driven) joint on the opposite mirrored axis, as per your selection. For most situations, the X-axis will be the default symmetry axis, especially when rigging creatures facing the Front view. The driven joint is connected to the source joint via a symmetry constraint that connects the *Translate*,

FIGURE 3.17 Joint tool options menu

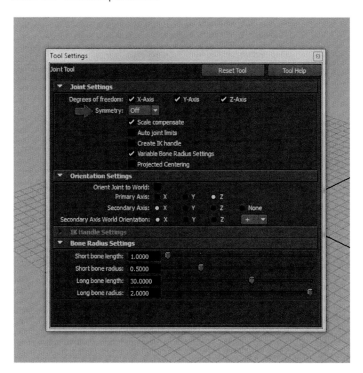

FIGURE 3.18 New symmetry function for joints

Rotate, Scale, Rotation Order and *Joint Orient* attributes. And to make the deal even sweeter, a new type of snapping option has been added called **Snap to Projected Center**. You can find it on the snapping buttons toolbar or by selecting the Projected Centering checkbox in the Joint Settings. This snapping function will position either joints or locators in the center of the selected mesh. Setting up the joints on your creature with those two tools will greatly speed up the initial joint placement process.

To demonstrate these features, I will use the Base Man with Shoes (see figure 3.19) (found under Silo's Custom Primitives menu) as my model. I've applied a Smooth deformer on the mesh.

1. Open the Joint Tool Settings (**Skeleton > Joint Tool > □**).
2. Set **Symmetry: X-Axis**.
3. Check **Projected Centering** (or use the snapping option from the toolbar) (see figure 3.20).
4. Dolly close to the shoulders and start drawing the joints from the clavicle down towards the fingers (see figure 3.21).
5. As you set the finger joints, you can pickwalk up back to the wrist joint by pressing the up arrow key, and start another finger joint chain from there (see figure 3.22).
6. Press Enter when you have finished placing the joints. You'll notice that the mirrored chain is highlighted in pink and that there is a Symmetry Constraint connected to each symmetrical joint (see figure 3.23).
7. Any changes you now make on the source joints will reflect on the driven joints—be it positioning, deleting or rotating.

To break the symmetry connections between the source and driven joints, you can use the following methods:

*   Delete the *symmetryConstrain* node directly from the Outliner or Hypergraph.
*   RMB-click on a selected joint (source or target) > **Break Symmetry**.
*   Select **Edit>Delete by Type >Constraints**.
*   To break all symmetry constraints, select the hierarchy from the root joint of the chain and apply one of the above methods.

There are a few drawbacks to using the Snap to Projected Center method, the biggest being that joints are not perfectly aligned to one another, especially if they will be using IK solvers. Point in case, drawing a joint between shoulder and elbow—unless the geometry is tube-like—and does not change girth/radius along its length; when using this snapping function, there will be a slight offset between the elbow joint and the shoulder joint (see figure 3.24). Certain joint alignments need to be placed on a flat plane in order to solve properly when they are manipulated with IK handles, or it might cause some issues during rigging (see figure 3.25). A good example of this are

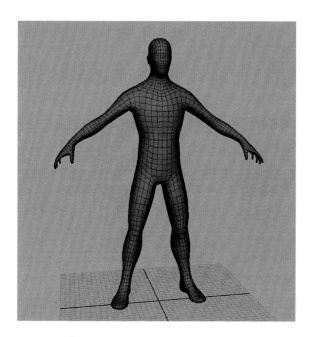

FIGURE 3.19 **Base man default mesh**

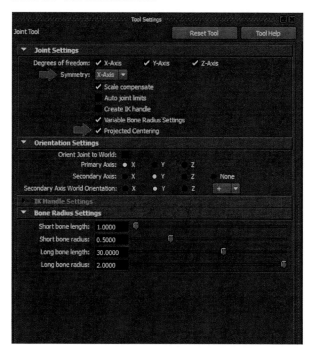

FIGURE 3.20 **Symmetry options in the joint tool menu**

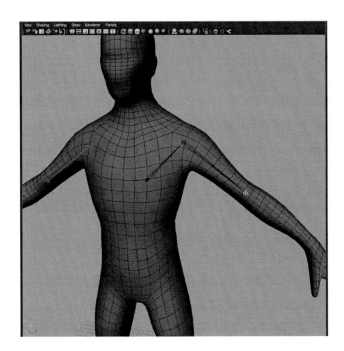

FIGURE 3.21 Drawing symmetrical joints on the model

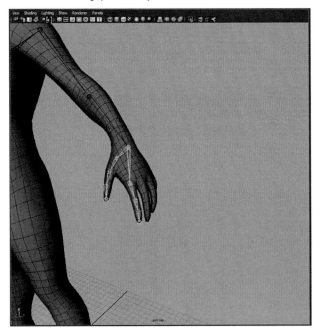

FIGURE 3.22 Pickwalk down the finger joints using the arrow keys

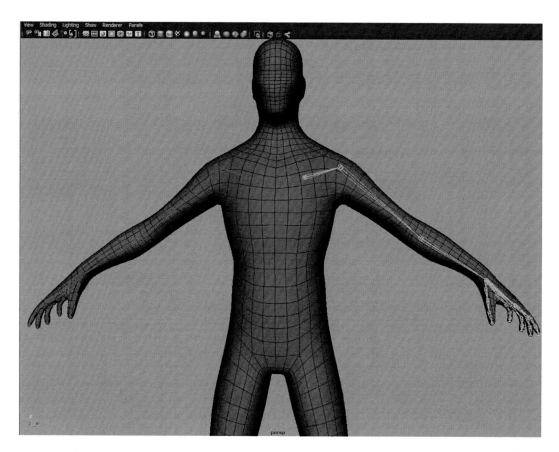

FIGURE 3.23 Finished symmetry on joints

Pole Vectors, used typically to control the orientation of knees and elbows on a character. But, it is definitely a welcome addition to the rigging arsenal provided by Maya out of the box.

Joint Orientation

One of the most important aspects of setting joints in Maya is to understand the concept of joint orientation. When an object is created in Maya, by default its pivot point is aligned to the World axis. Joints, on the other hand, have the ability to have their pivots created based on user input through the Orientation Settings and by drawing the subsequent joints in the chain. To explain this, we'll use a typical leg joint setup (see figure 3.26). To properly see the joint orientations, first click on the root joint in the chain and then select **Edit > Select Hierarchy**. Once all the joints are selected, select **Display >**

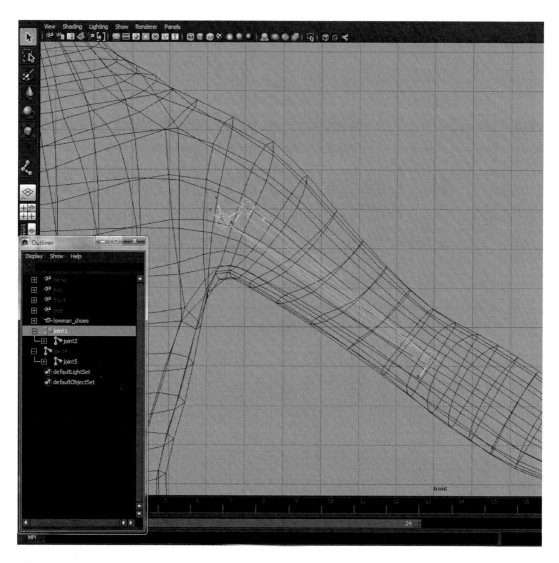

FIGURE 3.24 **Unaligned joint rotations**

Transform Display > Local Rotation Axes. This will display the actual orientations of the axes on the selected joints. What we see in figure 3.25 is the default XYZ joint orientation set by the Joint Tool settings.

Taking a closer look, we can see that the X-axis (red) is going down the length of the joint, pointing toward the next joint in the chain. The Y-axis (green) is

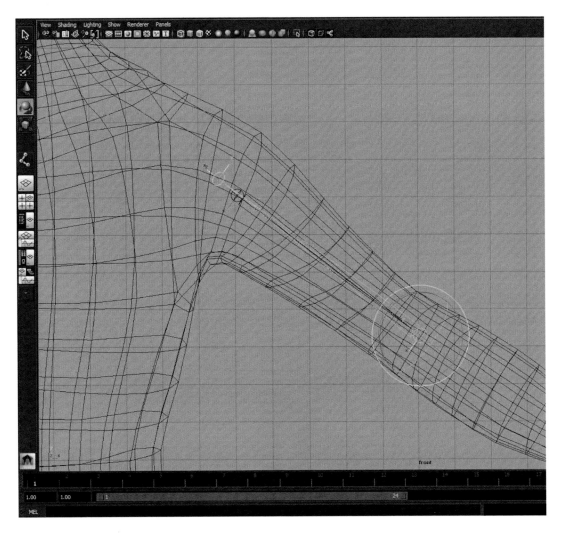

FIGURE 3.25 **Aligned rotations**

set perpendicular to the X-axis, and pointing upwards, towards the positive-Y in World orientation. The Z-axis, the third axis in the orientation, gets placed automatically at a 90-degree angle, based on the settings of the first two axes. A couple of things you'll notice in this leg setup (see figure 3.27):

1. The joint orientation in the knee is reversed.
2. The last joint (toe joint) is aligned to the World.

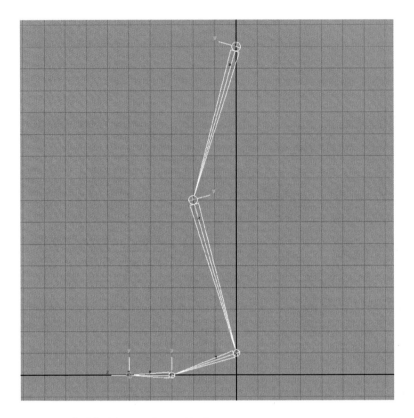

FIGURE 3.26 Basic leg joint setup from a side view

First, let's take a look at the Orientation Settings options we have available and see what we're dealing with:

- **Orient Joint to World**—by checking on this checkbox, all of the joint orientations will align themselves to the World axis, regardless of their orientation alignment.
- **Primary Axis**—this option sets which axis will point down the length of the bone toward the next joint in the chain. It's known also as the *twist axis*.
- **Secondary Axis**—the axis selected in this option will act typically as the relative *up axis* in the chain.
- **Secondary Axis World Orientation**—sets the direction the Secondary axis will point. That is also the reason why the Secondary Axis is relative, since it does not necessarily point in the World's up axis (typically Y-axis), but rather at the local orientation set in this option. You can select either the positive or negative of that axis.

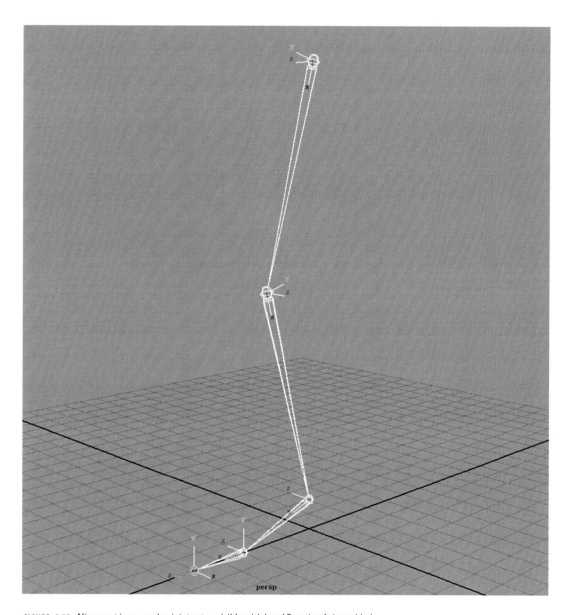

FIGURE 3.27 **Alignment issues on leg joint setup visible with Local Rotation Axis enabled**

Sounds a bit confusing, but bear with me for a bit longer and this will become clear. Now, since we already drew the joint chain, it wouldn't make sense to redraw a whole new chain every time to modify the joint orientations. The good folks who developed Maya have provided us with a useful tool called

Orient Joint (**Skeleton > Orient Joint>**□). You'll notice that it has the same settings as the Joint Tool, with a couple more checkboxes and a visibility toggle for the local axes (see figure 3.28).

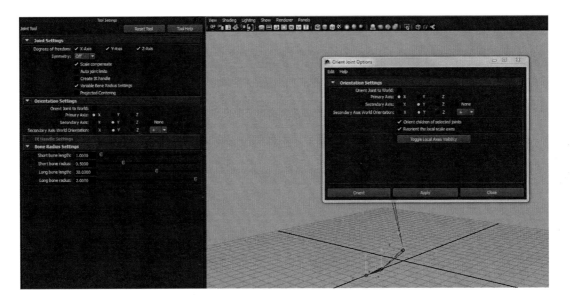

FIGURE 3.28 Orient joint tool options compared to joint tool

NOTE: The Orient Joint Tool options have evolved to their current look since Maya 2012. Prior to that version, the orientations were based on radial buttons with the different combinations (i.e., XYZ, YZX, ZXY, etc.).

We can change the primary axis to any of the three and create a variety of combinations. Some riggers prefer setting the Y-axis as the primary (Y-down) and the Z-axis as the secondary to match the traditional axis orientation. In other words, twist along the Y-axis, and Z-axis faces forward perpendicularly. It might also be a requirement from some game engines and motion capture setups. In some cases, the Z-axis might be the twist axis. Make sure you know the final output medium where the rig will be exported to, as well as any specific requirement of that software, if any. For the purpose of this book, we will stay with the default XYZ orientation, unless there is a reason to change it.

NOTE: The last joint in the chain does not get affected when orienting the joints, since it has no other joint to orient itself to. If you do want to orient it the same way as its parent joint, setting the Secondary Axis to None *should* work. As of Maya 2012, it doesn't for some reason. If by the time you are reading this, it still has not been updated, here's a quick fix:

Select the end joint and open the Attribute Editor. Look for **Joint > Joint Orient** values and enter a zero for the X, Y and Z values.

If you wish to automate this process, here's a quick MEL script that you can place in your custom shelf tab. Select the end joint, and run this script:

// set the Joint Orient values of the selected joint to zero

```
string $lastJnt='ls -sl';

for ($sel in $lastJnt) {

        setAttr($sel+".jointOrientX") 0;

        setAttr($sel+".jointOrientY") 0;

        setAttr($sel+".jointOrientZ") 0;

}
```

The diagrams below show how the different settings affect the joint orientation of our leg chain example:

1. **Orient Joint to World**—all axes are aligned to the World orientation (see figure 3.29).
2. **YZX +Z**—a common setup. If you look at the joint orientation, you'll see that the Y-axis is the twist axis and the Z-axis is the up axis. Since the Secondary Axis World Orientation is set to +Z, the Z-Axes are all facing forward (see figure 3.30).
3. **ZXY−Z**—a custom orientation setup. Here, the Z-axis goes down the length of the bone, the X-axis is the up axis, and the world orientation is set to −Z (negative Z), so it's facing toward the back of the leg (see figure 3.31).

As you can see, once the principle behind the joint orientation is clear, you can set up the joint chains to behave exactly as you wish.

The importance of keeping the local rotation axes of the joints facing in the same direction is to ensure proper joint rotation during rigging. A good example to illustrate this is an unfurling action, similar to what a spine or a finger would do. Take a look at figure 3.32. This chain was drawn using the default joint orientations in the Side view. As you can see, the rotation axes in the Y are not properly aligned. If you select the joint hierarchy starting at the root (**Edit > Select Hierarchy**) and rotate all the joints in the Z-axis, you'll get a weird unfurling like in figure 3.33.

There are a few ways of fixing this. You can use the Orient Joint tool, and change the Secondary Axis World Orientation to +X. This will make the Secondary Y-axis face in the direction of +X, and align all of the rotations

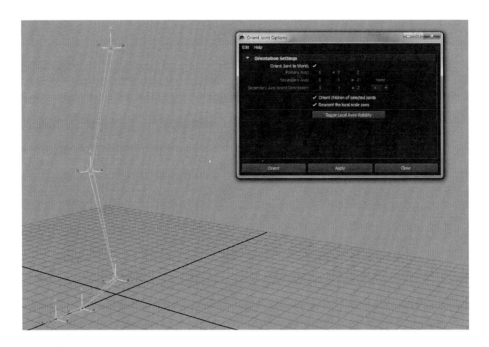

FIGURE 3.29 **Orient joints to world option**

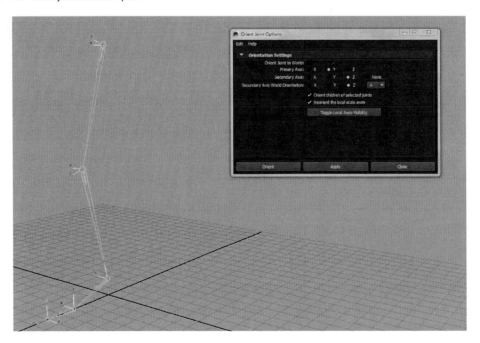

FIGURE 3.30 **Orient joints to YZX +Z orientation**

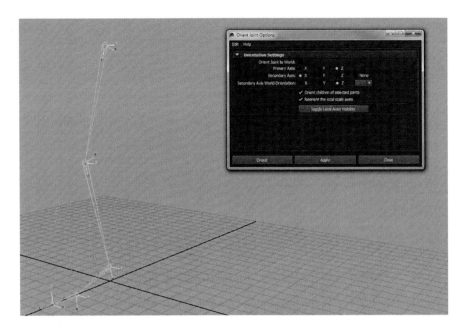

FIGURE 3.31 Orient joints to ZXY—Z orientation

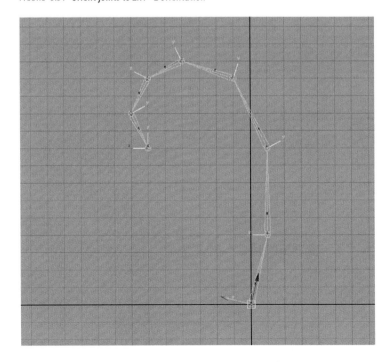

FIGURE 3.32 Unfurling joint chain with default Local Rotation Axis position

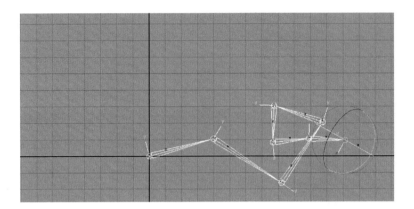

FIGURE 3.33 **Unaligned unfurling. Looks painful!**

properly. Mind you, if you want to rotate the joints now, you won't do so on the Z-axis as before, but rather on the Y-axis. Make sure you align all the joint orientations *prior* to rigging, since it will affect how the rig behaves, especially if you add driven keys, expressions or scripts.

Another way to do so is via direct manipulation of the Local Rotation Axis. Select the joint chain, go into component mode and click on the "**?**" icon in the filters on the toolbar. Select the rotation axis you want to modify and rotate it to match the orientation you wish. It works, but unfortunately, eyeballing was never the most precise of methods.

A much more efficient way—with perfect precision and a huge time saver if you have to repeat the action on multiple joints—is to write the following MEL line after selecting the local rotation axes:

```
rotate -relative -objectSpace 180 0 0;
```

What this command does is rotate the local rotation axis relative to the joints position (*-relative* flag) around the object-space axis (*-objectSpace* flag), 180 degrees on the X, and 0 degrees on the Y and Z axes. In other words, since the X-axis is the axis going along the length of the bone, it will rotate around itself 180 degrees, effectively flipping the Y-axis, reversing its position (see figure 3.34).

> **NOTE:** The Python command is very similar, but since we haven't yet discussed setting up Python for Maya, we will stick with basic MEL commands for the time being.

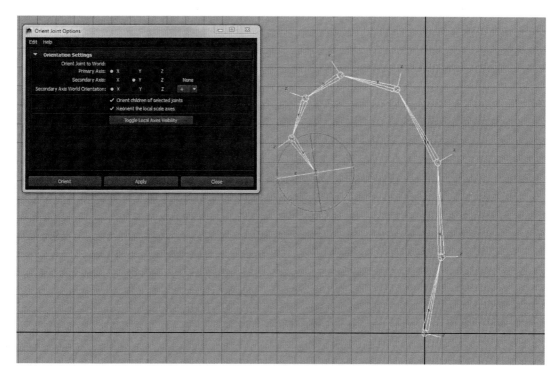

FIGURE 3.34 **Aligned unfurl joint orient tool**

Kinematics

The motion of joints in Maya is split between two camps: forward kinematics (FK) and inverse kinematics (IK).

With FK, the movement of the joint chains is done via *rotation*, starting at the root of the chain and moving down the joints' child nodes. Think of the wooden articulated artist's model figure or an action figure toy—the ones you used to play with, not the ones still shrink-wrapped and collecting dust in your closet, awaiting the famous "I'll-sell-them-on-eBay-and-be-super-rich" day. Let's say you wanted to pose your action figure like Rodin's famous *The Thinker* pose (see figure 3.35). Here is a verbal breakdown of the actions you would potentially take with an FK setup:

- You would rotate the thighs upward first, and then bend the knees.
- You would then lean the torso and head forward a bit, rotate the right shoulder so it's jutting out.
- Then you would bend the right elbow so it touches the left knee, and rotate the wrist inwards to point at the face.

- The left shoulder would be rotated outward a bit, and the left elbow bent so as to rest on the left leg.

If you followed all of this, you would have noticed that all the motion started from the core and extended out toward the extremities.

FK is great to show arcing, natural movement like the swinging of a pendulum or an arm in a character. It falls short, though, when you want to keep the joint

FIGURE 3.35 Rodin's *The Thinker* sketch

chains locked in place, for example like leaning in and pushing against a wall. This is where inverse kinematics comes into the picture.

In order to move joints via inverse kinematics, you first need to create a special handle to enable it. The default is the IK Handle Tool. You choose between which joints the IK handle will be created and connected. An end effector node (the driver node of the IK chain) will be created and sit on the last joint you selected, and the motion will be controlled through the IK handle via *translation*. The effect on the joint chain will differ depending on the type of IK solver you choose.

Some prefer IKs since they are easier to pose, but the interpolation between each key set on an IK handle is linear. You lose the arcing motion of the FK chain, since you are now translating the IK handle from one point to another in a straight line. To give the illusion of an arc, multiple keys will have to be set in an arcing shape.

As for keeping joints in their place, this is where IK handles shine. The IK handle can be locked in place through a constraint to a control object, and the root of the chain will move in relation to that locked point.

> **NOTE:** Depending on your 3D software package of choice, the equivalent to Maya's IK-Handles might be approached differently. Read the documentation that came with your 3D software in order to get comparable results.

There are a couple more types of useful IK solvers available. For example, the IK Spline Tool allows you to move a chain of joints by modifying the CVs of a NURBS curve. Another useful but somewhat hidden IK solver is the Spring Solver. This IK solver helps when rigging creatures or objects with multiple joints like insects or reversed-kneed creatures (usually found in demonic lore and such, or mistakenly assumed by mammals such as cats, dogs and horses that walk on the equivalent of the ball of our foot). To enable the IK Spring Solver in the IK Handle Settings menu, type the following command:

```
ikSpringSolver;
```

It will now appear in the dropdown for types of available IK's with the **IKHandleTool**.

Attaching Meshes to Joints

Joints, on their own, won't do much for your creatures and rigged objects. They have to be connected to the mesh in some form for them to be effective.

There a few ways of achieving this, some of which we've already discussed above:

1. **Parenting**—parenting the mesh to the joints is probably the quickest way of checking if the underlying skeleton works as planned. This method works great with non-organic objects made up of multiple pieces. They should ideally be grouped together in a logical construction and then parented to the relevant joint. For organic characters, usually low-resolution, proxy characters will be created—having the exact same dimensions and volume as their final high-resolution equivalent—and segmented around the main joint points. With this method, layout artists and animators can start blocking out the shots, while the final mesh and rig gets updated. The main drawback is that there isn't any mesh deformation, so keep that in mind.

2. **Constraints**—similar to the parenting method described above, but this time the mesh is constrained to the joints, keeping the hierarchies separated from each other. Takes a bit longer to setup, but you can use some of the more advanced constraint tools for additional control.

3. **Skinning**—Skinning is the process of attaching a mesh to a skeleton. It is probably the most common type of mesh deformation with the use of joints, since it offers the most amount of flexibility—pun intended. The setup is more time consuming and complex than the other methods, but the end results will be as detailed as you make them.

There are two types of skinning available in Maya: Direct skinning and indirect skinning. With direct skinning, the mesh is bound directly on the joint. With indirect skinning, a deformer such as a lattice or a wrap deformer gets bound to the joint, and in turn they affect the underlying mesh.

In the case of direct skinning, the vertices on the mesh get weighted to the joints around them. Each binding type affects how the mesh will react to the joint deformations as well as how they are manipulated once bound.

> **NOTE:** As of Maya 2015, *the rigid binding option has been removed*. It can still be accessed, although only through scripting. To emulate a rigid type of binding on your meshes using smooth binding, make sure the Maximum Influence is set to 1.
>
> If you're using a previous version of Maya, the rigid binding section will still be relevant. Keep in mind also that game engines *do not* do well with rigid binding, so your best option is to stick to smooth binding and paint the weights. Binding will be discussed in greater detail in Chapter 6.

In figure 3.36 you will see two polygon cylinders in a scene, both bound to an identical joint structure, but one is a smooth bind, while the second is a rigid bind. Both meshes were bound with the default smooth and rigid bind settings. Select the middle joint of each chain and rotate 35 degrees on the Y-axis of each.

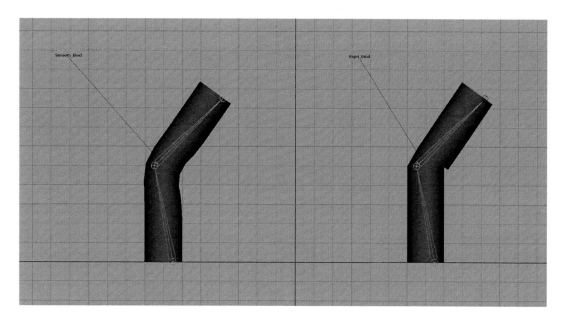

FIGURE 3.36 **Rigid and smooth bind cylinders**

You'll see that the smooth-bound cylinder bends and deforms the mesh in an almost organic, rubber-like way. On the other hand, the rigid bound cylinder has a much harsher bend, and part of the geometry actually begins to intersect itself.

Smooth Binding

The smooth bind method allows the mesh to be influenced by several joints. The influence area can be painted on interactively using the Paint Skin Weights Tool (**Skin > Edit Smooth Skin > Paint Skin Weights Too l> □**) or by using the Component Editor (**Window > General Editors > Component Editor**).

To smooth bind a mesh to a skeleton, select the skeleton chain followed by the mesh you want to bind and select **Skin > Bind Skin > Smooth Bind > □** (see figure 3.37). The Smooth Bind Options window will open up and offer a variety of options to affect how the joints will affect and influence your selected mesh. You can read a detailed explanation of each of the options in Maya's help menu.

FIGURE 3.37 **Smooth bind options**

In figure 3.38 (using Maya 2014 for this example) you can visually see the influence of the joints on the cylinder's vertices by enabling the Paint Skin Weights Tool. Older versions of Maya were limited to showing this information only in a greyscale ramp, but now you have the option to see it as a color ramp. It's a matter of personal preference and does not affect the functionality of the tool. To see the falloff skin weight colors, make sure that color ramp is checked under the Gradient rollout. Using the default settings, we can see that the hotter the color, the higher the influence of the joint on the vertices. As the colors begin to cool, the influence diminishes, until it there's no effect anymore. There is an option that takes any vertices with small weight values and normalizes them fully to the joint. These small weights, for the most part, have an insignificant effect on the mesh deformation. On the other hand, they can slow down the skin processing. You can prune them to speed up the processing time and keep the weights more even. This tool is found under **Skin > Edit Smooth Skin > Prune Small Weights >** ☐. You can change the prune value according to each specific situation. Prunes are also good for low-fiber diets.

The Paint Skin Weights Tool uses Maya's Artisan interface, so if you have a pressure-sensitive tablet, you can have finer control over weight painting. You can also set all the selected vertices in an object to 100% to a specific joint, which will prevent from blending influences, making it look like a rigid bind. Speaking of. . .

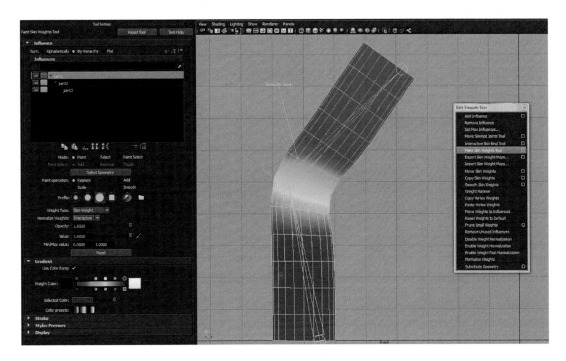

FIGURE 3.38 Smooth weight paint tool with a colored ramp

Rigid Binding

As mentioned earlier, if you're using a version prior to Maya 2015, you can
still use the rigid binding option from the menu. As opposed to its smooth
counterpart, this method limits mesh points to be influenced by only one
joint at a time. The most common way of editing the rigid weights is through
the use of the Component Editor (**Window > General Editors > Component
Editor**). You select vertices or CVs on your mesh, and, with the Component
Editor open, you select the Rigid Skins tab. Each one of the vertices/CVs
selected will have a weight value beside it, under the column representing the
joint cluster it's connected to.

Another way to change the influence of an area of a rigid bind is through the
use of flexors, found under **Skin > Edit Rigid Skin > Create Flexor**. Flexors are
deformers that allow finer control over the vertices and CVs. Some of those
deformers are based on lattices, while others are sculpt and cluster deformers.

There is a way to also paint weights on a rigid bound mesh. Select **Edit
Deformers > Paint Cluster Weights Tool > □**. It follows a similar setup as the
smooth bind painting, but you don't have the joint hierarchy present like the
smooth bind. Instead, under the Paint Attributes rollout, select the joint you
wish to influence by clicking the *jointCluster.weights* button (see figure 3.39).

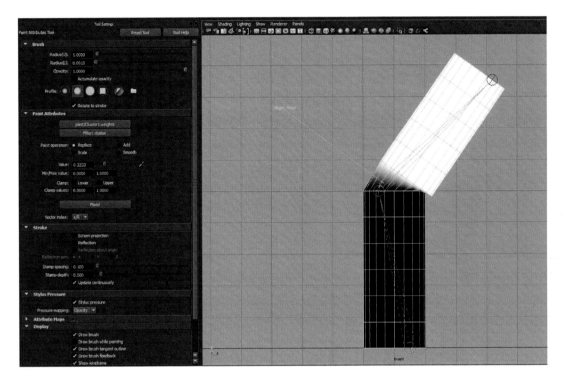

FIGURE 3.39 Rigid bind paint attributes tool

Introduction to Scripting

Up until this point we've discussed some of the main rigging concepts necessary to put a rig together. There are a few more which we will cover as we proceed, including driven keys and expressions. Right now, I would like to focus on both parts of our wonderful brains and get into the truly technical aspects of rigging—scripting!

The mere mention of scripting or writing any type of code tends usually to invoke some kind of instinctive primal feelings of revulsion and fear in many an artist. It's almost anathema to the creative spirit. Yes, scripting can be a daunting, intimidating and frustrating experience. But if understood properly, it can be a formidable tool in the creative arsenal of 3D creation. Rigging is but one aspect of it, and once harnessed, scripting can be used along any segment of the production pipeline.

Scripting can be divided into two main sections. The first is to automate and speed up repetitive tasks. Any action that has to be done time and again can, in most cases, can be scripted. The second part of scripting is to write custom tools that will help production, and enhance the default functionality of the 3D toolset.

The scripting process can be as simple as writing a single command in the Command Line or be as complex as running a full suite of scripts referencing each other and running off a remote server. The limits fall only within what you decide you want your scripts to do.

Scripting in Maya

Maya currently offers two methods of writing scripts: The original Maya Embedded Language (MEL) scripting language, as well as the more recent introduction of Python (since version 8.5).

MEL is fully integrated with Maya in the sense that any action you do within the program will trigger a MEL function representing that action. It might call a direct MEL command such as creating a polygon cube (*polyCube;*) or call an existing MEL script to extrude a polygonal face on that polygon cube (*performPolyExtrude 0;*). Maya's user interface is an amalgamation of MEL scripts working together, executing and updating the actions done within the program. One of the biggest strengths of MEL is that most commands implemented within Maya will be echoed in the **Script Editor**. This offers a glimpse into the inner workings of Maya and can increase your understanding of MEL scripting as you gain experience with the language.

Another one of the advantages of MEL is that it offers a wide legacy of scripts that have been written since Maya first came out. You can find online an enormous amount of MEL scripts which you can dissect and learn from (www. creativecrash.com is a great resource for MEL scripts). As well, you can go into your Maya installation folder and look at the **scripts** directory. In there, you will find the core scripts that run the Maya interface and see what went into making the various tools and options offered in the program.

> **WARNING**: make sure you copy those MEL scripts or folders first in a separate location **before** you start mucking around with them. You don't want to break Maya.

Once you familiarize yourself with the workings of MEL, it is a relatively simple scripting language to pick up and work with. It uses a similar syntax to the C-language family, meaning ending code lines with a semi-colon, curly brackets to define procedures and identifying variables with the $ sign in front of them.

Python, while relatively a newcomer to Maya, has been around for years and has an extended and loyal community supporting it. A very important distinction to be aware of is that while MEL is uniquely tied to work *only* with Maya, Python can be used completely as a standalone language. Because of Python's flexibility, support and adoption in the VFX industry, it has become one of the main scripting languages that connect studio pipelines between multiple software packages.

Python does have a few advantages over MEL as a scripting language, including that it:

1. Is object-oriented as compared to MEL's procedural scripting style
2. Has an extended set of data-types compared to MEL's limited one
3. Has access to Maya's Application Programming Interface (API) for deeper integration with Maya's core engine
4. Has large and comprehensive standard and user-created libraries of pre-built code and references that can greatly improve its functionality
5. Has great control over data types, especially arrays, lists, dictionaries
6. Has "clean" visual formatting (although some people might see this as a disadvantage due to its rigidity)

Now, unlike MEL, you cannot simply call Maya commands directly into a Python editor and expect them to work. You first have to import the correct modules prior to coding in order to have access to them. Python is effectively a wrapper around MEL, allowing the use of the Python scripting power but still following the command-based approach of MEL. In other words, think of a MEL in disguise—albeit with a faster, stronger and more flexible disguise.

There is also an additional way to script for Maya through Python, which is getting more and more exposure with each version of Maya. It is called PyMEL. PyMEL combines the power of Python but is organized in a more intuitive and clearer manner. It has obvious advantages such as brevity of code and clarity. As MEL, though, it is specific only to Maya. It is well worth exploring, though.

Options, options . . . it's wonderful! In the next few sections we will discuss both scripting languages in more depth and talk more about their advantages and limitations. We will also discuss how they build on each other to offer an unprecedented amount of control over Maya. Admittedly, more and more TDs and technical artists are choosing the Python way because of its power, but knowing and understanding how MEL works will allow you to take full advantage of Maya's capabilities and understand it better. Personally, I would take the time to familiarize myself with both flavors of Maya's scripting languages in order to have the ability to choose when to use one or the other, depending on the needs and circumstances called for in the production.

MEL

Scripting with MEL would probably be the easiest and most straightforward way to start taking advantage of Maya's power. Let's start with the basics and see where that takes us.

As mentioned earlier, most of the commands executed in Maya will be echoed in the Script Editor (**Window > General Editors > Script Editor**). Open the Script Editor, and then create a default polygon cube. You will see the following command appear in the history panel:

```
polyCube -w 1 -h 1 -d 1 -sx 1 -sy 1 -sz 1 -ax 0 1 0 -cuv 4 -ch 1;
// pCube1 polyCube1 /
```

In the viewport, translate the cube on the X-axis 6 units, and then rotate it on the Y-axis 30 degrees. You'll see a sequence of commands appearing, including the following two lines:

```
move -r -os -wd 6 0 0 ;
rotate -r -os 0 30 0 ;
```

The first action ran the command to create the cube. The second sets of commands reflect the transformations on the cube to their new position. Let's take a look at the way these commands are constructed. This will also help us later when we analyze the Python angle of things.

Looking at the *polyCube* command, we see that it is made up of the command itself, which tells Maya to create our polygon cube in the viewports, followed by a sequence of flags that set specific parameters on the command and ending with a semicolon. The flags in MEL are preceded by a dash and are typically echoed with their short form version. For example, the flag *w* stands for *width*, *h* for *height*, etc. Sometimes flags will have arguments following them, setting values or conditions. Another important aspect of the MEL syntax is that commands or flags that are made up of multiple words are camel-cased, meaning they always start with a small letter, and each subsequent word has its first letter capitalized. For example: *polyCube*, *reflectionAboutOrigin*, *polySphericalProjection*.

You will find a list of all commands and their corresponding flags in Maya's Help under **Help > MEL Command Reference**. It's a searchable, very comprehensive and detailed help system—so do make sure to make use of it when you're unsure about the inner workings of a specific command. A very useful feature in the help system is the list of scripting examples related to the command in question, found at the bottom of each page.

The Script Editor

Maya's Script Editor is a good place to start delving into the arcane arts of script writing. It is divided into two sections. On top, we have the history panel that updates the actions taken by Maya as commands are processed and executed. At the bottom we have the input panel, which is where code can be entered. There are two tabs in the input panel, one for MEL scripts and the other for Python. Needless to say, make sure the correct code type you enter is in the proper tab, otherwise it won't work.

Let's start by customizing the Script Editor to get the most out of it. Tear off the Command menu and add a check on the following options (see figure 3.40):

- Show line numbers
- Auto-close braces
- Command Completion
- Show Tooltip Help

The first two options are self-explanatory. Line numbering greatly helps with keeping track of where actions are occurring in our script and with debugging errors. Closing braces can prevent the annoyances of having your script not executing properly because of a forgotten bracket somewhere . . . something we are all guilty of doing at some point or another. The last two items are optional, but if you're starting out with MEL, it's a good way to see the commands and flags available as you type them. You can turn off those two options once you feel comfortable with the coding process and are more familiar with the different flags and arguments.

There are a few ways to execute commands via the Script Editor. In the input area, type the following:

```
polyCylinder -radius 10 -height 3;
```

If you press the "Enter" key on the keyboard, your cursor will move one line down. Bring up the cursor to the end of the line you just typed and now press "Enter" on your numeric keypad. Two things will happen. The first is that the command you entered disappeared, and the second is that a flat polygonal cylinder got created in the viewport.

The command worked, but the line of code we entered is now a distant memory—at least until you press undo and bring it back to life again. Do so now, and delete the cylinder from the viewport and in the input area to bring the code back. To run the code and keep it in the Script Editor, you can do one of two things:

1. Highlight the code, and press "Enter" from the numeric keypad (or CTRL-Enter).
2. Press the Execute All icon (double arrows) (see figure 3.41).

FIGURE 3.40 **Options on script editor**

If you want to get help about specific commands, you can highlight the command, RMB and select **Quick Help** from the dropdown menu. The Quick Help window will open up on the right of the input area and show all of the flags and arguments available for that specific command. Double-clicking those flags will add them to the command line, including the arguments needed to be populated.

> **NOTE:** The Quick Help, for the time being, shows commands and flags in MEL syntax only.

FIGURE 3.41 Highlighted code and Execute All button

MEL 101

Commands can be used on their own, but can also be attached to variables. Variables are like containers that hold information and can be called within the script. In MEL, variables are identified by different data types, as illustrated below:

- **Integers**—whole numbers, both positive and negative, without any decimals (i.e., 1,2,-738, 43, -64, etc.)
- **Floats**—numbers with decimal points (i.e., 4.56, 1.00, -78.904, etc.)
- **Strings**—alphanumeric characters (i.e., "The meaning of life is 42")
- **Vectors**—a combination of 3 floating point values (i.e., <<1.618, 3.14, 9.8>>)

In MEL, variables are preceded by a **$**-sign. In order to define a variable, it must be first declared. For example, to declare an integer variable:

```
int $meaningOfLife;
```

To store information in the variable, we'll use the = (equal) sign to assign it:

```
$meaningOfLife = 42;
```

For string variables, the value is placed between two sets of quotes:

```
string $wonderland = "Down the rabbit hole.";
```

If you highlight and run the line above, this is what Maya will output in the history window:

```
// Result: Down the rabbit hole. //
```

This tells us that the variable has been acknowledged, so to speak. To actually send back feedback and help in debugging our scripts, MEL offers a very useful command called the print command.

Enter this command in the line beneath $wonderland:

```
print $wonderland;
```

The result will be the value of the string. The print command is great for debugging scripts, where you can have it keep track of the actions taking place as the script is being executed.

Integer, float and string variables contain only one value per variable. In programming languages, there is a special type of variable that can hold multiple values, called an array. Arrays are defined by square brackets following the variable name.

```
string $elvenRaces[];
$elvenRaces={"Wood","Drow","Moon","Sun","Wild","Sea"};
```

As opposed to Python, MEL arrays can hold only values of the *same data type*. To populate arrays in MEL, you encompass the values in curly brackets:

Arrays are based on an index-0 system, meaning that the first value in the array has an index of 0, the second has an index of 1, the third an index of 2 and so on. For example, if you want to call out the "Moon" value, you would type the following:

```
print ($elvenRaces[2] + " elves are known to be impulsive by nature.");
```

The result will show:

```
Moon elves are known to be impulsive by nature.
```

Notice that the values in the print statement were encompassed by parentheses, and the textual element was added to the array variable with a + (plus) symbol. You'll see more examples of this throughout the book.

Arrays don't have to be populated with values from the beginning. They can be left as empty arrays and values added to them later on. These are called dynamic arrays. The next example will put this concept in practice, as well as introduce one of the most useful commands in Maya: ls.

ls stands for "list". Depending on the flags enabled when running the command, it will return the names and/or name types of objects in the scene.

Create a new scene and duplicate a handful of polyCubes in it. Select them with your cursor, and type the following in the Script Editor:

```
$selObj[]='ls -selection';
```

First, notice the backticks ' ' surrounding the ls command. You can find them to the left of the 1-key on your keyboard, along with the ~ (tilde) key. Anytime a command is put between backticks, it tells Maya to execute that command and return the action to the variable it is paired to. In our example, this command will list the objects you selected in the viewport (the DAG nodes—remember those?), and place them in the $selObj array. One thing to remember is that they will be listed in the order you've selected them. The list of flags this command has is quite comprehensive and you can filter through a wide variety of selections.

As you start scripting, either for yourself or for a team-based production, it's always good practice to comment your scripts in order to clarify and explain what went into them. Below, you'll find a couple of ways of commenting your MEL scripts:

```
// This is a commented line in MEL. You will see these quite often
/* This is a commented block. To close it, you simply have to use the reversed form of
the comment, like so. . . */
```

Anatomy of a Script

One of the staples of scripting is the ability to loop the code to affect a sequence of objects or variables. Let's say that you want to turn all selected objects into wireframes while the viewport is still in shaded mode, and prevent them from being rendered at render time. To make things a bit more interesting, let's assume that there is a child node attached to our main selected objects. In figure 3.42, you'll see 4 cubes, with spheres in each one of them parented to the cubes. The view is in X-ray mode so you can see through for your convenience, and so you can validate the veracity of said statement.

In the next example we will go step-by-step and detail the breakdown of a simple script.

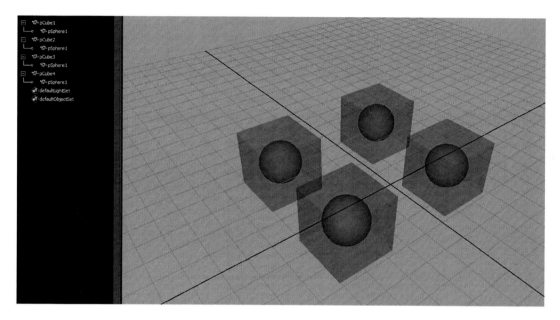

FIGURE 3.42   PARENTED SPHERES AND CUBES

```
// Create the selection array variable
string $selected[]='ls -sl';
```

Next, we start the loop. We will use a *for-loop* which is a specialized loop geared to work with array iterations. The format is: **for (element in array) {repeatable action;}** . The element variable does not have to be pre-defined.

```
for ($object in $selected){
    // repeatable action
}
```

Before we get into the details of the *for-loop*, there's one thing to remember for this exercise: the visibility attribute affects the Transform node of the object. So in this case, if we were to hide the visibility attribute, it would also affect the child nodes, turning them into wireframes as well. We want to affect only the Shape node of the object, while leaving the child nodes as they are. For this, we will need to drill down the Transform node and use the listRelatives command to get to the Shape node. Here's what we should have so far:

101

```
// Create the selection array variable
string $selected[]='ls -sl';
for ($object in $selected){
    string $shapeObj[]='listRelatives -shapes $object';
    // Print the shape nodes of all the selected objects
print $shapeObj[0];
}
```

The reason we use $shapeObj[0] is that in this case, the element in the *for-loop* iterates only one object at a time. And since our indices are 0-based, it is the first and only number in the loop.

The next command we will add to our script is the setAttr command. It stands for "set attribute" and allows us to change an attribute on the object in question. In this case, we will first override the **Drawing Overrides** option and, second, turn off the shading option. And, while we're at it, we'll also turn off the **Primary Visibility** of the cubes so they don't render. The zeroes and ones at the end of the setAttr lines, in this particular case, stand for "off" and "on". You can use this script to create polygonal control characters for your rigs (see figure 3.43).

```
// Create the selection array variable
string $selected[]='ls -sl';
for ($object in $selected){
    string $shapeObj[]='listRelatives -shapes $object';
    // Print the shape nodes of all the selected objects
    print $shapeObj[0];
    setAttr ($shapeObj[0]+".overrideEnabled") 1;
    setAttr ($shapeObj[0]+".overrideShading") 0;
    setAttr ($shapeObj[0]+".primaryVisibility") 0;
}
```

There are other types of *for-loops*, but we will discuss them as needed. All these loop types will make an appearance again as we discuss Python scripting in-depth a bit further in the book.

The true power of scripting comes from combining commands into contained functions. In MEL these functions are called procedures. Simple scripts can run with no defined procedures—especially if they're being run directly from the Script Editor or as a custom button from the shelf tabs. Yet, if you want to define a script, save it and re-use it in Maya, you will need to start defining procedures to call and execute the code in them.

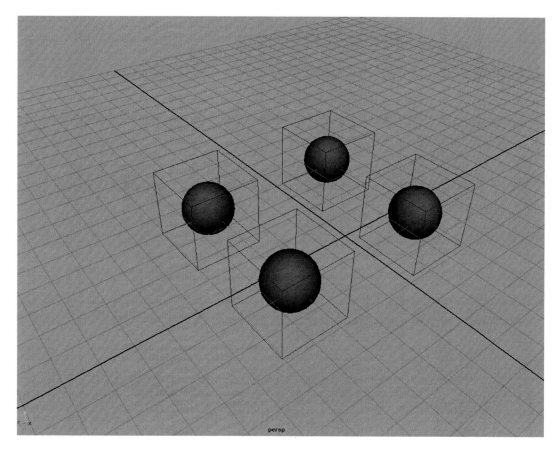

FIGURE 3.43 **End result of *for-loop* overriding the visibility of the cubes (shown as wireframe)**

Think of each procedure as a cog in a machine, with each cog in charge of certain behaviors or calculations. When combined together, these cogs execute their dedicated function and make the machine run smoothly and effectively. You can define in your script, for example, a procedure that will create the GUI and user interaction, a procedure for error checks, and specific procedures for each type of calculation you want Maya to run on your objects.

There are two types of available procedures: local and global. Local procedures are the default, and they are declared as follows:

```
proc procedureName() {
    // executable code
}
```

The difference between local and global procedures is that local procedures can be called only within the scope of the script in which they were created. Global procedures, on the other hand, can be called and made available from anywhere. As an example, you can have a library of custom scripts, where *scriptA.mel* calls on a global procedure defined by *scriptE.mel*. You can combine global and local procedures within a MEL script, depending on the functionality you are looking to achieve. To make a script *global*, simply type the word *global* in front of *proc*.

> **NOTE:** A local procedure cannot be declared in the Script Editor. Instead, it has to be specified in an external script file. In other words, every procedure and variable created and executed in the Script Editor becomes global and remains accessible in memory, until you shut Maya down.

Here's a very basic procedure used to create a simple polygon cube:

```
proc cubeMaker(){
    polyCube -name "myCube";
}
```

Highlight the procedure, and press **CTRL-Enter**. The procedure is now in memory. If you type cubeMaker in the command line (make sure it's set to MEL), you'll see a cube show up in the viewport, going by the name of "myCube". Run the procedure again, another cube—this time with the number 1 appended to its name—will show up. You can repeat that command as many times as you want, and a new "myCube" will appear, each uniquely identified by the number attached to its name. Yawn! Ok, let's make this a bit more interesting. Let's say we want to specify how many cubes we want to create, and then translate and rotate those cubes based on their creation sequence, and throw some other fun stuff in there:

```
proc cubix(int $num){
    for ($i=0;$i<$num;$i++){
        polyCube -name "cubix";
        // divide $i by 2 and assign it to $x
        $x=$i/2;
        // move and rotate each cube in worldSpace according to
        // the function declared in X,Y,Z axes
        move -ws ($x*'cos $i') $i ($x*'sin $i');
        rotate -ws ($i*30)($i*40)($i*50);
        }
}
```

Execute the script (pay attention to the backticks around the *cos* and *sin* commands!) and enter the following in the MEL command line: *cubix 100.*

Guess what? I don't think we're in Kansas anymore (see figure 3.44)!

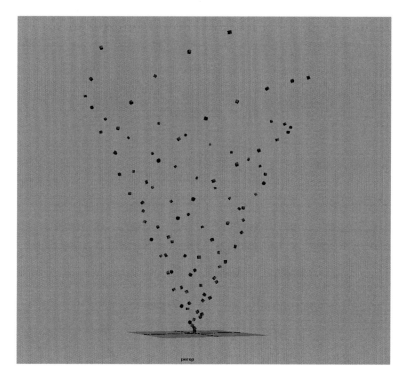

FIGURE 3.44 **Cubix tornado created through the script**

Procedures can also return statements. Place the type of variable you want to be returned before the procedure name. Here's a basic example:

```
proc string myName(string $first, string $last){
    return ("My name is " + $first + " " + $last + ".\n");
}
```

Run the procedure, this time putting your first and last name after *myName* as follows:

```
myName("yourfirstname","yourlastname");
```

The return statement will display the data you entered within the sentence.

105

> **NOTE:** the **\n** after the period is called an escaped character. When certain characters are placed after a backslash, Maya interprets them in a different way. For example, in our case, it means *newline*. This means that once the line is printed, it will go down to a new line.
>
> Some other escaped characters:
>
> \r   carriage return
>
> \t   tab
>
> \"   prints double quotes
>
> \\   prints a backslash

Saving the Script

As with most things in Maya, there are multiple ways of running your scripts. The first is to save the script on a shelf. In the Script Editor, highlight your script, then MMB-drag the highlighted code to the shelf. Maya should be able to identify the script language automatically. If not, you'll be prompted to save it either as MEL or Python. The one disadvantage of this method is that you are copying the full script into the shelf button, and it might make it awkward to edit and debug.

A better way is to save your scripts as individual files. The most straightforward way is to highlight your code in the Script Editor, go to **File** > **Save Script**. . . Maya will prompt you where you want to save your script, with the default *.mel* extension. There are 3 "scripts" folders available for you to save your scripts into, all under the ***<Users\<name>\Documents\maya>*** directory (in Windows). I personally save it under the "prefs" folder, but you can use any of the three. For me, saving it in that location means that I can back that folder up and zip it or email it so I can keep all of my custom scripts, icons and shelves all under one directory.

> **NOTE:** For Mac or Linux, check for the relevant location of those folders in the documentation.

It is customary to save your script with the name of your main procedure. Looking at the **cubix** example a couple of pages back, you can save the file as *cubix.mel*. It is also recommended to make the procedure global before saving it, so it can be accessed at any time, otherwise you might get a "Cannot find procedure "<name>" error. Another common practice is to put your initials in front of your procedures. With the amount of scripts available out there, you never know if someone might have used the same naming convention as you did. By using your initials, you reduce the chance of name conflict from happening.

For example, this would be the final version of the **cubix** script, set as a global procedure:

```
global proc eaCubix(int $num){
    for ($i=0;$i<$num;$i++){
        polyCube -name "cubix";
        // divide $i by 2 and assign it to $x
        $x=$i/2;
        // move and rotate each cube in worldSpace according to
        // the function declared in X,Y,Z axes
        move-ws ($x*'cos $i') $i ($x*'sin $i');
        rotate-ws ($i*30)($i*40)($i*50);
    }
}
```

In this case, I would save it as eaCubix.mel.

As a quick aside, writing short scripts in the Script Editor might be sufficient, but if you are planning on doing heavy-duty script writing, seriously consider using a fully featured text editor or a dedicated Integrated Development Environment (IDE). As I mentioned in the introduction, I use Eclipse as my main scripting environment—especially with Python.

Once your MEL script is saved, there are a few steps you must first do before it is ready to be run:

1. **Rehash**—when saving a script while Maya is open and running, you must first refresh and update Maya's list of existing scripts. To do so, type the *rehash* command in the command line. Closing and opening Maya will automatically update the script list, but it's a counter-intuitive method.
2. **Source**—if you decide to change the content of your script after you've saved it, Maya won't update it automatically. You have to use the source command to do that. The format is source <filename>.mel.

We talked briefly earlier about dragging and dropping your script to the shelf as a button, and the potential disadvantage of saving a long script as such. An efficient method, instead, would be to save the script as a .mel file and create a shelf button with the source command and the procedure name. Using our previous script as an example:

```
source cubix.mel; cubix;
```

This way, if you ever need to make additional changes to the script, it will run with the updated changes.

This was but a tiny fraction of what can be accomplished with MEL scripting. In the following sections and chapters we will expand our scripting scope using Python, with the occasional MEL command thrown in for flavor or simple convenience, as needed.

Python

I found that one of the best ways to learn a tool or related concept is to jump right in and immerse myself in it. In this next section, we will create the first production script for the *Tin* game. This script will allow us to easily create gears and cogs (a must in anything vaguely mechanical). Although it is not a rigging script per se, this will introduce some of the basic concepts of scripting with Python.

> **NOTE:** One extremely important point to mention . . . Python is an indent-based language, so the indentation order is critical, otherwise it will throw errors back. Due to the layout and formatting of this book, some of the code will wrap across the margins and will look wrong, especially with Python. The code shown here is only for example purposes. Please go to the companion website at www.thetingirl.com and download the properly formatted code for review.
>
> If you see a set of triple arrows at the end of a line of code (i.e., >>>), it means the code actually continues on that same line.

Python, like MEL, can be used as a procedural language. This means that it can run a sequence of contained subroutines or functions, each running a specific action in a top-down sequence. On the other hand, the strength of Python can be truly leveraged when used as an object-oriented programming (OOP) language, thus allowing the creation of modular objects that can be used and reused throughout the script(s). We will explore OOP further along in upcoming chapters. For now, in this first script, we will transition gently into Python using the procedural approach. This will offer a good introduction to the language as well as help transition those of you who do have previous MEL experience, to see and compare the language differences and approaches. The key right now is to note the syntax differences in the way Python calls the Maya commands and their respective flags.

In order for Maya to recognize the Python scripts, there are a couple of small things to enable in the interface. First, in the command line, click on the word "MEL" to change it to "Python" (see figure 3.45). Now Maya will know that you are entering Python commands. Just make sure to switch back if you go back to MEL at any point.

FIGURE 3.45 **MEL/Python command line**

Next, in the Script Editor, you'll notice the two types of tabs above the input area. Obviously, the Python one is the one we want. To create additional tabs, RMB-click in the input area, select "New tab. . ." from the radial menu and then choose the scripting language you wish to code in.

Unlike in MEL, where the core Maya commands are built in the scripting language—in Python they have to be explicitly imported. We will use the import command to do so:

```
import maya.cmds
```

This action will load Maya's core commands module and allow us similar access as we would have in MEL. For example, to create a simple polygon cube, we will type:

```
maya.cmds.polyCube()
```

The one drawback in this method is that you'll have to prefix every Maya command with maya.cmds in front of it. Not too worry; there is a more elegant way to do so using an alias:

```
import maya.cmds as mc
```

In this way, we will be using mc as an alias for maya.cmds.

> **NOTE:** You can use any alias you want, but it's recommended to stick with some of the standards to prevent confusion in case you wish to share your scripts. Another typical alias used when importing Maya commands is "cmds" (which you will find in Autodesk's documentation). Another method is to do completely away with aliases and use:
>
> ```
> from maya.cmds import *
> ```

This will bring all of Maya commands into the top-level namespace and there is no need to prefix it with anything. The possible drawback is that there might be a slight chance of conflict between Maya commands and Python commands. Caveat emptor! I personally prefer to use "mc".

Now, to create our polygon cube with the mc alias, this time we will simply type:

```
mc.polyCube()
```

NOTE: In Python, every Maya command is followed by a set of parentheses. Empty parentheses are the default command, while the command's flags will be within those parentheses. And just to reiterate one more time: Indentation is very important when scripting with Python.

Our First Python Script—tgpGears

Fire up your IDE of choice and type the following lines:

```
import maya.cmds as mc
from random import *
from functools import partial
```

We will be importing commands from the random module, which we will make use of further down in our script. This is one of the ways Python stays trim and light, by allowing users to bring in only the commands they need, rather than loading into memory everything including the proverbial kitchen sink.

As well, we will import the partial command from a Python module called functools. According to the Python documentation, functools allows "for higher-order functions: functions that act on or return other functions". For our purposes, the partial() function in this module will offer the ability to pass additional arguments to a callback function, for example when calling a function triggered by a radio button.

Navigate to your Maya scripts directory and *save the file* as tgpGears.py. In the next lines, we will create our first function. Functions in Python are the equivalent of procedures in MEL. I usually tend to create the first function with the name of the script and use it as a kind of gateway for other functions in case I need to check for necessary plugins, references, load UI's, etc.

NOTE: In Python, comments are preceded by the # (hash) symbol. To comment a block of lines, you can either use three ' ' (single) or """ (double) quotes before and after the commented block.

```
# Start main tgpGears function
def tgpGears():
    print "loading tgpGears UI"
    tgpGearsUI()
```

The def command defines the name of the Python function. In this particular case, our function will print the statement in the Script Editor and run the tgpGearUI function, where we will create the user interface for our gear maker script.

Creating the GUI

For the interface we will use Maya's ELF (Extension Layer Framework) commands. These are special commands that allow the creation of custom interface elements.

NOTE: An alternate method of creating interfaces in Maya with Python is by using the QT Designer application. It offers a WYSIWYG layout, rather than coding the GUI elements. We won't cover its use in this book, but feel free to read the documentation and try your hand designing GUIs with it.

This is the basic frame of our interface:

```
# Start UI function
def tgpGearsUI(*args):
    # check if window exists, and if yes, delete
    gWin="tgpGearsWin"
    if mc.window(gWin, exists=True):
        mc.deleteUI(gWin, window=True)
    elif mc.windowPref(gWin, exists=True):
        mc.windowPref(gWin, remove=True)

    # create UI
        mc.window(gWin, title="TGP Gear Maker", widthHeight=(326,330),
```

```
sizeable=False, menuBar=True, minimizeButton=True,
maximizeButton=False)

# build the UI elements . . .
# display the window
mc.showWindow(gWin)
```

When creating UI widget elements, Maya passes on automatically an additional number of arguments to the function. The *args argument inside the tgpGearsUI() function acts as a general catch-all for those unspecified number of arguments. This will help us prevent argument-related errors in the future.

We first have to check if the window already exists and if it is open in the viewports. Without this check, Maya would have thrown an error stating that the window is not unique. To prevent this from happening, we check if our window exists. If it does, then we run the deleteUI command to remove it. We will also check for the window preferred attributes such as size and position, and remove them in order to reset the window to its default size.

Next is where we create the actual UI window. The various flags and their descriptions can be found under Maya's **Help > Python Command Reference**. Use the search bar for the specific command you're looking for. Finally, we display the window using the showWindow command. Remember to save your file!

As opposed to MEL, we don't have rehash or source commands in Python. Instead, we will load our script by opening the Script editor and typing the following lines in a Python tab:

```
import tgpGears
reload(tgpGears)
tpgGears.tgpGears()
```

We first import our script into Python. The reload command is there to refresh the script, if you will. It's similar in action to the MEL source command in the sense that if you update the code, it will always load the latest version of the script, rather than what was originally loaded into memory the first time it was executed. The last line tells Python which function from the script to load. Highlight the code and execute it. You should see an empty UI window floating above the viewports (see figure 3.46).

NOTE: You might want to make a shelf button from those lines for convenience. After you highlight them, MMB-drag and drop those lines on one of your Maya shelves. You can now simply click on that button to run the script.

FIGURE 3.46 **Empty UI window**

Our next feature will be to create a drop-down menu that will reset our UI to its defaults. Go back to the script and type the following after the `mc.window(. . .)` command:

```
# create menu
mc.menu(label="Edit")
mc.menuItem(label="Reset", command=tgpGearsUI)
```

The "Edit" option will appear under our window title. When clicked, the "Reset" command will be offered. Executing it will call the `tgpGearsUI()` function, in effect reloading the script.

The next few lines will complete the creation of the UI elements of our script. They will focus on creating the various buttons, sliders, and input fields in our gears script. The commands are self-explanatory for the most part, calling for the various interface controls, their position within the UI framework, and any default values they might start with, and calling additional functions via commands. In the case of `tgpCheckType`, this is where the Python `partial` command comes into play, allowing for calling another function and passing a condition argument to it. We'll discuss that further down.

One thing to note—*make sure to give each and every one of the interface commands a unique name!* This will greatly help with querying the controls, getting information from them or piping information back. For the sake of brevity, the shortened versions of the flags have been used in most instances (i.e., *v* instead of *value*). Below is the full `tgpGearsUI()` function.

```
# Start UI function

def tgpGearsUI(*args):

    # check if window exists, and if yes, delete
    gWin="tgpGearsWin"
    if mc.window(gWin, exists=True):
        mc.deleteUI(gWin, window=True)
    elif mc.windowPref(gWin, exists=True):
        mc.windowPref(gWin, remove=True)

    # create UI
    mc.window(gWin, t="TGP Gear Maker", wh=(326,330), s=False, mb=True,
        mnb=True, mxb=False)

    # create menu
    mc.menu(label="Edit")
    mc.menuItem(label="Reset", command=tgpGearsUI)

    # build layout

    mc.columnLayout("mainColumnLayout", adj=True, rs=5)
    mc.radioButtonGrp("gearAxis", l="Gear Axis: ", la3=["X","Y","Z"],
        nrb=3, sl=2,cw4=[150,30,30,30],
```

```
        cal=[(1,"right"),(2,"center"),(3,"center"),(4,"center")])

mc.radioButtonGrp("gearBody", l="Gear body: ", la2=["Hollow","Solid"],
      nrb=2, sl=1, cw3=[150,50,50], cal=[(1,"right"),(2,"center"),(3,"center")],
      onc=partial(tgpChangeType))

mc.rowColumnLayout("optionsRCL",nc=2, cw=[(1,150),(2,100)],
      cal=[(1,"right"),(2,"center")])

mc.text(label="Name of gear set: ")
mc.textField("gearNameField", text="gearSet")

mc.text(label="Number of teeth: ")
mc.intField("gearTeeth", min=6, v=12)

mc.text(label="Gear radius: ")
mc.floatField("gearRadius", pre=2,v=5)

mc.text(label="Gear inner radius: ")
mc.floatField("gearInRadius", enable=True, pre=2,v=2)

mc.text(label="Gear Height: ")
mc.floatField("gearHeight",pre=2,v=2)

mc.setParent ('..')

mc.floatSliderGrp("gearToothL",l="Tooth length: ", cw3=[150,50,100],
      cal=[(1,"right"),(2,"center"),(3,"center")],
      f=True, pre=2, min=0.1, max=1.00, v=1.00)
mc.floatSliderGrp("gearToothW",l="Tooth width: ", cw3=[150,50,100],
      cal=[(1,"right"),(2,"center"),(3,"center")],
      f=True, pre=2, min=0.1, max=1.00, v=0.80)

mc.floatSliderGrp("gearToothH",l="Tooth height: ", en=True,cw3=[150,50,100],
      cal=[(1,"right"),(2,"center"),(3,"center")],
      f=True, pre=2, min=0.1, max=1.00, v=0.75)

mc.intSliderGrp("gearCaps", l="Number of body caps: ", cw3=[150,50,100],
      cal=[(1,"right"),(2,"center"),(3,"center")],
      f=True, min=1, max=5, v=3)

mc.rowColumnLayout("buttonsRCL",nc=2, cw=[(1,160),(2,160)],
      cal=[(1,"center"),(2,"center")])
```

```
mc.button("createBtn",w=150,h=40,al="center",l="Create Gear",c=tgpUserGear)
mc.button("rndBtn",w=150,h=40,al="center",l="Random Gear",c=tgpRandomGear)

# display the window
mc.showWindow(gWin)
```

If we try running the script right now, we will encounter an error, stating the following:

```
# Error: global name 'tgpChangeType' is not defined
# Traceback (most recent call last):
#   File "<maya console>", line 3, in <module>
#   File "C:/Users/. . ./Documents/maya/2015-x64/prefs/scripts\tgpGears.py", line 23,
    in tgpGears
#     tgpGearsUI()
#   File "C:/Users/. . ./Documents/maya/2015-x64/prefs/scripts\tgpGears.py", line 49, in
    tgpGearsUI
#     mc.radioButtonGrp("gearBody", l="Gear body: ",la2=["Hollow","Solid"],nrb=2,sl=1,
      cw3=[150,50,50],cal=[(1,"right"),(2,"center"),(3,"center")],onc=partial(tgpChangeType))
# NameError: global name 'tgpChangeType' is not defined #
```

Our script is looking for functions that we have not created yet (tgpChangeType, tgpUserGear, tgpRandomGear). When it doesn't find them within the code, it throws back those errors to let us know.

Let's fix that by creating those functions now. Enter them below the block of code we entered earlier and use the pass command in the body of each of the functions. The pass command creates a null operation—in other words, it doesn't do anything—and works great as a placeholder for future code that will go in the function.

```
def tgpChangeType (*args):
    # the pass command acts as a placeholder for the code
    # that will populate the function
    pass

def tgpUserGear(*args):
    pass

def tgpRandomGear(*args):
    pass
```

Now, if we run the script again, we will see our UI in all of its UI-like glory (see figure 3.47).

FIGURE 3.47 **Populated UI window**

Querying the GUI Values

Great! Now it's time to get those gears in working order. Our next function will check if we are creating a hollow or a solid gear. If the user selects *Hollow*, the **Gear inner radius** option will be available for modification. If *Solid* is selected, it will be greyed out. This process is actually related to one of the key components of good scripting, which is checking for potential user errors. The last thing you want your script to do is crash because of an unanticipated user function.

As mentioned above, the tgpChangeType function was called via the partial command. In it, the variable checkBody is assigned to the radioButtonGrp command **gearBody** that was created in the UI function. The main difference now is that instead of creating the UI buttons, it actually is querying (using the q, or query flag) which of the buttons was selected.

If the query of checkBody returns our first selection (*hollow gear*), then the UI stays unchanged and accessible to the user. This is done by setting the enable flag to true. On the other hand, if the second option (*solid gear*) is selected, then the option is greyed out. In this case, enable is set to false. The else command works well in a situation where a true/false condition exists. For multiple options, you can use the elif command (else-if).

```
def tgpChangeType (*args):
    checkBody=mc.radioButtonGrp("gearBody",q=True,select=True)
    if (checkBody==1):
        mc.intSliderGrp("gearCaps",edit=True, minValue=1)
        mc.floatField("gearInRadius",edit=True,enable=True)
    else:
        mc.intSliderGrp("gearCaps",edit=True, minValue=2)
        mc.floatField("gearInRadius",edit=True,enable=False)
```

The role of the next function in our script is to query all of the values from the UI and attach them to variables. Those values will then be passed to a function that will determine the type of gear that will be created and apply the relevant calculations to it.

The key aspect of this function is to pass those variables as arguments to the next function in our script, as seen in the last line of the following segment.

```
def tgpUserGear(*args):

    gBody=mc.radioButtonGrp("gearBody",q=True,select=True)
    gearSetName=mc.textField("gearNameField",q=True,text=True)
    gRad=mc.floatField("gearRadius", q=True, v=True)
    gInRad=mc.floatField("gearInRadius", q=True, v=True)
    gTeeth=mc.intField("gearTeeth",q=True, v=True)
    gHeight=mc.floatField("gearHeight", q=True, v=True)
    gTL=mc.floatSliderGrp("gearToothL",q=True, v=True)
    gTW=mc.floatSliderGrp("gearToothW",q=True, v=True)
    gTH=mc.floatSliderGrp("gearToothH",q=True,v=True)
    gCaps=mc.intSliderGrp("gearCaps",q=True,v=True)

    # pass the variables as arguments to the tgpCheckGearType function

    tgpCheckGearType(gBody,gearSetName,gRad,gInRad,gTeeth,gHeight,gTL,gTW,gTH,gCaps)
```

NOTE: I've prefixed the variable names with a **g** (for gear). It's just a habit of mine to keep continuity—and uniqueness—within the script. You'll find that as you develop your own coding practices, you'll come up with your own ways of doing things.

Remember when we started our script, we imported the `random` module? The next section will make use of it in order to generate random values, instead of the user entered values. The first step will be to populate each variable with a random value—including the minimum and maximum ranges of each value. Once each variable is defined, we will provide a visual feedback to the user and update the UI with the generated values. This way, in case the user likes the end result that was randomly created, they will be able to recreate or tweak it to their taste.

To update the UI fields, the `edit` (or its short form "e") flag is used to change the pre-existing values.

```
def tgpRandomGear(*args):

    # create random values for each UI element

    gBody=randint(1,2)
    gearSetName=mc.textField("gearNameField",q=True,text=True)
    gRad=round(uniform(2,7),2)
    gInRad=round(uniform(gRad-0.25,gRad-2),2)
    gTeeth=randint(7,16)
    gHeight=round(uniform(0.5,3),2)
    gTL=round(uniform(0.7,1),2)
    gTW=round(uniform(0.5,1),2)
    gTH=round(uniform(0.7,1),2)
    gCaps=randint(2,5)


    # update the values when using the random gear function
    mc.radioButtonGrp("gearBody", edit=True, select=gBody)
    mc.floatField("gearRadius", e=True, value=gRad)
    mc.floatField("gearInRadius", e=True, value=gInRad)
    mc.intField("gearTeeth", e=True, v=gTeeth)
    mc.floatField("gearHeight", e=True, v=gHeight)
    mc.floatSliderGrp("gearToothL", e=True, v=gTL)
    mc.floatSliderGrp("gearToothW", e=True, v=gTW)
    mc.floatSliderGrp("gearToothH", e=True, v=gTH)
    mc.intSliderGrp("gearCaps", e=True, v=gCaps)
```

```
# pass the variables as arguments to the tgpCheckGearType function

tgpCheckGearType(gBody,gearSetName,gRad,gInRad,gTeeth,gHeight,gTL,gTW,gTH,gCaps)
```

The previous couple of functions were similar in scope, both passing the gear values to the next function block, but each obtaining that information from different sources.

Creating the Gears

With the gear values firmly in place, the next phase of the script will focus on creating the 3D geometry of the gear.

```
def tgpCheckGearType(gBody,gearSetName,gRad,gInRad,gTeeth,gHeight,gTL,gTW,gTH,gCaps):

    # create a set
    if mc.objExists(gearSetName):
        print (gearSetName + " exists.")
    else:
        mc.sets(name=gearSetName)

    # get the axis
    gearAxis=mc.radioButtonGrp("gearAxis",q=True,select=True)
    gX = tgpGetAxis(gearAxis)

    # subdivision of polyPipe is twice the number of gear teeth
    gSubd=gTeeth*2

    if (gBody == 1):
        gStart=gSubd*(gCaps+1)
        gEnd=gSubd*(gCaps+2)-1

        # function to create a hollow gear
        tgpHollow(gearSetName,gRad,gInRad,gX,gStart,gEnd,gSubd,gHeight,gTL,gTW,gTH,
                gCaps)

    elif (gBody == 2):
        gStart=gSubd*gCaps-gSubd
        gEnd=gSubd*gCaps-1

        # function to create a solid gear
        tgpSolid (gearSetName,gRad,gX,gStart,gEnd,gSubd,gHeight,gTL,gTW,gTH,gCaps)
```

The first part of this particular function deals with the creation of a set in which we will place all of our script-generated gears. If the set already exists in the scene, the user is notified. Otherwise, a new set is created using the text field entry. Sets are a wonderful way of keeping your scenes all neat and tidy, and offer some additional functionality in terms of selections and setups.

The next section code section sets a variable to check the axis in which the gear will be created. The UI radio buttons get queried, and a new function—tgpGetAxis—gets called with that variable as an argument.

The rest of the function checks if the gear selection was a hollow or solid. Based on that information, the formula sets the start and end faces of the geometry to extrude the gear teeth from and passes it to the relevant function to generate the gear model itself.

Let's analyze the next bit of code. Until now, especially if you are familiar with MEL, you might have noticed that so far the majority of the commands in the script were very similar to MEL's own structure—apart from the obvious difference of Python's syntax. The tgpGetAxis function in the next segment will introduce us to a Python feature called dictionaries.

A dictionary in Python acts as a container that—unlike other lists which hold sequences of single items—holds paired items. The first item is the key to the second item's value.

Before detailing the workings of our particular dictionary in this script, we have to figure out what Maya does when a polygonal object is created and its axis of creation is modified from the defaults. Create a polygon cylinder, and from the options, change the axis from the default Y-axis to the Z-axis.

If you check the Script Editor, you'll see the following line:

```
polyCylinder -r 1 -h 2 -sx 20 -sy 1 -sz 1 -ax 0 0 1 -rcp 0 -cuv 3 -ch 1;
```

The detail we're looking for is the—*ax* flag. Notice that it has three values that follow it, one for each orthographic axis. In this case, both the X- and Y-axes have a value of zero, while the Z-axis has a value of 1.

If you recall also when we created the UI, the *gearAxis* radioButtonGrp had 3 label values—"X", "Y","Z". Each one of those labels has an index number attached to them, ranging between 1 and 3. For our example, we need to pipe in the correct 3 values into our axis flag when the gear geometry gets created. In cases like these, dictionaries really shine and make scripting very straightforward and clean.

As mentioned earlier, in the previous function, we queried the value of *gearAxis* and passed that on as an argument when we call the current tgpGetAxis function. The argument should give us a value between 1 and 3 depending on the selection.

We then create a variable that defines the keys in our dictionary. Key 1, which corresponds to the X-axis, will have a value of 1, 0, 0. Following this setup, we apply the second and third keys in the dictionary.

Lastly, we create a set of *if* statements that match the selected axis to their proper values, and that information is sent back to our previous function—tgpCheckGearType using a return statement. Very useful, these return statements. . .

```python
def tgpGetAxis(gearAxis):
    # create a dictionary with the axis values
    axisOpt = {'1': [1,0,0], '2': [0,1,0], '3': [0,0,1]}
    if (gearAxis== 1):
        return axisOpt["1"]
    elif (gearAxis==2):
        return axisOpt["2"]
    elif (gearAxis==3):
        return axisOpt["3"]
```

To complete our script, we will create the last two functions that actually build the geometry for the gears. All of the information we have collected and processed in the earlier functions will now be sufficient to tweak the primitive polygon meshes and turn them into our gear assets. Both functions work identically to each other, the difference being that tgpHollow uses a pipe primitive while tgpSolid uses a cylinder primitive.

```python
def tgpHollow(gearSetName,gRad,gInRad,gX,gStart,gEnd,gSubd,gHeight,gTL,gTW,gTH,gCaps):
    print ("Hollow gear")

    # create a polygon pipe primitive using the argument values
    # flags: radius, height, thickness, axis, subdivisionCaps,subdivisionsAxis, name
    hGear=mc.polyPipe(r=gRad, h=gHeight, t=gInRad,ax=gX,sc=gCaps,sa=gSubd,n="hGear01")
    mc.sets(hGear[0],add=gearSetName)

    # clear the any current selection and create a loop to calculate the number of
    # teeth in the gears
    mc.select(clear=True)
    for teeth in range(gStart,gEnd, 2):
        mc.select(hGear[0]+".f[{0}]".format(teeth), add=True)
```

```
    # extrude each face (tooth) according to the preset values
    mc.polyExtrudeFacet(ltz=gTL, ls=(gTW,gTH,0))
    mc.select(clear=True)

def tgpSolid(gearSetName,gRad,gX,gStart,gEnd,gSubd,gHeight,gTL,gTW,gTH,gCaps):
    print ("Solid gear")

    # same as hollow, except use a cylinder primitive
    sGear=mc.polyCylinder(r=gRad,h=gHeight, ax=gX,sc=gCaps, sa=gSubd,name="sGear01")
    mc.sets(sGear[0],add=gearSetName)

    mc.select(clear=True)
    for teeth in range(gStart,gEnd, 2):
        mc.select(sGear[0]+".f[{0}]".format(teeth), add=True)

    mc.polyExtrudeFacet(ltz=gTL, ls=(gTW,gTH,0))
    mc.select(clear=True)
```

The code is pretty straightforward. Once the flags for the primitive geometry are set and the number of gear teeth is known, a *for-loop* is created to select the relevant faces and extrude them out.

String Formatting in Python

The interesting—and very useful—Python functionality present in these few lines of code is the .format() method.

String formatting allows us to do complex variable and value substitutions in our code. It takes a bit of getting used to if you come straight from MEL, but once you get the hang of it, it sure beats concatenating strings hands down!

Here's a quick example of the. format() method:

```
name="Leaf"
job="tree mechanic"
drill=2
saw=1

print "My name is {0} and I'm a {1}. I have {2} power tools".format(name,job,drill+saw)
# result

My name is Leaf and I'm a tree mechanic. I have 3 power tools.
```

The values are placed between curly {} brackets (note that they are 0-indexed) and called in sequential order from within the .format() method at the end of the string. There are many other ways to substitute the values, which are too many to cover in this Python introduction.

This method is set to replace the older way of string substitution that used the % (modulo) operator. Here's the same example as above using this method:

```
print "My name is %s and I'm a %s. I have %i tools" %(name,job,wrenches+hammer)
```

At first glance, it looks the same, if not even simpler. The % operator can be combined with a variation of suffixes to represent various argument types, i.e., %s for string, %f for floats, %d for integers, etc. You will probably encounter quite a few examples of code still using this method, but according to the good folk developing Python, it is being deprecated and the use of .format() is encouraged when writing code from Python v2.6 and up. Some of the advantages the .format() method has over the % operator include added flexibility in terms of operations and re-using of arguments.

> **NOTE:** You can find the full documentation of Python commands at docs.python.org.

Congratulations! The script is complete and ready to be run in Maya. With this we complete the rigging overview chapter. The process of scripting touched on a few basic but important foundation concepts that will help you build more complex tools. This will aid you with the rigging—and general—pipelines found in 3D productions.

Chapter 4
Scripting Mechanics

Engineering the Fantastic

The act of solving puzzles can be one of life's most fascinating aspects. And I'm not talking about only us humans, either. Ever watched a parrot trying to figure out how to untie a knot, or a mouse work its way through a maze? Puzzles are everywhere, from mind-bending logical conundrums to simple actions like using a clothespin to hold a nail you need to hammer into a wall. They're all puzzles in their way, and getting to that "Aha!" moment (not the band, but then again—it was the 80s!) In this chapter, we are going to take that innate curiosity and use it to solve mechanical rigging puzzles.

A good way to help your audience relate to the fantastic mechanical creations that might spring out of your creative mind is to have some elements of them grounded in our day-to-day reality. In other words, if you theoretically could build your 3D mechanical creature or construct in real life, how would you go about putting it together? If you conceptualize your mechanical designs with enough "engineered" elements that give the impression that they are functional to the operation of your construct, the element of suspension of disbelief will be much easier for your audience to accept. I find that if you can envision and work out the mechanical aspects behind your model, the model itself, as well as its functionality, will be much easier to put together as well as control in a rig.

Our first task will be to create a rigging setup for pistons and springs. These, like the gears we made in the last chapter, are the basic fundamentals of most things mechanical. We see them everywhere, from the engines in the cars we drive, the self-closing doors in our apartments and houses, the retractable pens we write with and the fascinating inner workings of hand watches. Extrapolating those concepts, we can also easily imagine their functions in massive robots and mechs, wild steampunk vehicles and tiny magical clockwork creatures—pistons, springs and gears make the world go round, literally!

Python's Object-Oriented Programming

As we start writing the tools to create said mechanical elements, we will begin to explore Python's object-oriented programming (OOP). To recap from Chapter 3, a procedural programming language such as MEL lets us take data and pass it down as a sequence of ordered functions in order to be processed and implemented. It follows a top-down approach, meaning the scope of the data gets evaluated first in a general, high-level manner, and then it's handed on to smaller procedures, each in charge of a specific set of functions.

Object-oriented programming, in general, allows us to bundle together both data and functionality together in one object. We can then use that object, or call an instance of it and make additional changes to it without having to rebuild the original object from scratch. We will focus specifically on how Python approaches OOP in this book. I highly recommend you read more in depth about object-oriented programming in the documentation offered at www.python.org. Another great resource for all coding-related questions can be found at www.stackoverflow.com.

Classes in Python

The power of OOP comes with its use of classes. Think of a class as a modular template that defines how an object—which can be literally anything—will behave, as well as its default parameters. Once that class is created, it can be instanced and is fully independent of the originating class itself. In other words, the class provides the core DNA, if you will, of the object. Once instanced, that original DNA can be modified and built upon to create additional functionality through inheritances and polymorphism.

Here's a basic example. Let's create a class called *Book*. This class will define the make-up of a typical book which will include the book type, page size, cover and binding style.

We first define the class name *Book* followed by the *(object)* base class. Next, we initialize the class using the method *__init__(self)*: The *(self)* argument refers to the current instance of the class we're creating. Following the initialization of the class, we then set the various arguments that will make up our main class. They're set to *None* to establish that no value has been assigned to the arguments. The *self* argument in front of the variable names makes them unique to each instance of the class we call.

Next, we create a new method that will print the sentence, filling in the arguments in their relevant spot using the *format()* string method. That is all for our Book class.

```
class Book(object):
    def __init__(self):
        self.type=None
        self.pages=None
        self.cover=None
        self.binding=None
```

```
    def bookType(self):
        # code base would go here. . .
        print ("This is a {0} with {1} pages. It has a {2} cover and a {3} binding.").
    format(self.type,self.pages,self.cover,self.binding)
```

We can now use the Book class and instance it as a paperback class, hardcover class, magazine class, etc.

```
class Paperback(Book):
    def __init__(self):
        self.type="paperback"
        self.pages="small"
        self.cover="soft"
        self.binding="glue"

class Hardcover(Book):
    def __init__(self):
        self.type="hardcover"
        self.pages="large"
        self.cover="hard"
        self.binding="stitch"

class Magazine(Book):
    def __init__(self):
        self.type="magazine"
        self.pages="oversized"
        self.cover="soft"
        self.binding="glue"
```

When we define the instance classes, we name them and then call the Book base class within the parentheses. After we initialize the instance classes, the arguments get populated with their relevant data and are ready to be created.

If we were to run the Book class, we would get this result:

```
Book().bookType()
>>> This is a None with None pages. It has a None cover and a None binding.
```

Now running the instance classes:

```
pb=Paperback()
pb.bookType()
```

```
>>> This is a paperback with small pages. It has a soft cover and a glue binding.
hc=Hardcover()
hc.bookType()
>>> This is a hardcover with large pages. It has a hard cover and a stitch binding.
. . .
```

As you can see from this very simple example, once you set up the base class, it saves you from retyping the same code over and over. All you need to do is modify the argument data and the rest falls into place. You can find many more examples that explain the various advantages of using classes in the Python documentation. It is well worth learning how they work and expanding your understanding of Python (Google is your good friend in this case). As we write and explore the scripts in this book, I will explain how and why they are set up in such a way—which hopefully will help you understand further how the classes work and how you can modify them to write your own custom scripts and tools.

You might have noticed that I've been calling def as methods and not functions as we did in the last chapter. In a nutshell, methods and functions are basically the same, with this exception: a function can be called by name from anywhere outside the class and is independent, while a method is explicitly tied to the class. Same with variables: in a class they are referred to as attributes. I know, confusing.

NOTE: A word about self argument: it's incredibly useful when you want to retrieve the content of a unique instanced attribute throughout the class. Think of it as being similar to MEL's global variables. In other words, if you plan on storing the value of that attribute in order to pass it around multiple methods, then prefix it with the self argument. Otherwise, if it's going to be localized and used only within a specific method, there is no need to make it a self argument. There are many ways to go about this. With experience you'll know which one to use for your needs.

Building a GUI Framework

A good example of where to use classes would be when creating GUIs for your scripts in Maya. Rather than having to recreate interfaces for every script you write, you can create a standardized GUI framework by making it into a class, and then calling and modifying it depending on the needs of your script. In the following pages, we will see how to create such a GUI class. Once the basic principles are understood, any type of custom GUIs can be created for your specific scripting needs.

Let's plan the GUI framework first of all. There's nothing like a good scribble to get your thoughts lined up in a row. For this particular GUI framework we will need a main window, which will include a custom number of tabs. Each tab will correspond to a particular creation function. There will be two constant buttons (Create and Cancel) that will always be present regardless of which tab is selected, as well as a small info section (see figure 4.1).

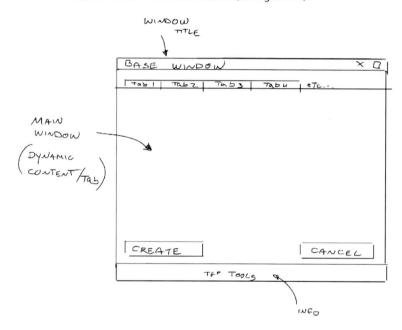

FIGURE 4.1 **Diagram of tabbed GUI**

Create a new Python file and navigate to the default Maya scripts folder (typically found in your *C:\Users\name\Documents\maya\version\scripts* folder) and save the script as *tgpBaseTabUI.py*. We start our script, as always, by importing the *maya.cmds* into Python:

```
import maya.cmds as mc
from functools import partial
```

Defining the UI Class

Next we define the class and initialize it with our default argument values, followed by a call to the self.createUI() method:

```
class BaseTabUI(object):
    def __init__(self):
```

129

```
            self.window="uiWindow"
            self.title="Base Window"
            self.winSize=(500,330) #default starting window size

            # the number of tabs has to equal the tab names
            self.numberOfTabs=4
            self.name=["firstTab","secondTab","thirdTab","fourthTab"]
            #create a dictionary for the tabs
            self.tabs={}

            self.createUI()
```

You'll notice that the self.tabs variable is set as an empty dictionary. This will enable us to dynamically create and populate the tabs and call their function later on.

This next method is the meat and potatoes of the UI class where all the elements are created and placed.

```
def createUI(self,*args):

    #check if window and prefs exist. If yes, delete

    if mc.window(self.window, exists=True):
        mc.deleteUI(self.window, window=True)
    elif mc.windowPref(self.window, exists=True):
        mc.windowPref(self.window, remove=True)

    # error check if the numberOfTabs is equal to the name[]
    if (self.numberOfTabs!=len(self.name)):
                mc.warning("# of tabs and names are not equal!")
                pass
    else:

            #create the main window UI
            self.window=mc.window(self.window, title=self.title,
            widthHeight=self.winSize,
            sizeable=False, menuBar=True,
            mnb=True, mxb=False)

            # #### UI code goes here ####

    #show the window
    mc.showWindow(self.window)
```

The first section of the `createUI()` method deals with an error check in the script. It looks to see if there already exists an instanced GUI window of this class. If the window already exists, it is deleted. Next, the numerical value of the tab argument is matched against the string value of the named tabs. The `len()` function returns the number of items in an object, be it a list, a string or a tuple. If there's a discrepancy, the user is warned. If no errors are found, a new instance of the window is created using the `showWindow` command (see figure 4.2).

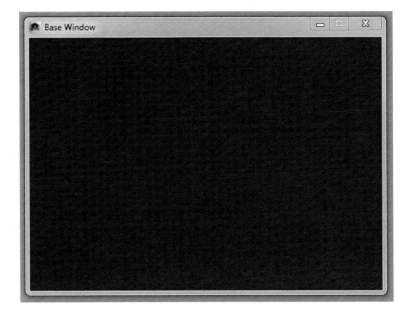

FIGURE 4.2 **Empty framework (blank UI)**

We will now start building the various tab layouts and prepare them so that they can then be populated with custom content. Insert the following code, replacing the commented "UI layout code goes here" above the `showWindow` command. Type the following bit of code (note that it still should be indented under the `else` command:

```
self.mainForm=mc.formLayout(numberOfDivisions=100)
self.tagLine=mc.text(label = "Tin Girl Tools")
self.tabs["uiTabs"]=mc.tabLayout(innerMarginWidth=20,
                                 innerMarginHeight=20,
                                 parent=self.mainForm)
```

The first thing we'll do is to setup a formLayout variable within our window to place the various tabs and components. The formLayout is probably the most flexible and powerful layout option that Maya offers (imagine a gridded sheet of paper that allows you to precisely position elements on it). Having said that, and referring to that old cliché of "with great power comes great. . .", it does take a bit of getting used to working with the formLayout. Although I found that once you get its idiosyncrasies, it makes sense. The formLayout is, by default, subdivided into 100 units. That makes it straightforward to position things around. Think of working with percentage values.

The next line creates a text command, which we will use to label our tool title section. Following that, we define the dictionary self.tabs key using the tabLayout command as a value. This will set the inner margin width and height for all of our dynamically created tabs. Also, it states that the parent layout of the tabs is our self.mainForm layout. Because of the dynamic behavior of the tabs, the use of Python's dictionaries becomes very handy. Each tab will be assigned a dictionary key and value, and then positioned within the main formLayout.

The next segment of our script brings us back to our formLayout, but this time we edit it and start placing our UI elements in the form. In this particular case, we will attach to the form both the tagline and the tabs placements.

```
#attach UI elements to mainForm layout
    mc.formLayout(self.mainForm, edit=True,
        attachForm=(
            (self.tabs["uiTabs"],"top",0),
            (self.tabs["uiTabs"],"left",0),
            (self.tabs["uiTabs"],"right",0),
            (self.tabs["uiTabs"],"bottom",30),
            (self.tagLine, "left", 0),
            (self.tagLine, "right", 0)
            ),
        attachControl=(
            (self.tagLine,"top",10,self.tabs["uiTabs"])
            )
        )
```

The attachForm command allows the placement of the UI elements on the form itself. We've set a buffer of 30 pixels from the bottom of the GUI to our uiTabs in order to give us space to place the tagline. The right and left values for the tagline allow us to center its location on the form between the side edges. Using the attachControl command, we attach the top of the tagline to the uiTabs, with a buffer of 10 pixels. So now, regardless of the size of our window, the tagline will always be 10 pixels beneath the tabs [See figure 4.3].

> **NOTE:** A useful tip to see how your various layouts shape up as you're setting them up is to give them each a unique background color using the *backgroundColor = (float,float,float)* flag (short form is *bgc*). All of the Maya layout-related commands have that flag as an option. It greatly helps with visualizing how the layouts fit with one another and can help with troubleshooting. Here's an example of the full GUI window using different backgrounds to illustrate the layout structure (see figure 4.4).

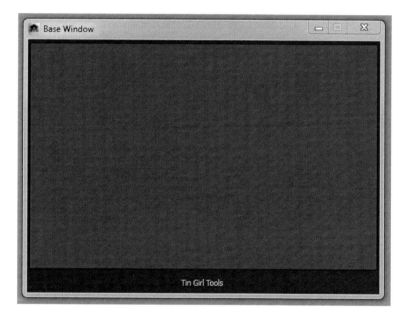

FIGURE 4.3 **Empty framework with tagline**

The next code segment will allow us to dynamically create the tabs for our GUI and set them up with an empty layout that later can be populated with custom content.

```python
#dynamically create number of tabs
for x in range(self.numberOfTabs):

    self.tabForm=mc.formLayout(bgc=(0.21,0.21,0.21))

    #rename tabs according to name array
```

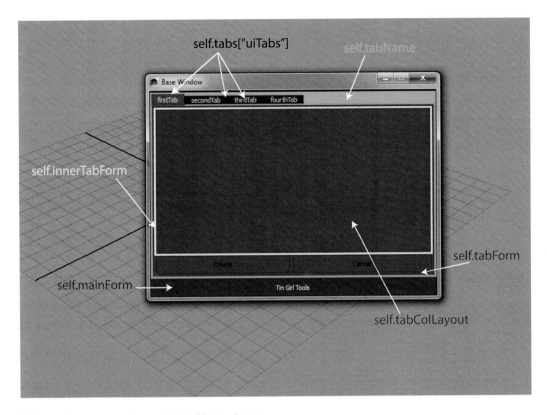

FIGURE 4.4 **Using colors to better see individual layout elements**

```
self.tabName=mc.tabLayout(self.tabs["uiTabs"],edit=True,
                          tabLabel=(self.tabForm,self.name[x]),
                          parent=self.mainForm)

self.currentName=self.name[x]

self.innerTabForm=mc.formLayout()

mc.formLayout(self.tabForm, edit=True,
              attachForm=(
                          [self.innerTabForm,"top",3],
                          [self.innerTabForm,"left",3],
                          [self.innerTabForm,"right",3],
                          [self.innerTabForm,"bottom",36]
                                )
                )
```

We start by creating a for-loop based on the `numberOfTabs` variable established in the `__init__()` method. Each tab will have its own *formLayout*, compliments of the `self.tabForm` variable. The background color has been darkened slightly for visual aesthetics using the `bgc` flag. The tabs are then assigned a variable and renamed according to the `self.name` variable established above, using the `tabLayout` command. The `tabLayout` command is a child of the `mainForm` layout.

A variable holding the current name of the tab is then established followed by another `formLayout` to hold the content of the tab. This new `formLayout` (`self.innerTabForm`) is attached to the main `tabForm` layout. There's a 3-pixel margin all around, except for the bottom, which has a 36-pixel margin. This is to accommodate the common buttons present in each tab, which we will get to it shortly. Continue by adding the following lines to your script:

```
#columnLayout for each tab
self.tabColLayout=mc.columnLayout(rs=5,parent=self.innerTabForm)

#create custom UI elements
self.createCustom(self.currentName)

mc.formLayout(self.innerTabForm,e=True,
                    attachForm=(
                            (self.tabColLayout,"top",3),
                            (self.tabColLayout,"left",3),
                            (self.tabColLayout,"right",3),
                            (self.tabColLayout,"bottom",3)
                            ))

mc.setParent("..") #for self.tabColLayout
mc.setParent("..") #for self.innerTabForm

#create common UI elements
self.createCommon(self.currentName)

mc.setParent("..") #for self.tabName
```

The *formLayout* is a very precise and flexible option, but you will find that it can get quite tedious having to position every single element on the form. For simple and straightforward scripts, you can get away with using some of the less complex layout options Maya has to offer. In this case, we will fall back to the good old *columnLayout*. It's a basic and effective way of getting GUI information in a top-down order, which is what we will be using for these examples. You can always modify this later for your own purposes.

Each tab will now have a dedicated *columnLayout*, with a row spacing of 5 pixels between elements. The next line—*self.createCustom(self.currentName)*—calls the method that populates the custom content of the tab. For the time being it is being left as a "blank" method, but once the class is instantiated, you will be able to add various GUI elements and commands into it.

This is followed by attaching the *self.tabColLayout* to the *self.innerTabForm* layout, leaving a 3-pixel border all around. Finally we use the *setParent* command to assign each layout to the layout above it in the hierarchy. We do that twice, for the *tabColLayout* and *innerTabForm* layouts, then we call the *createCommon* method—to place the Create and Cancel buttons—and we wrap up the loop with a final *setParent* command to attach it to the *tabName* layout.

Add the following methods to your code, below the *showWindow* command. It's to make sure Maya doesn't return errors when it calls the methods we set above. Pay attention that the new methods are indented in the same line as the *def createUI(self,*args)* method previously typed. We're also adding a print statement in the methods so we can get feedback from the pressed buttons and make sure everything is working as it should.

```
def createCommon(self,name,*args):
    #create common UI elements for all class instances
    pass

def createCustom(self,name,*args):
    #create custom UI elements per class instance
    print ("Custom UI elements for {0}".format(name))
    pass

def createButtonCmd(self,name,*args):
    # override create command
    print ("Create command pressed in {0}".format(name))
    pass

def cancelButtonCmd(self,*args):
    #close the window
    mc.deleteUI(self.window,window=True)
```

It's time to put this script into action. Save your script (that goes without saying), open the Script Editor in Maya and type the following lines:

```
import tgpDefTabUI as bt
reload(bt)
bt.BaseTabUI()
```

I recommend making a button and putting this on your shelf for convenience. Once you run it, you should have this window pop up on the screen (see figure 4.5).

FIGURE 4.5 **Base UI with tabs in place**

Adding Button Functionality

In the final piece of code we will revisit the *createCommon()* method and update it to complete our GUI class script with the creation of the common buttons. These buttons—for this particular example—will be constant in all of the tabs and will execute or cancel the function called on each tab.

```
def createCommon(self,name,*args):

    #create common UI elements for all class instances
    #create default buttons
    self.cmdButtonsSize=((self.winSize[0]-30)/2,30)
```

```
self.createButton=mc.button(label="Create",
                            width=self.cmdButtonsSize[0],
                            height=self.cmdButtonsSize[1],
                            command=partial(self.createButtonCmd,
                                            self.currentName))
self.cancelButton=mc.button(label="Cancel",
                            width=self.cmdButtonsSize[0],
                            height=self.cmdButtonsSize[1],
                            command=self.cancelButtonCmd)

#attach buttons to tabForm
mc.formLayout(self.tabForm, e=True, af=([self.createButton,"left",5],
[self.createButton,"bottom",5],
[self.cancelButton,"right",5],
[self.cancelButton,"bottom",5]
),
ac=([self.cancelButton,"left",5,
self.createButton])
                    )

return
```

The script should by now be self-explanatory. First we set an argument that establishes the size of the buttons by taking the width of the GUI window (remember, *self.winSize* has two arguments, width and height defined as [0] and [1] respectively), subtract 30 pixels from it, and divide it by 2. The height we set to 30 pixels.

The *self.createButton* deals with the creation of the "Create" button (thank you, Captain Obvious!). Here we finally get to use the *partial()* function which will let us pass arguments through the Maya *command* flag, in this case calling the *self.createButtonCmd* method and passing it the *self.currentName* argument.

Following up, we create the "Cancel" button, which will ultimately call the *self. cancelButton* method. Note that we don't have to use the *partial()* function since we're not passing any arguments this time.

Last but not least, we attach the buttons to our *self.tabForm* layout and wrap it up with a *return* command. If you run the script, you should see the following in your Maya screen (see figure 4.6).

We've written our first Python GUI class! In the next section we will put it to use and create our custom tools.

FIGURE 4.6 **Completed UI**

Creating tgpMechanix

With our framework in place, we can start building our **tgpMechanix** toolset. In this example we will create two tabs—one to create springs and the other to create pistons. As we proceed with the script, you'll notice that both springs and pistons use a similar starting point but then diverge to create each unique rig.

Create a new Python script and save it as *tgpMechanix.py.* We will start by importing the following modules and classes into our script.

```
import maya.cmds as mc
from math import *
from functools import partial
from tgpBaseTabUI import BaseTabUI as UI #import our base class as UI
```

NOTE: Notice that in the math module, we are importing an * (asterisk). This means that all of the commands in the module will be accessible at the root level. Sometimes that can cause conflicts if different modules use the same command names, but for our purposes, we should be ok. Another way of importing that module with a namespace would be:

```
import math
```

So if we want to use the square root command, it will have to be entered as `math.sqrt()`

If you know ahead of time which commands to import from the module, you can do that as well:

```
from math import sqrt, pow
```

Referencing the UI Class

Start by defining the class and the __init__ function:

```
class MechanixUI(UI):
    def __init__(self):
        self.window="uiWindow"
        self.title="tgpMechanix"
        self.winSize=(330,250)
        self.numberOfTabs=2
        self.name=["Spring","Piston"]

        #create a dictionary for the tabs
        self.tabs={}
        self.createUI()
```

Our *MechanixUI()* class is referencing the *tgpBaseTabUI()* class—which is now known as *UI*. The variables are replaced with the values we want to use for our script such as size, number of tabs and names. We then call the *self.createUI()* function. The great thing about this is that we don't have to worry about the interface itself, since it's being called by the *UI* class and populated with our updated variables. We are going to focus solely on the specific functions that deal with our script.

Now, if you recall from the *UI* class, we had a *createCustom()* method as a temporary placeholder. We are going to overwrite it with the code that will populate each tab window with the correct and relevant information, based on our selection.

```
def createCustom(self,name,*args):
    #populate tab names
    self.tabVer=mc.tabLayout(self.tabs["uiTabs"],edit=True,
                                tabLabel=(self.tabForm,"{0}".format(name)))
    self.rigType=("{0}".format(name))
```

```
    #customize the UI to match the rig type
    if (self.rigType==self.name[0]):

        mc.text(label="1. Create positioning locators")
        self.posButton=mc.button(label="Position Locators",
                        w=(self.winSize[0]-16),
                        h=40,
                        command=partial(self.checkObj,self.name[0],
                                    "radius_CTRL","setSpring")
                        )
        mc.text(label="2. Adjust radius of spring")
        mc.text(label="3. Click Create")

    elif (self.rigType==self.name[1]):

        mc.text(label="1. Create positioning locators (at full piston
                extension)")
        self.posButton=mc.button(label="Position Locators",
                        w=(self.winSize[0]-16),
                        h=40,
                        command=partial(self.checkObj,self.name[1],
                                    "topRod_CTRL","setPiston")
                        )
        mc.text(label="2. Adjust radius & position of top piston rod")
        mc.text(label="3. Adjust radius & position of bottom piston rod")
        mc.text(label="3. Click Create")
```

For this script example, we will be making a lot of use of the **name** variable in order to keep track of the various actions and calls. We start first by populating the tabs with t In the next part of this method, we are going to introduce heir relevant names, as set in the __init__(self) method. For clarification, **name [0]** is *Spring* and **name [1]** is *Piston*. The goal of this example also is to try and save on creating multiple methods that do similar and repetitive actions.

The self.rigType is a name array, holding both of our named rig variables. Depending on the tab we choose, the relevant name[#] is called, where we prompt the user to position the locators for either the spring or piston and build the button to generate the locators and radius controls. The command attached to the buttons will send us to a new method that will check if spring or piston guide locators already exist by checking for specific objects in the scene.

Error Checks

Before we continue, I'd like to take a few moments and talk about checking for errors in your scripts. Good coding practice calls for writing tight and robust code that will be streamlined, fast and efficient and that can handle user and/ or code errors. Now, this is obviously a personal choice, especially if you are writing little mini scripts for yourself where you know exactly what is going on and can debug things on the fly. But with larger and more complex scripts, or when creating scripts that you will share with a team or community, adding error checks can help you keep track of what is going on and prevent user error.

Having said that, one of the biggest drawbacks to adding error checking to your code is that the script size will increase—sometimes by a lot—and you will have to play the role of a field general with a magic crystal ball to try and anticipate as many potential error situations as might be introduced through the misuse of your script. Yes, misuse—as in pressing buttons in the wrong sequence or closing the script window prematurely and then reopening it and realizing that none of the variables have been initialized properly and other scary stuff like that.

Regardless, I personally think it's a good habit to put those error checks in place. Error check functions can be very simple or can be large, complicated, procedural endeavors. I'll go with the simple and to-the-point school of thought and mention different ways of recycling code to optimize our coding Zen. Throughout the book, you will notice the repetition of certain functions and methods that include error checks. You can collect these little utility scripts into a general toolkit and call upon it when needed. It's especially useful as you build a larger suite of scripts.

Creating a Utility Section

Getting back to our script, let's create a "MISC" section in which we will write mini utility methods to help out with our main script. The first one of those utilities will be the *checkObj* method mentioned above. The reason for this particular error check is to check that there is only one set of guides present in the scene.

```
###########################
# MISC. SECTION     #
###########################
#check if objects exists procedurally
def checkObj(self,name,checkObjName,runFunc,*args):
    getFuncName=format(runFunc)
```

```
    if (mc.objExists(checkObjName)):
        mc.warning("{0} guides already exist!".format(name))
    else:
        # note, this getattr function is a python function, not Maya!
        self.callFunc=getattr(self,getFuncName) #will return self.getFuncName
        self.callFunc()
    return
```

The functionality of this method is very straightforward. It uses the Maya *objExists* command to check if an object is present in the scene. Let's take another look at the initial command that sent us here:

```
command=partial(self.checkObj,self.name[0],"radius_CTRL","setSpring")
```

We have the name of the function (in this case, *spring*), the specific object to look for (*radius_CTRL—which we will create shortly*) and the name of the function to run (*setSpring*).

If the condition is false, it prints out a warning to the user. If the condition is true, the script calls on a Python command called *getattr* (note: it's different that Maya's *getAttr!*). The simplest explanation of this function is that it allows us to call a method based on a custom string. In this case, we want to call the *self.setSpring()* method. The *getFuncName* variable receives the value of the *runFunc* input and stores it. But, if we tried to simply call it by replacing the *getFuncName* variable, we would have gotten an error stating that there is no such name.

In this case, *getattr* takes what's in the parentheses and creates a method out of those custom values; in other words *getattr(self, getFuncName)* effectively becomes *self.getFuncName()* which translates to *self.setSpring()*.

The Connectors

The core drivers of these scripts are the connectors that allow us to position the start and end points of our springs and pistons. The idea is to create two locators, connected by a curve to help visualize the link between them (see figure 4.7). These locators will drive the dynamic functionality of the springs and pistons we will create.

```
def set_connector(self,name):

    #create locators
    self.baseLoc=mc.spaceLocator(name="baseLoc_{0}".format(name)[0]
```

```
self.topLoc=mc.spaceLocator(name="topLoc_{0}".format(name))[0]

#create the connecting curve
self.conCurve=mc.curve(name="conCurve_{0}".format(name),
                    degree=1, p=[(0,0,0),(0,0,0)])
mc.setAttr(self.conCurve+".template",1) #template the curve

#move topLoc to arbitrary position at y=10
self.topPos=mc.move(0,10,0,self.topLoc)

#connect the curve between the locators
mc.connectAttr(self.baseLoc+".t",self.conCurve+".cv[0]", force=True)
mc.connectAttr(self.topLoc+".t",self.conCurve+".cv[1]",force=True)

#create distanceNode
self.dNode=mc.createNode("distanceBetween")

#attach the distanceNode between the locators while calculating
#worldSpace values
mc.connectAttr(self.topLoc+".worldMatrix[0]",self.dNode+".inMatrix1",
            force=True)
mc.connectAttr(self.baseLoc+".worldMatrix[0]",self.dNode+".inMatrix2",
            force=True)

return
```

We begin by creating the two locators and naming them accordingly. The *[0]* at the end of the line assigns the transform node of the locator to the variable. Next, we generate the curve and set its degree to 1 (linear) and define two points at the origin. We also enable the *template* attribute to the curve so it won't be selectable in the viewports.

The top locator is arbitrarily moved 10 units on the Y-axis. This value can be modified depending on your needs. We now connect each of the two curve CVs to the appropriate locators by using the *connectAttr* command.

In the next part of this method, we are going to introduce a very useful utility node called **distanceBetween**. We could use the Distance Tool in Maya (**Create > Measure Tools > Distance Tool**), which will provide us with this value, but using it as part of a script can be cumbersome since it creates additional nodes and locators. The **distanceBetween** node offers a simple way to pipe in two inputs (*point1* and *point2*) and calculate the distance between them. There is a small drawback to doing that, though. If we know that we

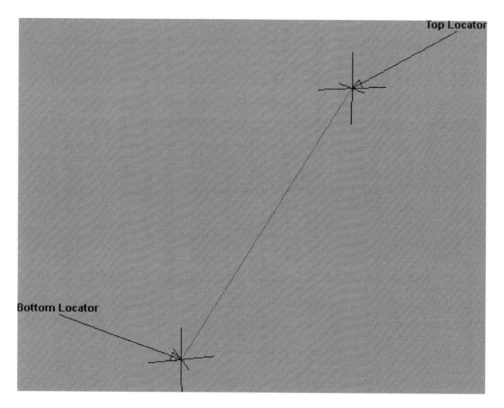

FIGURE 4.7 **Creation of locators and curve**

will use only use objects that will stay at the root level (i.e., not parented to anything else), then using the default inputs from the ***distanceBetween*** node will work. But since rigging is like cooking and you add one thing to another and mix them together and hope for the best result, chances are that some of the objects used will be parented to others, thus providing us with incorrect values due to changes between local and world spaces.

A way to fix this is to connect the output ***worldMatrix*** of our locators to the ***inMatrix*** input of the ***distanceBetween*** node. This will guarantee that, regardless of the parenting setup our locators will have, it will calculate the world space position of the locators. Once this is done, the distance between our two control locators will be reflected in the values returned to the *self. dNode* variable.

Making the Spring

In this section we will go over the creation of the actual spring geo and hooking it up to our dynamic controllers. The piston section further down this chapter will be similar in scope. There are two parts to this process:

1. Setting up the position of the custom controllers
2. Creating the rig components and geometry of the object

We first start by defining and positioning the custom controllers, as seen in the code below.

```
def setSpring(self,*args):
    #define name
    self.springName="spring"

    #create a set to put all of the spring elements inside
    self.springSetName="spring_SET"
    if mc.objExists(self.springSetName):
        print (self.springSetName + " exists.")
    else:
        mc.sets(name=self.springSetName)
    #call the set_connector method to build the guides
    self.set_connector(self.springName)

    #create radius circle
    self.radCntrl=mc.circle(name="radius_CTRL",c=(0,0,0), nr=(0,1,0), sw=360,
                                            r=3, d=3, ut=0, tol=0.01, s=8,
                                            ch=1)
    #create springRadius attribute
    mc.addAttr(self.radCntrl, sn="sr", ln="springRadius", k=1, defaultValue=3.0,
                                            min=0.1, max=15)

    #connect the springRadius attribute to the circle
    mc.connectAttr("radius_CTRL.springRadius","{0}.radius".format(self.radCntrl[1]))
```

The initial part of this method creates a set in which we will place all of the elements related to the spring creation. Sets are extremely useful for quick object selection and keeping the 3D scenes organized. There's a quick name check to see if the set already exists and creates it if it's not present. We then call the *self.set_connector* method to build the guides as discussed above, piping in the *spring* name. The radius controller shape is then created, which will allow us to visually adjust the radius of the spring. A custom attribute called *springRadius* is then added to the controller itself.

```
#position radCntrl between locators and aim
mc.pointConstraint(self.baseLoc, self.topLoc,self.radCntrl[0])
mc.aimConstraint(self.topLoc,self.radCntrl[0],aimVector=(0,1,0))

#lock and hide all default attributes
self.lockHide(self.radCntrl[0])

#create tmp group for easy deletion
mc.select(self.baseLoc,self.topLoc,self.conCurve,self.radCntrl)
self.selSpringObjs=mc.ls(sl=True,type="transform")
#print self.selSpringObjs
self.createTmp(self.selSpringObjs)
```

The above section of the script starts by constraining the radius control between the two locators, both for position and aim. To keep things neat and clean, we will remove all unnecessary channels from the radius control using a custom method to do so for us, which we will explore very shortly.

The last bit of code for this section creates a temporary group that houses all of our guide controllers. By doing this, we will create an error check setup that prevents the user from "forgetting" controllers and other script-related objects in the scene. This check will refer to that group and remind the user to delete the guides or continue with creating the rig. Type the code for the *createTmp()* in the MISC. section:

```
#create tmpGrp
def createTmp(self, selection,*args):
    if (mc.objExists("mxTmp_GRP")):
        mc.parent(selection,"mxTmp_GRP")
        mc.select(clear=True)
    else:
        mc.select(selection)
        self.tmpGrp=mc.group(name="mxTmp_GRP")
        mc.select(clear=True)

    return
```

This brings us to the end of the *self.setSpring* method. We are now going to add another utility function to our MISC. section. This method will lock and hide the default transforms of the selected object.

```
#lock & hide object transform attributes
def lockHide(self, obj):

    toLock=[".tx",".ty",".tz",".sx",".sy",".sz",".rx",".ry",".rz",".visibility"]
    for locked in range(len(toLock)):
        mc.setAttr ((obj+toLock[locked]),lock=True, k=False, channelBox=False)
    return
```

We start by creating a list of the default transform attributes. We then create a for-loop, set to the length of attributes in the list and, using the *setAttr* command, lock and hide those attributes from the object. You can try a variation of this script where only selected attributes are locked and hidden by piping in those attributes as a list to the method header. As you can see from the examples above, these types of small utility scripts that automate repetitive functions are the bread and butter of technical artists. Start building your own little library of miscellaneous tools. Before you know it, you'll see how much more productive and faster your interaction with the 3D software is, allowing you to focus more on the creative aspect rather than endlessly clicking your way to frustrating, repetitive actions. I'd wager that it would be more fun to click your way through a dungeon crawl in a hack-n-slash game than manually changing the attributes of 100 poly cubes.

OK, on to the last segment of our spring tool creation. In this section we will focus on the building of the actual spring and hooking it up with the create button in the GUI.

```
#create the spring
def makeSpring(self,*args):
    self.springRadius=mc.getAttr("{0}.springRadius".format(self.radCntrl[0]))
    #get diameter (width)
    self.upWidth=self.springRadius*2
    #create base spring mesh using polyHelix
    self.springBase=mc.polyHelix(c=20,h=4,w=self.upWidth, r=0.2,sa=24,sco=24,
                        sc=0,ax=(0,1,0),rcp=0,cuv=3,ch=1,
                        name="springGeo")
```

We first get the value of the *radius_CTRL* and get the proper diameter value by multiplying that number by 2. For this example we will be using Maya's *polyHelix* primitive. This method is only one of the myriad of ways available to create spring-like objects and spirals. Some methods work better than others, and you might have to revisit this for your own needs. For the purpose of this script, we will stick to this method since it's the most straightforward.

```
mc.pointConstraint(self.baseLoc,self.topLoc,self.springBase[0])
mc.aimConstraint(self.topLoc,self.springBase[0],aimVector=(0,1,0))

#connect height attribute of helix to distance node
mc.connectAttr("{0}.distance".format(self.dNode),"{0}.height". format(
            self.springBase[1]),force=True)

mc.delete(self.radCntrl)
```

The spring geometry is constrained to both of the guide locators, and the height of the spring is matched to that from the distance between the locators.

```
mc.select(self.baseLoc,self.topLoc,self.conCurve,self.springBase)
#select all spring parts
self.selection=mc.ls(sl=True)

#loop through the parts and rename/renumber them accordingly
for x in self.selection:
        mc.rename(x,(x+"_#"))

#create a group for the springs and number it incrementally
self.springGrp=mc.group(name="spring_GRP_#")
#delete tmp group
mc.delete(self.tmpGrp)
#add GRP elements to set
mc.sets(self.springGrp, add=self.springSetName)
```

This last bit organizes our geometry and guides into a group and connects it to the set we've created in the *setSpring()* method earlier.

NOTE: Using the pound (#) character within a string variable between quotes tells Maya to increase the numbering of an object. If no previous object exists, the numbering starts at one. You can pad the numbering by adding additional pound characters. For example: "**myGeo_###**" will return *myGeo_001* and increase sequentially. Note that it differs from using that same character as a comment prefix.

Assign Functionality to the Buttons

We're almost there. We now need to assign the *Create* button and make sure it runs the proper function in the tab.

```
def createButtonCmd(self,name,*args):
    selName=("{0}".format(name))
    if (selName==self.name[0]):
        #check that spring has been created
        if mc.objExists("radius_CTRL"):

            #pass info to create spring
            self.makeSpring()
        else:
            mc.warning("Spring guides are missing!")
    elif (selName==self.name[1]):
        #check that spring has been created
        if mc.objExists("topRod_CTRL"):

            #pass info to create piston
            self.makePiston()
        else:
            mc.warning("Piston guides are missing!")
```

Starting with a simple object check, we assure that the relevant objects are in place (both for springs or pistons) and call up the appropriate method. If the condition is not met, a warning is shown to the user. The next button to take care of now is the *Cancel* button:

```
def cancelButtonCmd(self,*args):
    # 1. check if guides are present in tmp_GRP
    # 2. if yes, prompt user to proceed with cancellation or return back to script
    if (mc.objExists("mxTmp_GRP")):
        confirmStatus=mc.confirmDialog (title="Confirm exit",
                                        m="Guides present! Exit?".
                                        button=["Yes","No"], defaultButton="Yes",
                                        cancelButton="No", dismissString="No")
        if confirmStatus=="Yes":
            mc.delete(self.tmpGrp)
            mc.deleteUI(self.window,window=True)
    else:
        mc.deleteUI(self.window,window=True)
```

Most cancel functions simply close down the script GUI. In our case, we want to make sure that we also clear up any remnants of the files we've created. One issue that arises if we simply close the GUI and don't remove the guidelines is that the next time the script is opened the guides will come up as present through the object check. Yet, since the script is looking for the proper variables to create them—which by now have been purged from memory—it will return an error. By creating a confirmation dialog that kicks in if certain conditions are met—in our case, looking for the *mxTmp_GRP* group that holds all of our guidelines—we can prevent that error from happening. It's basic, but it works. The goal here is to raise awareness to potential common pitfalls that could arise while running the script and provide solutions to them while finding that balance between usability and going overboard. Of course, not everything can be anticipated or taken care of (like closing the GUI window manually, which will override our cancel conditions), but at least try to cover the common errors.

The spring section of our *tgpMechanix* script is ready. Save your script, and let's test it out in Maya and see it in action.

As before, type the following in the Script Editor and make a button for your shelf:

```
import tgpMechanix as mx
reload(mx)
mx.MechanixUI()
```

The script should come up on your screen (see figure 4.8), ready to be tested. Position the locators and then create the spring. Moving the *topLoc* and *baseLoc* locators will stretch out the spring (see figure 4.9). You can now parent or point-constrain the locators to any other object and have a dynamic spring ready to be animated. If you want to change the default geometry of the spring to meet your specific requirements, click on the *springGeo*, open the **Attribute Editor** and select the *polyHelix* tab. Needless to say, do not delete the history of the spring, or you'll lose the dynamic attributes.

Making the Piston

The process of scripting the piston generator is very similar to that of the spring generator. We are, once again, using the locators as guides. This time, though, we will have two controls on the guide curve. One will represent the diameter and position of the outer piston shell, and the other—the inner shell position and diameter.

The piston rig itself is based on using a couple of joint chains with IKs on them, pointing at each other. The IK handles are point-constrained to the opposite locator (i.e., top IK to bottom locator and vice versa), along with an aim-constraint. This guarantees the joint chains will always follow and point at each other. Again, like most things in Maya, there are many ways and

FIGURE 4.8 **Finished spring script**

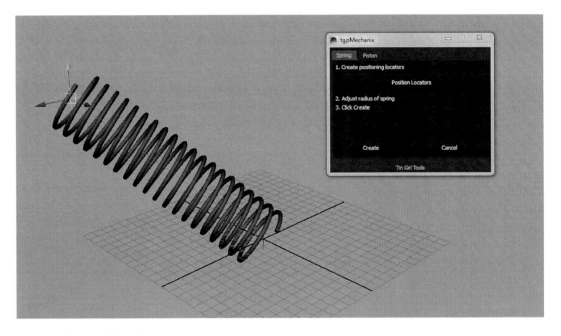

FIGURE 4.9 **Spring script in action**

approaches to get similar results. This particular workflow allows you to easily swap the stand-in geometry created by the script and replace it with your own custom geometry.

```
###########################
# PISTON SECTION      #
###########################


def setPiston(self,*args):

    self.pistonName="piston"

    #create a set to put all of the piston elements inside
    self.pistonSetName="piston_SET"
    if mc.objExists(self.pistonSetName):
        print (self.pistonSetName + " exists.")
    else:
        mc.sets(name=self.pistonSetName)

    #create guides
    self.set_connector(self.pistonName)

    #create control circle
    self.topRod=mc.circle(name="topRod_CTRL",c=(0,0,0), nr=(0,1,0),
                                    sw=360, r=2, d=3, ut=0, tol=0.01, s=8, ch=1)

    self.botRod=mc.circle(name="bottomRod_CTRL",c=(0,0,0), nr=(0,1,0),
                                    sw=360, r=2, d=3, ut=0, tol=0.01, s=8, ch=1)

    #create radius and position attributes
    mc.addAttr(self.topRod, sn="tpr", ln="pistonRadius", k=1,
                                    defaultValue=3, min=0.1, max=15)
    mc.addAttr(self.topRod, sn="tpos", ln="position", at="double", k=1,
                                    defaultValue=0.45, min=0, max=1)
    mc.connectAttr("topRod_CTRL.pistonRadius", "{0}.radius".format(self.topRod[1]))

    #connect POC node and clean channelBox
    self.pocCon(self.pistonName, self.topRod)
    self.lockHide(self.topRod[0])

    #rinse and repeat for bottom rod
    mc.addAttr(self.botRod, sn="bpr", ln="pistonRadius", k=1,
```

```
                                        defaultValue=4.0, min=0.1, max=15)
    mc.addAttr(self.botRod, sn="bpos", ln="position", at="double", k=1,
                                        defaultValue=0.5, min=0, max=1)
    mc.connectAttr("bottomRod_CTRL.pistonRadius","{0}.radius".format(self.botRod[1]))


    self.pocCon(self.pistonName, self.botRod)
    self.lockHide(self.botRod[0])


    #create tmp group for easy deletion
    mc.select(self.baseLoc,self.topLoc,self.conCurve,self.topRod,self.botRod)
    self.selPistonObjs=mc.ls(sl=True,type="transform")
    print self.selPistonObjs
    self.createTmp(self.selPistonObjs)
```

The two control circles with custom attributes are created. The main difference between placing the control circles on the curve for the spring guides and the piston guides is whereas with the spring guides we used a point-constraint to keep the control circle exactly between the two locators and locked it's translation, with the pistons we need them to move along the curve, even while the locators are being moved around. Using a point-constraint won't meet those requirements. Instead we are going to use a very useful utility node called the *pointOnCurveInfo* node. We'll create another mini utility function in the MISC. section of our script called *pocCon()*. Type the following:

```
#connect control to curve
def pocCon(self,name,ctrl):
    #create pointOnCurve node
    pocNode=mc.createNode("pointOnCurveInfo",name="POC_{0}".format(name))
    #connect POC to connector curve and ctrl
    mc.connectAttr(self.conCurve+".worldSpace",pocNode+".inputCurve", force=True)
    mc.connectAttr(pocNode+".position", ctrl[0]+".translate", force=True)
    mc.connectAttr(ctrl[0]+".position", pocNode+".parameter", force=True)


    #tangent constrain to curve
    mc.tangentConstraint(self.conCurve,ctrl[0], aim=(0,1,0), upVector=(0,0,1),
                    wut="vector", wu=(0,1,0))


    return
```

This method will accept the name of the piston and the relevant control and then connect the *pointOnCurveInfo* node to the curve. Its position will be determined by the values dialed by the controller.

Ok! We're almost there, I promise. A couple more short methods and we're done. The first method will collect all of the information from the locator guides and call the second method to actually generate the joints and stand-in geometry for the pistons. Here we go!

```
def makePiston(self):

    #get radius & position channels from rods
    self.topRodRadius=mc.getAttr("{0}.pistonRadius".format(self.topRod[0]))
    self.topRodPos=mc.getAttr("{0}.position".format(self.topRod[0]))

    self.botRodRadius=mc.getAttr("{0}.pistonRadius".format(self.botRod[0]))
    self.botRodPos=mc.getAttr("{0}.position".format(self.botRod[0]))

    #get position of locators and controllers

    self.topLocPos=mc.objectCenter(self.topLoc,gl=True)
    self.topRadiusPos=mc.objectCenter(self.topRod[0],gl=True)

    self.botLocPos=mc.objectCenter(self.baseLoc, gl=True)
    self.botRadiusPos=mc.objectCenter(self.botRod[0],gl=True)

    #create a group for the piston
    # use Maya's #-sign to automatically add a number to the value,
    #instead of adding a counter
    self.pistonGrp=mc.group(em=True,name="piston_GRP_#")

    #create joints between locators

    self.setJoints(self.topLocPos, self.botLocPos, self.topRadiusPos,
                        self.topLoc,self.baseLoc, self.topRodRadius,
                        "topRod",self.pistonGrp)

    self.setJoints(self.botLocPos, self.topLocPos, self.botRadiusPos,
                        self.baseLoc,self.topLoc, self.botRodRadius,
                        "botRod",self.pistonGrp)

    #delete control curves
    mc.delete(self.topRod,self.botRod)

    #select piston controls
    mc.select(self.baseLoc,self.topLoc,self.conCurve)
```

```
#select all piston parts
self.selection=mc.ls(sl=True)
#loop through the parts and rename them accordingly
for x in self.selection:
        mc.rename(x,(x+"_#"))

#parent to piston group
self.newSel=mc.ls(sl=True)
mc.parent(self.newSel,self.pistonGrp)
#delete tmp group
mc.delete(self.tmpGrp)
#add GRP elements to set
mc.sets(self.pistonGrp, add=self.pistonSetName)
mc.select(clear=True)
```

The key part here is calling the *setJoints()* method, located halfway through, which will work out all of the magic. And here it is:

```
def setJoints(self,rootPos,endPos,ringPos,rConstLoc,bConstLoc,radius,jntName,pGroup):

    #thickness of pipe wall
    thickness = radius/3

    #clear selection
    mc.select(clear=True)
    #create joints
    joints=[]

    joints.append(mc.joint(position=rootPos,name=(jntName+"_root_JNT_#")))
    joints.append(mc.joint(position=ringPos,name=(jntName+"_end_JNT_#")))

    mc.joint(joints,edit=True,orientJoint="xyz",zeroScaleOrient=True,
                secondaryAxisOrient="yup")

    #create IKhandle
    self.pistonIK=mc.ikHandle(sj=joints[0], ee=joints[1],
                                            name=(jntName+"_IK_#"))

    #parent to locators
    mc.parent(joints[0],rConstLoc)

    #constrain to locators
```

```
mc.pointConstraint(bConstLoc,self.pistonIK[0])

#calculate distance between 2 points
distance = sqrt (pow((rootPos[0]-ringPos[0]),2) +
                 pow((rootPos[1]-ringPos[1]),2) +
                 pow((rootPos[2]-ringPos[2]),2))

#create pipe rod (polyPipe bug. . . must double the height)
self.rod=mc.polyPipe(r=radius,t=thickness,h=(distance*2),
                     sa=20,ax=(0,1,0),cuv=3,ch=1,sc=0,
                     name=(jntName+"_geo_#"))

#move pivot point to origin
mc.xform(pivots=(0,(distance/-2),0))
#aim and parent to joints
mc.pointConstraint(joints[0],self.rod[0])
mc.aimConstraint(joints[1],self.rod[0],aimVector=(0,1,0))

#clear the list
del joints[:]

mc.select(self.pistonIK[0],self.rod[0])
mc.ls(sl=True)[0]
toGroup=mc.group(n=jntName+"_GRP_#")
mc.parent(toGroup, pGroup)

return
```

There are a few things going on here. We begin by setting a variable for the thickness of the stand-in pipe geometry. You can change that number according to your needs. The next few lines deal with creating our dynamic piston skeleton. We set an empty list to the variable *joints*. We then use the Maya *joint* command to create the joints that stretch between the locator and the position of the appropriate ring control. To connect the joints together, we utilize the Python *append* command. Finally, the joints are properly oriented. Once they are in place, we attach an IK handle between them.

The next segment connects thjoints, IK and locators together via parenting and point-constraints. And now, this is where the real fun begins! In order to create the proper height of the stand-in geometry, we have to calculate the distance between the base joint and the position controller. To do so, we'll use some good old-fashioned Euclidean math. The basic formula to find the distance between two points (in one dimension) is:

$$d(a,b) = \sqrt{(a-b)^2}$$

In other words, the distance between points *a* and *b* is the square root of *a* minus *b* squared. The same principle holds for 3D space, except that we have to calculate all 3 axes. In this case, the formula is:

$$d(a_{xyz}, b_{xyz}) = \sqrt{(a_x - b_x)^2 + (a_y - b_y)^2 + (a_z - b_z)^2}$$

In Python, we use the *sqrt* and *pow* math commands we imported at the head of our script to recreate the distance formula and assign it to the *distance* variable. This variable is then inserted in the Maya *polyPipe* command.

NOTE: Due to a bug in the *polyPipe* command, the height shows up as half the intended value. To correct it, we have to double the *distance* variable in order for it to work properly. If this bug gets fixed and suddenly the geometry appears twice its intended length, change it to *h=distance*.

In the last part, we move the pivot of the geometry to the origin where they are created by default, and then point and aim constrain them to the joints. We wrap it up with some grouping clean up, and done (see figure 4.10)! Save your work and try it out (see figure 4.11).

You have successfully completed the **tgpMechanix** script. Review the code, and make sure to refer to Maya's *Python Command Reference* in the Help

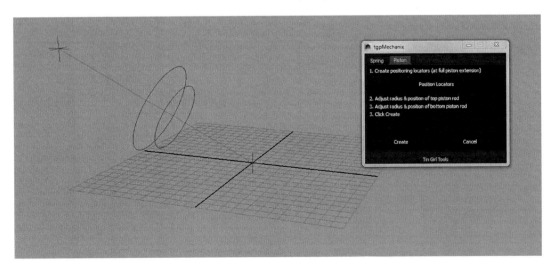

FIGURE 4.10 **Piston script**

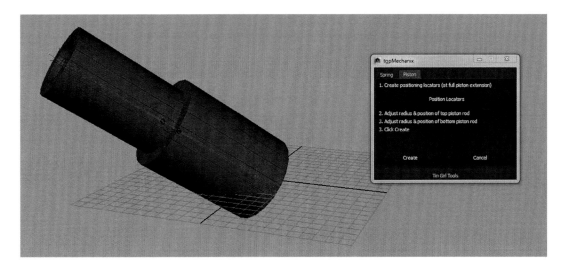

FIGURE 4.11 **Piston script in action**

menu in case you need further explanation on the commands we used or any of the related flags.

And Now for a Lite Version of the GUI Framework. . .

The GUI framework we just covered included the option to use multiple tabs and create a unified GUI for related scripts. Oftentimes, though, you'll find you'll need to create much simpler GUIs for your scripts, which involve a single panel with a few options. Below you will find the code for a simple, base GUI. It's very similar in structure to the *BaseTabUI()* we wrote above, with a few omissions. Save it as *tgpBaseUI.py* in your *scripts* folder.

```
import maya.cmds as mc
from functools import partial

class BaseUI(object):

    def __init__(self):

        self.widgets={}
        self.window="baseWindow"
        self.title="Base Window"
```

```
    self.winSize=(500,350)

    self.createUI()

  def createUI(self,*args):

    #check if window and prefs exist. If yes, delete

    if mc.window(self.window, exists=True):
      mc.deleteUI(self.window, window=True)
    elif mc.windowPref(self.window, exists=True):
      mc.windowPref(self.window, remove=True)

    #create the main window UI
    self.window=mc.window(self.window, title=self.title,
              widthHeight=self.winSize,
              sizeable=False, menuBar=True,
              mnb=True, mxb=False)

    self.mainForm=mc.formLayout(numberOfDivisions=100)

    self.tagLine=mc.text(label = "Tin Girl Tools")
    self.mainColumnLayout=mc.columnLayout(rs=5,bgc=(0.21,0.21,0.21))

    #attach UI elements to mainForm layout
    mc.formLayout(self.mainForm, edit=True,
          attachForm=(
              (self.mainColumnLayout,"top",0),
              (self.mainColumnLayout,"right",0),
              (self.mainColumnLayout,"left",0),
              (self.mainColumnLayout,"bottom",30),
              (self.tagLine,"left",0),
              (self.tagLine,"right",0)
            ),

          attachControl=(
              (self.tagLine,"top",
               10,self.mainColumnLayout)
              )
        )

    #create custom UI elements
    self.createCustom(self)
```

```
   mc.setParent("..")

   # CONSIDER USING IF NECESSARY
   self.createCommon(self)
   mc.setParent("..")

   #show the window
   mc.showWindow(self.window)

def createCommon(self,*args):

   #create common UI elements for all class instances
   #create default buttons
   self.cmdButtonsSize=((self.winSize[0]-30)/2,30)

   self.createButton=mc.button(label="Create",
               width=self.cmdButtonsSize[0],
               height=self.cmdButtonsSize[1],
               command=partial(self.createButtonCmd)
               )

   self.cancelButton=mc.button(label="Cancel",
               width=self.cmdButtonsSize[0],
               height=self.cmdButtonsSize[1],
               command=self.cancelButtonCmd)

   mc.formLayout(self.mainForm, e=True, af=([self.createButton,"left",5],
                     [self.createButton,"bottom",35],
                     [self.cancelButton,"right",5],
                     [self.cancelButton,"bottom",35]
                      ),

                  ac=([self.cancelButton,"left",5,
                    self.createButton])
       )

   return

def createCustom(self,*args):
   #create custom UI elements per class instance
   print "Custom window"
```

```
def createButtonCmd(self,*args):
  # override create command
  print "Button"

def cancelButtonCmd(self,*args):
  #close the window
  mc.deleteUI(self.window,window=True)
```

We have covered quite a bit of concepts in these last few pages, but if you break them down into small components, you'll notice that there is a basic logic behind everything. This is one of the main goals of this book—to show how to break down a series of events into logical steps and bring them together in a unified format. Once you get comfortable with scripting your tools, you will probably find that there are faster, better, more "Pythonic" ways of doing things. Keep exploring the language and learn good coding practices, as your scripting skills improve.

Chapter 5
Rigging Mechanoids

Rigging Meep

We are ready now to tackle our first foray into creature rigging. Meep will be the first character we will tackle. Being a mechanical creature, the focus will initially be on the concepts of joint placements, joint behaviors, controllers and custom joint attributes and functionalities without worrying about enveloping the mesh and creating the deformations associated with organic creatures. As we proceed, we will write and use small utility scripts to help us out with the rigging process. This will give us a solid foundation as we move onto the character of Leaf later on in the book.

Rigging Pre-Flight

Planning the functionality of your rig ahead of time is a good strategy to prevent frustration, wasted time and ineffectual yelling at your monitor out of annoyance. Taking a page out of a pilot's manual, the importance of a pre-flight check can help provide necessary and relevant information for the behavior of the rig, flag potential problems and pitfalls prior to the production stage, and give you an excuse to wear aviator sunglasses. That last item is optional, by the way.

Here is a general list of recommended steps to follow before starting the rig process. Feel free to add steps (or ignore some) depending on your particular project requirements:

1. **Clean mesh**—Once your model is finished, make sure to delete history (**Edit > Delete by Type > History**) on all of the relevant mesh parts. Should you need to keep history on parts of your geometry that have deformers applied to it, you can delete the non-deformer history (**Edit >Delete by Type > Non-Deformer History**). The less "garbage" your mesh has, the better it will behave during the rigging process.
2. **Center pivots**—Always a useful thing. Unless, of course, you need the pivots of your mesh to be at a specific position.
3. **Delete hidden geometry**—If any part of the mesh will never be seen, delete it. It's surprising how often this step gets ignored. Easier to UV too.
4. **Scale mesh**—Set the proper scale of the mesh prior to starting to rig based on your project's parameters. Technically, scaling the rig is doable,

but why tempt the fates? Also, make sure that if the rig is going to be exported to another software package the scale units match.

5. **UV maps**—It's preferable to have your mesh UV-mapped before beginning to rig. It will help with flagging stretching textures when bound. It also signals that the mesh is finalized and ready to go (for the most part. . . there are always surprises). Having said that, there are ways of UV-mapping a bound and rigged mesh after the fact.

6. **Start pose**—Establish the proper pose for rigging your character. Will it be a T-pose (arms out) or an A-pose (relaxed shoulders and elbows slightly bent)? Make sure the model is properly set according to your project's guidelines. If it's for a cinematic, you might consider a general neutral pose. For a game, figure out the common default pose your character will be in most of the time and arrange the model accordingly.

7. **Proxy geometry**—In cinematic productions, sometimes the need for a low-resolution proxy mesh that provides real-time feedback to the animators is crucial. Review the need for a proxy geometry for your project, and should you need one, prepare the proxy mesh and set it to the same scale and volume of your final bind mesh.

Sketching Out the Rig

Another very useful way of planning your rig is to draw it out on paper (or its digital equivalent). It frees you from the confines of working in the 3D software and allows you to make notes and modifications on the fly. Drawing it out will also greatly help visualize the positioning of the joints within the rig and help with some of the guesswork and potential limitations your rig might have (see figure 5.1). This step will become very handy once you start rigging more complex characters and having to deal with proper anatomy, muscle movement and range of motion.

> **NOTE:** Some 3D tools offer a "grease pencil" function that will allow you to doodle and sketch on top of your viewport.

Which Rig? Bind vs. Control

A common misconception in creature rigging is to build—if I may use this cliché—one rig to rule them all. It works in some cases, but it can cause unnecessary complexities in the rig. A good practice is to create at least two separate rigs: one which will be bound to the geometry and the other(s) to control it. If you take into consideration all the deformations the mesh has to go through to be smoothly animated, you might realize you'll need a very specific joint setup to enable that level of fluidity, including influence objects, blendshapes and muscle systems. For example, if you are dealing

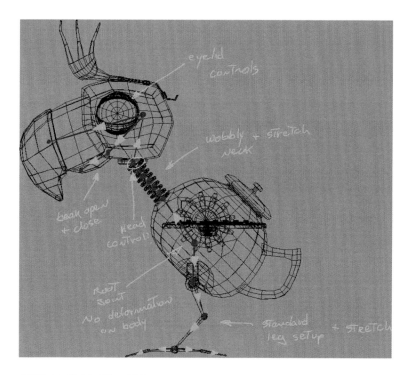

FIGURE 5.1 Sketch of Meep's joints

with a character modeled with a lot of body mass and jiggly bits, the bind rig to provide proper deformations is going to be vastly different than a rig for a stickman character. On the other hand, the animation (or control) rig should be lean, fast and easy to use, while offering quick feedback to the animator. It should be able to easily control the bind rig and offer a range of options to allow the animator to reach the desired poses.

Another situation where this is especially true is rigging creatures for the current slew of game engines in the market. Complex control rigs with constraints, expressions, IKs and utility nodes will not always translate properly inside the game engine. The best solution is to build a base bind rig that will be exported to the engine, and manipulate it via the control rig. Make sure to follow the requirements (and limitations) of the game engine as you prepare the bind rig. The control rig, on the other hand, can be as simple or complex as you need it to be.

Analyzing the Rig Behavior

The rig of Meep will focus around four main sections: the legs, the wings, the neck and head and an overall body controller.

1. **Legs**—the legs are based on a standard IK/FK leg rig, with a stretch option. The talons are made up of two articulated joints (see figure 5.2).
2. **Wings**—the wings are divided into two main parts:
   a. Attachment to the body—a control enables the wing to arc along the contour of the spherical body as well as enable an additional rolling function (see figure 5.3)
   b. Wing flap—the main flapping action is simulated via a sliding piston along a bar on the underside of the wing. The additional wing segments rotate along a hinge system (see figure 5.4).
3. **Neck and head**—the neck is made up of a spring with the ability to extend and compress. In addition, it has controls that enable it to wobble back and forth (like a bobble-head). The head is a simple rotational setup with further controls for the beak and eyelids (see figure 5.5).
4. **COG and Main**—the COG control holds together the wing and head controls, while the Main control moves the complete character and offers a scaling option (see figure 5.6).

Rigging the Legs

I personally prefer starting the rig with the creature's legs since that's usually the grounding point for the rest of the rig. Also, the legs are—typically—the easiest part of the rig to build. I find the complexity increasing as you move up the creature's body (assuming it's a biped or quadruped creature).

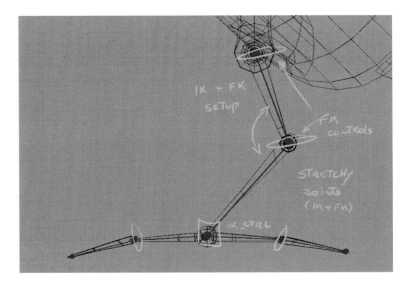

FIGURE 5.2 **Planning the leg setup**

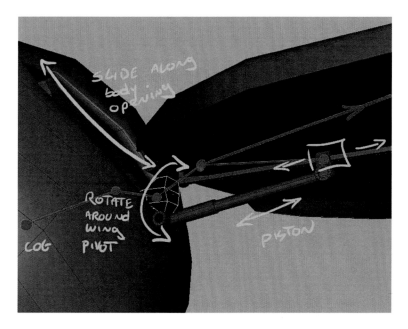

FIGURE 5.3 **Sketching the wing and body joint connection**

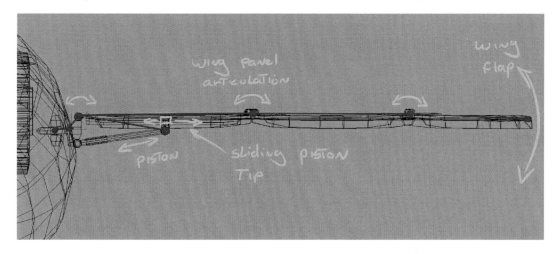

FIGURE 5.4 **Laying out the wing joints**

Meep's legs are roughly based on the skeletal structure of an actual bird (with plenty of creative freedom thrown in for good measure). In nature, birds typically walk on their toes, and through the evolutionary process, some of their bones have fused together to create their unique foot structure (see

167

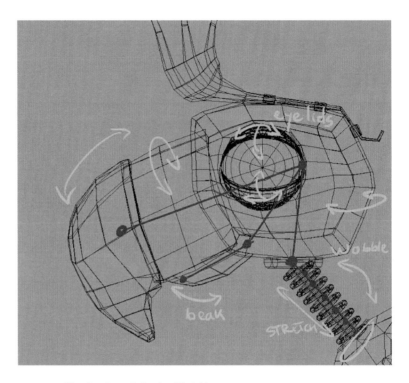

FIGURE 5.5 Planning the neck, head and facial features

FIGURE 5.6 Sketching the COG

figure 5.7). What looks like an inverted knee is actually the "ankle". The knee itself is usually hidden by feathers and rides high on the leg. For our purposes, Meep's knees have been omitted in the character design. Instead, all of the functionality of the leg rig will revolve around the foot and the upper leg.

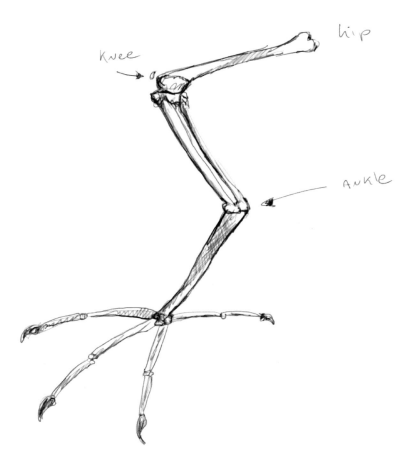

FIGURE 5.7 Sketch of a bird leg skeleton

Placing the Leg Joints

Because Meep is a non-standard type of rig, we will set the joints manually. Usually, when you will have to rig standard setups like bipeds or quadrupeds, automation of this process will come in handy and save a lot of time.

Load up **01_Meep_leg_setup.ma**. You'll find a prebuilt joint chain that will act as the foundation of our leg rig (see figures 5.8 and 5.9).

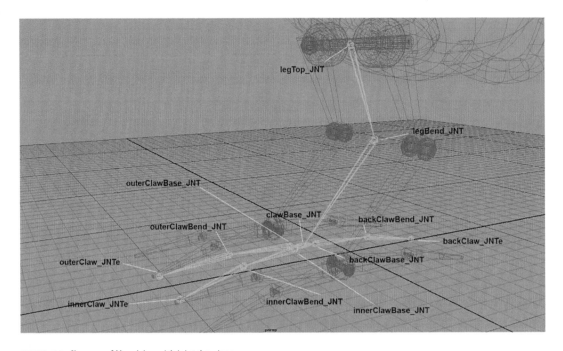

FIGURE 5.8 Close-up of Meep's leg with joint drawings.

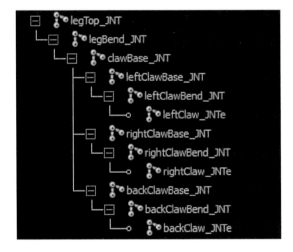

FIGURE 5.9 Leg joint names

The first thing to do is to check if our local rotation axes are facing the right way (*turn off the visibility on the GEO_LYR if it makes it easier to see*):

1. Select **legTop_JNT**.
2. Select the chain's hierarchy (**Edit > Select Hierarchy**).

3. Display the local rotation axis (**Display > Transform Display > Local Rotation Axis**).

> **NOTE:** If you haven't done so by now, create a couple of shelf shortcuts of these commands. You'll use them often. Create a new custom shelf (or select an existing one), go to the dropdown menu where the command is, press CTRL+SHIFT and then left-click on the command. A button representing your shortcut will appear on the shelf.

The goal is to set a consistent system of joint rotations throughout the rig. In our case, using the default joint orientation settings, we will establish that all rotations in the Z-axis will be up/positive and down/negative. Following this statement, we can see that all the joints are properly oriented, except for the **legTop_JNT** (and the end joints as well, but that's something we can ignore or fix using the workaround from Chapter 3) (see figure 5.10).

1. With the leg chain selected, enter **Component Mode**.
2. Select Miscellaneous Components (the question mark icon **"?"**).
3. Select the **legTop_JNT** Local Rotation Axis.
4. Type `mc.rotate(180,0,0,r=1,os=1)` in the Python command line.

> **NOTE:** Using the number "1" after the equal sign is equivalent to typing "True". Same goes to zero, which equals "False".

For the **baseClaw_JNT**, we'll make a small orientation change in the joint. There are two joint chains emanating from it, and by default, it will be oriented to the initial joint that was created after it. To fix that, we will select it and reset it's orientation to the world.

1. Select **baseClaw_JNT**.
2. Open the Orient Joint menu (**Skeleton > Orient Joint > □**).
3. Set "Orient joint to World", deselect all other checkboxes, and press the *Orient* button (see figure 5.11).

The joint chain is now properly oriented (see figure 5.12). Hide the Local Rotation Axis.

IK/FK Leg Setup

As mentioned earlier, we will create an IK/FK setup for the leg. The FK system will be ideal when Meep is flying and the legs will follow the main motion of the body. The IK leg setup on the other hand, will give us the proper control over the legs mainly when Meep is standing on a surface. We will use 3 separate joint chains, one for each of the IK and FK control setups, and one to bind the mesh. This is a true and tried method that offers quite a bit

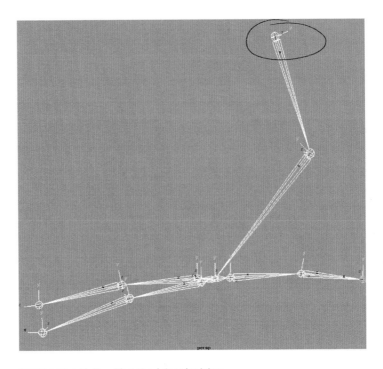

FIGURE 5.10 Initial Local Rotation Axis on leg joints

FIGURE 5.11 Orient joint options

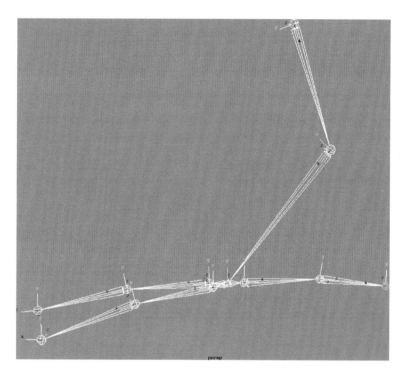

FIGURE 5.12 **Properly oriented joints**

of flexibility in rigging characters. Maya also offers a built-in IK/FK blend option within the IK Handle tool, which reduces the amount of joints in the scene, but introduces additional limitations by keeping the blending options connected to only one chain.

First, in the Front view, move the **legTop_JNT** so it fits inside Meep's leg (see figure 5.13). Duplicate the current joint chain for the FK and IK setups by selecting the **legTop_JNT** and pressing CTRL+D twice. Select one of the new chain's hierarchies (**Edit > Select Hierarchy**) and prefix the new chain with "*FK_*" (**Modify > Prefix Hierarchy Names**) and delete the "*1*" after. Do the same for the IK chain it (see figure 5.14). To the original joint chain, add the prefix "*BND_*". This will be our geometry bind chain. You should have now three unique and properly named joint chains.

We need to create a connection between the FK and IK control rigs and our main bind rig. The end result should be that as we switch between the control rigs, the transforms of the bind rig match the ones of the selected control rig. There are a few methods of achieving this result. A common one is to use constraints (orient, point and/or parent) between the control

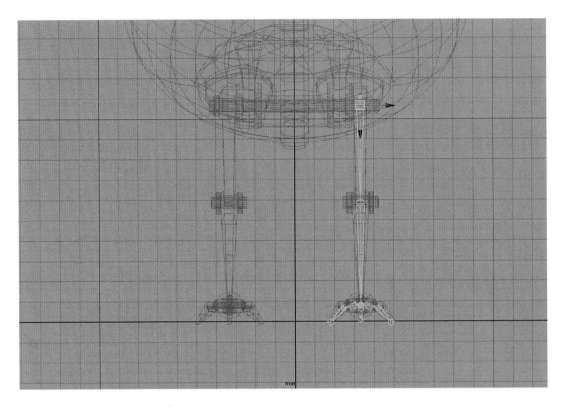

FIGURE 5.13 **Leg joint position in the front view**

and bind rigs, and then using driven keys for the switch. We will use instead utility nodes that are fast to setup, fast to evaluate and don't involve keying channels. Also, for the sake of simplicity, we will use Meep's **char_CTRL** for the location of the IK/FK switches. As you develop your own rigging systems, you can use any control you wish for this in your setups.

Setting Up the Switch

1. Select **char_CTRL** from the Outliner and turn the visibility on.
2. Create a *L_leg_IKFK* attribute (**Modify > Add Attribute...**) with a *minimum* of **0**; *maximum* of **1**; *default* **0** (see figure 5.15).
3. Press *Add* and repeat for the *R_leg_IKFK* attribute.

The utility node we will use to switch between the control rigs is the *blendColors* node. Even though its official purpose is to blend between two colors, it will accept any two inputs. We will use that to blend between the IK and FK control rigs and connect the output to our bind rig. This will have to be done for each joint, for both the Translate and Rotate transform channels.

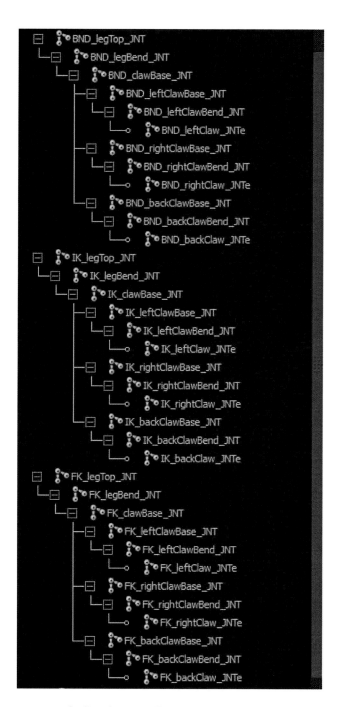

FIGURE 5.14 Duplicated joints into FK and IK chains

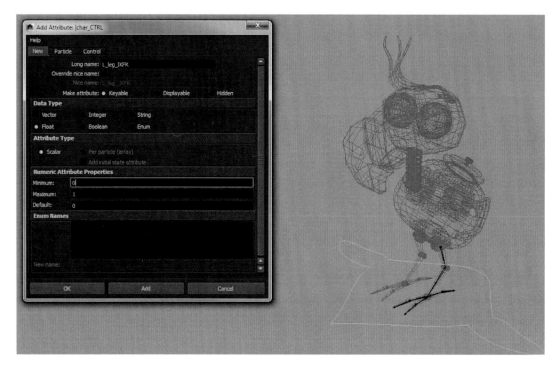

FIGURE 5.15 **Add IKFK switch attribute**

1. Select the **BND_legTop_JNT, IK_legTop_JNT and FK_legTopJNT**.
2. Open the **Node Editor** and add the selected nodes to the graph (see figure 5.16).
3. Press the *Tab* key and type ***blendColors*** in the text field. Press *Enter* to create the node. Rename it **rotate_BCN** (see figure 5.17).
4. Connect the output of **IK_legTop_JNT > Rotate** to **rotate_BCN > Color 2**.
5. Connect the output of **IF_legTop_JNT > Rotate** to **rotate_BCN > Color 1**.
6. Connect **rotate_BCN > Output** to **BND_legTop_JNT > Rotate** (see figure 5.18).
7. To check that the connections are working, select the **IK_legTop_JNT** and rotate it 45 degrees in the Z-axis. You'll see the **BND_legTop_JNT** hallway between the two control chains. The reason is that the *Blender* attribute **on rotate_BCN** is set to 0.5 (see figure 5.19).
8. Select the **char_CTRL** and add it to the **Node Editor**.
9. Connect the output of **char_CTRL > L_leg_IKFK** to **rotate_BCN > Blender** (see figure 5.20).

NOTE: Maya will automatically create *unitConversion* nodes to ensure different unit types connect with each other properly

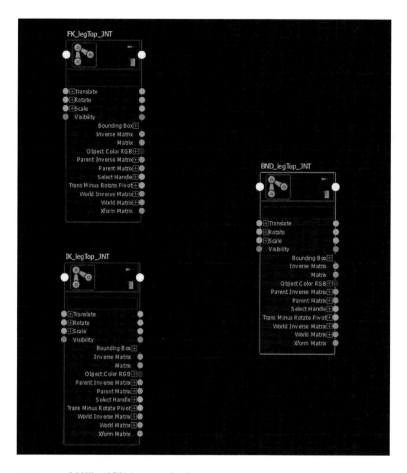

FIGURE 5.16 **Add IK and FK joints to node editor**

The rotation of the **BND_topLeg_JNT** chain is now split between the two control rigs, and the switch is now connected to the **char_CTRL**. When the value is at 0, we are in IK mode and in FK when the value is 1.

The same process has to be done now for the Translate channels. Create a new ***blendColors*** node, rename it **translate_BCN** and repeat as above, but use *Translate* instead of *Rotate* (see figure 5.21).

Excellent! All is working as it should. Now comes the annoying bit . . . we have to do that to all of the joints in the leg on both sides (minus the feet)! Oy vey! But, despair not, grasshopper, for by now you should be able to successfully tackle this conundrum with the scripting skills you have learned since embarking on this wondrous journey a couple of chapters back.

177

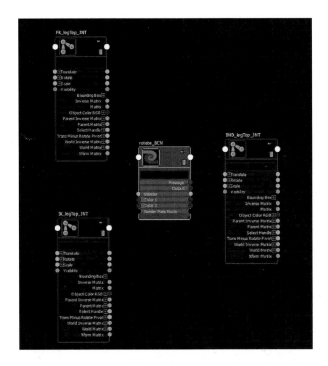

FIGURE 5.17 **Add rotate** *blendColor* **node**

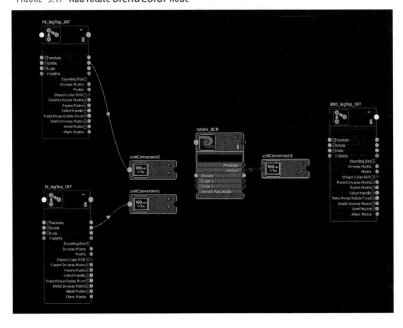

FIGURE 5.18 **Connect to** *rotate_BCN*

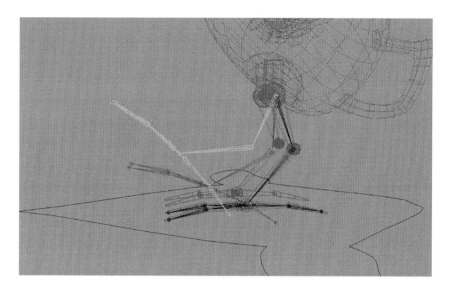

FIGURE 5.19 Blender at 0.5 showing halfway position of BND chain

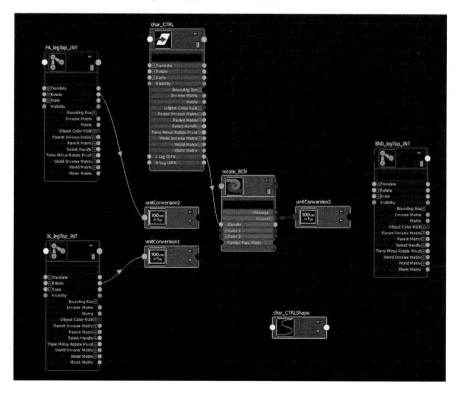

FIGURE 5.20 Connect blender to switch attribute

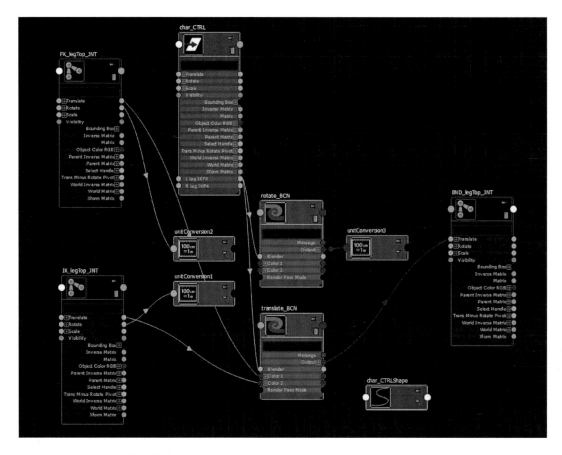

FIGURE 5.21 **Add translate** *blendColor* **node**

Let's break the script down into its components and see what we would need:

- Two source chains
- A target chain
- A blender control (can be optional since the blends will work regardless, but will have to be adjusted from within the *blendColor* node)
- Attributes to connect from sources to target
- Optional: include or exclude the end joint in the chain

At this stage, since we are dealing with straight transform attributes, focus on connecting **translate** and **rotate** attributes only. If you wish to make it a bit more encompassing, you can specify which particular channel to connect.

Give it a try. You can take a look at the included ***tgpBlendColor.py*** script if you need some help figuring it out.

Creating FK Leg Controls

Now that the switch option is in place, we'll focus on the FK side of things. Let's start by creating FK controls for our joints:

1. Create a circle control (**Create > NURBS Primitives > Circle >** □) and set its Normal Axis to Z; Radius of 1.
2. Rename it **FK_legTop_CTRL**.
3. Group it to itself and rename the group **FK_legTop_GRP** (see figure 5.22).
4. Snap **FK_legTop_GRP** to **FK_legTop_JNT**.
5. Select **FK_legTop_JNT** first, shift-select **FK_legTop_GRP** and parentConstraint (**Constraint > Parent >** □). Uncheck ***Maintain Offset*** (very important!) (see figure 5.23).
6. You'll notice **FK_legTop_CTRL** has rotated. That's due to the orientation of the group to the Local Rotation Axis of the joint.
7. Delete the parent constraint on **FK_legTop_GRP**.
8. Select **FK_legTop_CTRL** first, shift-select **FK_legTop_JNT** and orientConstraint (see figure 5.24).
9. Select **FK_legTop_JNT**, shift-select **FK_legTop_GRP** and pointConstrain (maintain offset should be unchecked).

Scripting tgpControlOrient

Rotating **legTop_CTRL** in the Z-axis will rotate now the joint chain properly. The groups will also be constrained to the position of the joints in space. Once again, having to do this to every single joint manually can be tedious. Here is a short script—***tgpCtrlOrient.py***—which will automate this setup for us. Make sure that ***tgpBaseUI.py*** is in your *scripts* folder, since it's the core of the GUI:

FIGURE 5.22 FK_ legTop_GRP

FIGURE 5.23 Disable maintain offset checkbox

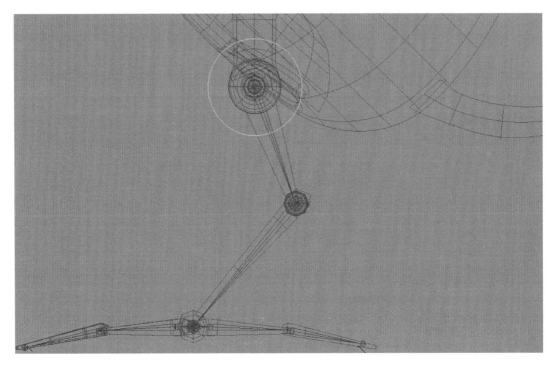

FIGURE 5.24 FK control topLeg_JNT

```
import maya.cmds as
from tgpBaseUI import BaseUI as UI

class tgpCtrlOrient(UI):
   def __init__(self):

      self.window="coWindow"
      self.title="tgpCtrlOrient"
      self.winSize=(250,210)

      self.createUI()

   def createCustom(self,*args):
      # create the GUI
      mc.text(align="left",label="Select the joints and pick a ctrl axis.")
      mc.radioButtonGrp("rbtns",labelArray3=["X","Y","Z"],
            cw3=(80,80,80), nrb=3,sl=3)
      mc.separator(st="in",w=250)
```

```
   mc.floatFieldGrp("cRad", cal=(1,"left"),nf=1,
           label="Enter radius of the controls: ",
           v1=1,pre=2,w=300)
   mc.separator(st="in",w=250)
   mc.checkBox("pCheck",label="Parent controllers")
   mc.checkBox("lhCheck",label="Show only rotation channels")


   mc.showWindow(self.window)

def createButtonCmd(self,*args):
     self.tgpMakeCtrl()
def tgpMakeCtrl(self,*args):
  # query the button selection
  axis=mc.radioButtonGrp("rbtns",q=True,select=True)
  getAxis=self.tgpGetAxis(axis)
  getRad=mc.floatFieldGrp("cRad",q=True,v1=True)
  gArray,cArray=[],[]
  # error check to make sure only joints are selected
  selJoints=mc.ls(sl=True,fl=True,type="joint")
  numJnts=len(selJoints)
  if numJnts==0:
    mc.warning("pick a joint!")
  else:
    for i in range (numJnts):

      # get joint position
      jntInfo=mc.xform(selJoints[i],q=1,t=1,ws=1)

      # look for "_JNT" in joint naming convention
      ctrlName=selJoints[i].split("_JNT")[0]

      # create curve controls and group it to itself
      ctrlCurve=mc.circle(name="{0}_CTRL".format(ctrlName),
            c=(0,0,0),nr=getAxis, sw=360,r=getRad,d=3,
            ut=0, tol=0.1,ch=1)
      ctrlGroup=mc.group(name="{0}_GRP".format(ctrlName))

      # create an array of controls and groups for parenting option
      gArray.append(ctrlGroup)
      cArray.append(ctrlCurve[0])
```

```
        # move groups to joint position
        mc.xform(ctrlGroup, t=(jntInfo[0], jntInfo[1],jntInfo[2]),ws=True)

        # parentConstrain groups to joints and delete constraint
        connect=mc.parentConstraint(selJoints[i], ctrlGroup,mo=False)
        mc.delete(connect)

        # orientConstraint joint rotation to curves
        mc.orientConstraint(ctrlCurve,selJoints[i])

        # pointConstraint groups to joints
        mc.pointConstraint(selJoints[i],ctrlGroup,mo=False)

    # parent controls
    getPcheck=mc.checkBox("pCheck",q=1,v=1) # checkbox enabled?
    getLhCheck=mc.checkBox("lhCheck",q=1,v=1)
    #if (getPcheck!=0):
    if getPcheck:
      for x in range (len(gArray)):
        try:
          mc.parent(gArray[x+1], cArray[x])
        except:
          mc.select(clear=True)

    # hide all channels except rotation
    if getLhCheck:
      for y in range (len(cArray)):
        toLock=[".tx",".ty",".tz",".sx",".sy",".sz",".visibility"]
        for locked in range(len(toLock)):
          mc.setAttr ((cArray[y]+toLock[locked]),
              k=False, cb=False)

def tgpGetAxis(self,axis):
  # create a dictionary with the axis values
  axisOpt = ['1': [1,0,0], '2': [0,1,0], '3': [0,0,1]]
  if (axis== 1):
    return axisOpt["1"]
  elif (axis==2):
    return axisOpt["2"]
  elif (axis==3):
    return axisOpt["3"]
```

The script offers a couple of additional options beyond what we discussed in the above example. Run it and do the following (see figure 5.25):

1. Enable the *"Show only rotation channels"* checkbox.
2. Select **FK_legBend_JNT** and click on the *Create* button (see figure 5.26).
3. For **FK_baseClaw_JNT**, change the radius to 2 and press *Create* (see figure 5.27).

FIGURE 5.25 tgpControlOrient window

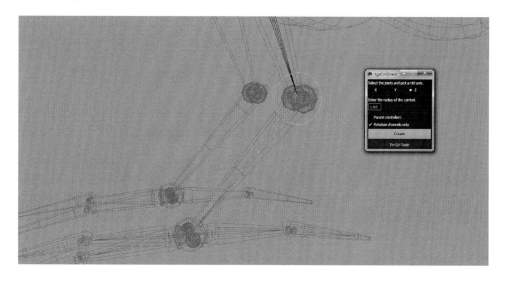

FIGURE 5.26 FK_legBend_JNT with controls

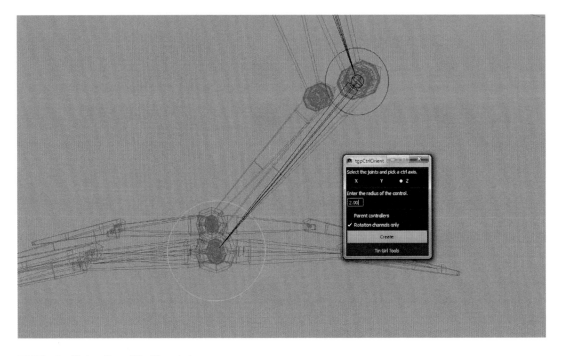

FIGURE 5.27 FK_baseClaw_JNT with controls

For the claws:

1. Select **FK_backClawBase_JNT** and **FK_backClawBend_JNT**.
2. Change the radius to 0.5.
3. Enable the *"Parent controllers"* checkbox.
4. Press *Create*.
5. Repeat for **FK_rightClawBase_JNT** and **FK_leftClawBase_JNT**.

You now should have a setup that looks like figure 5.28. Next, we will parent the controllers to each other and create a logical control hierarchy. The back, inner and outer *FK_clawBase_GRP* groups will be parented **to FK_clawBase_CTRL**. Its group, in turn, will be parented to the **FK_legBend_CTRL**, which, in turn, will be parented to the **FK_legTop_CTRL** (see figure 5.29).

A quick aside regarding controllers in general: think of them as safety buffers between the skeleton (and mesh if bound), and the overall rig functionality. A good rule of thumb is to try and not directly manipulate the joints. Rigs will break—take that as an inconvenient truth—but by creating a system of groups, locators and controllers between the actual joints and

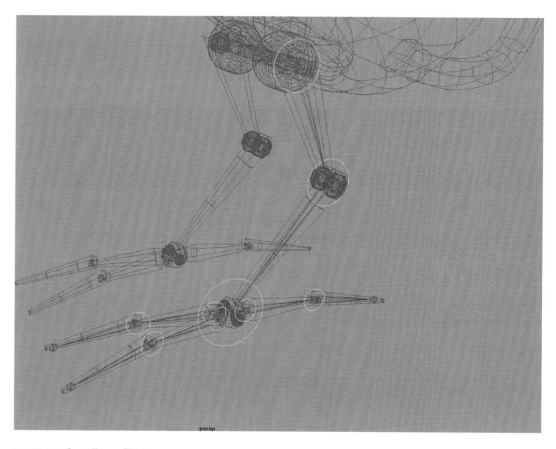

FIGURE 5.28 Controllers on FK joints

their manipulators, chances of repairing those breaks become a bit easier. Sometimes it can be simply a matter of reconnecting a lost node connection. If worse comes to worse, you might have to delete the controller and rebuild its connections from scratch. Even if that happens, the integrity of the joints (and mesh) *should* not be affected.

Stretchy FK Joints

A common option to offer in a rig is the ability to make it stretch. Squash and stretch, being one of the main principles of animation, can make a good pose look great as its animating from one position to another. Sometimes, using that bit of over-extension and exaggeration in the gesture will help the visual flow, regardless if it's rooted in realism of movement. We will add

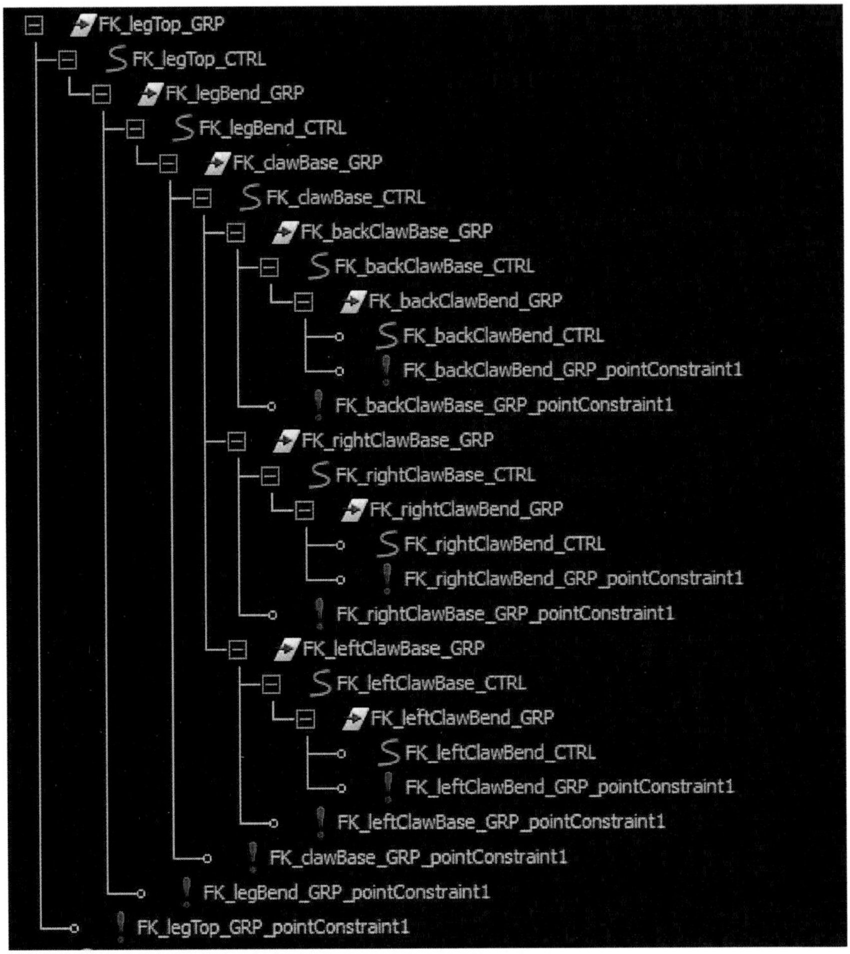

FIGURE 5.29 **FK control hierarchy**

this functionality to our FK leg chain, specifically to the **FK_legTopCTRL** and **FK_legBend_CTRL**. Chances are that you will rarely, if ever, have to actually stretch the feet themselves. There are two ways of stretching the joints. The first—and most common—is scaling the primary axis of the joint chain. It works, but sometimes problems arise if you parent geometry to it and apply rotations. The geometry will shear and it won't be pretty. A second option, which we will explore here, is to translate the child joint in the primary axis. This way it will move along its intended direction and won't negatively affect any of the objects that might be parented to it. Like anything in Maya, there are a myriad of ways of achieving the same result, be it using expressions, driven keys or utility nodes. For this example, we will again use utility nodes, since they're so much fun to use.

1. Select **FK_legTop_JNT**.
2. Change the default Rotate Order from **XYZ** to **XZY** in the Attribute Editor. By doing so, it will prevent our Z-axis rotations from being off-center if we rotate the leg around itself on the Y-axis.
3. Select **FK_legTop_CTRL**.
4. Add a new attribute called *stretch* with a float *minimum* of 0.1, a *maximum* of 3 and a *default* of 1 (see figures 5.30 and 5.31). The maximum value is the maximal stretch size of the joint. You can change that to reflect your project needs.
5. Select **FK_legTop_CTRL** and **FK_legBend_JNT**. Open the Node Editor and add selected nodes to graph (see figure 5.32).
6. Since we're using the X-axis as our primary joint orientation, select the **FK_legBend_JNT** and make a note of the translation value in the X-axis (see figure 5.33).
7. Create a *multiplyDivide* node and rename it *startLength_MDV* (see figure 5.34).
8. Open the attributes of the newly created *multiplyDivide* node. Verify the operation is set to *Multiply* and in the **input 1X** field, enter the translation X value of the **FK_legBend_JNT**.
9. Connect the **FK_legTop_CTRL > stretch > Output** to the **startLength_MDV > Input 2 > Input 2X** (see figures 5.35 and 5.36).
10. Connect the **startLength_MDV > Output X** to the **FK_legBend_JNT > Translate X** (see figure 5.37).

If you select the **FK_legTop_CTRL > Stretch** attribute and increase or decrease the value, you'll see the joint compressing or stretching out. Repeat the procedure with **FK_legBend_CTRL** and **FK_clawBase_JNT**.

The FK joints now should be working properly and have the ability to stretch. Now, the obvious question is. . . what about the mesh? How does it deform with this rig?

The question to ask is what is the end medium the rig will be used in? If it's a game engine, there is a high probability that your mesh will have to be bound to the skeleton. If it's for a cinematic, you can get away with also using parenting, constraints and deformers to attach the mesh to the joints.

For this particular example, we will bind the mesh as we complete Meep's rigging process later on in the chapter.

Creating IK Leg Controls

Start by hiding the FK joint chain and turning the visibility of the IK chain back on. We will create a foot control for the leg. Since there is a good chance we will be using IK as the main joint manipulation method, we will make this the main leg controller. We will also add functionality to it as we

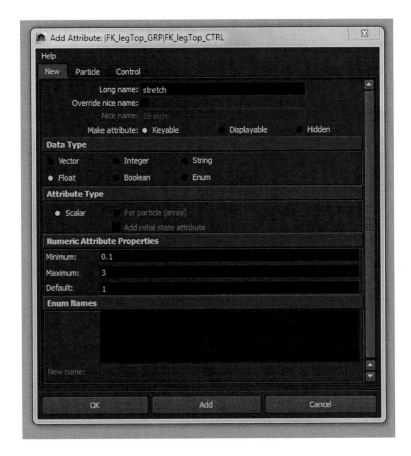

FIGURE 5.30 Setting the FK stretch attributes

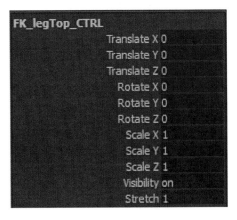

FIGURE 5.31 FK control stretch attributes properties

FIGURE 5.32 **FK stretch node editor setup**

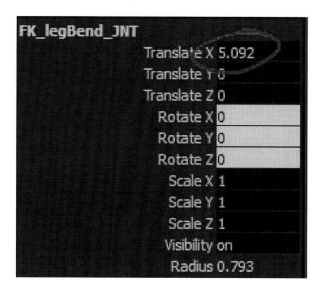

FIGURE 5.33 **Note the translation value in X**

FIGURE 5.34 **Add MDV node**

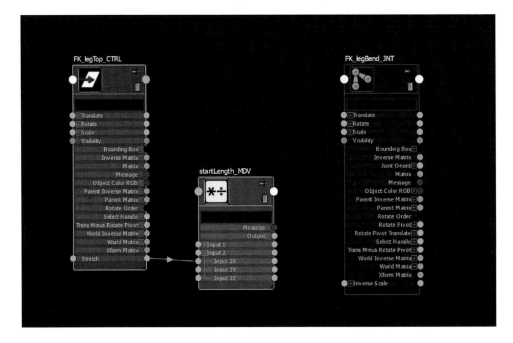

FIGURE 5.35 **Connect stretch to MDV**

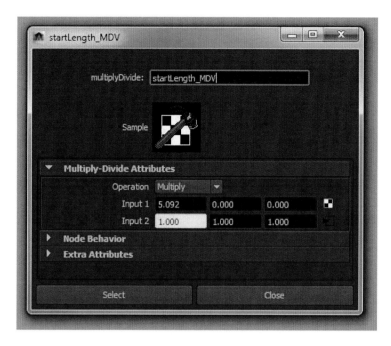

FIGURE 5.36 Inside MDV node with translate X value set in Input1

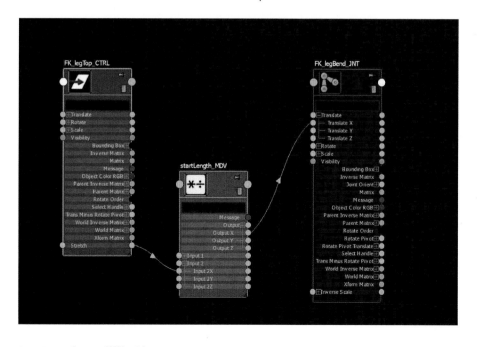

FIGURE 5.37 Connect MDV to joint

go along. You can use any type curve shape to represent your controller. Make sure it's clear and easily identifiable and selectable. For straight shapes, use a linear EP Curve (**Create > EP Curve Tool >** □) (see figure 5.38) and rename it **foot_CTRL**.

> **NOTE:** A great little script to generate control shapes can be found at the www.rigging101.com website—http//rigging101.com/free/melscripts/ rig101wireControllers.zip.

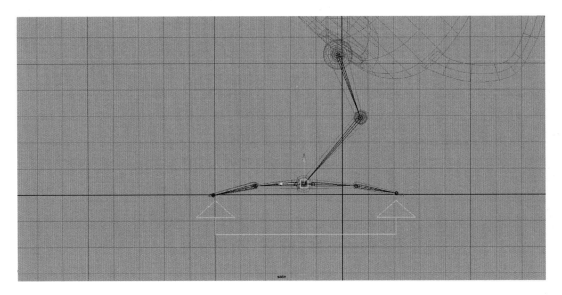

FIGURE 5.38 **Create foot control curve**

By default, the pivot point of the controller is created at the origin. We need to move it to a position on the leg that will make logical sense. You can move the **foot_CTRL** manually across the X-axis and then adjust the vertices of the controller or simply script it. We'll go with the latter option (which you can make into a shelf button or expand on with additional options).

Select **IK_clawBase_JNT** first, followed by **foot_CTRL** and run the following script:

```
sel=mc.ls(sl=True)
src=mc.xform(sel[0], q=True,ws=True,rp=True) #get first selected position
mc.xform(sel[1], ws=True, t=(src[0],src[1],src[2])) #move 2nd obj to first position
```

Freeze transformations after the control has been repositioned.

On to the IK setup:

1. Change the Rotate Order of the **foot_CTRL, IK_legTop_JNT, IK_legBend_ JNT** and **IK_baseClaw_JNT** from *XYZ* to *ZXY*.
2. Create a Rotate Plane Solver IK handle (**Skeleton > IK Handle Tool >** □).
3. Connect it between **IK_legTop_JNT** and **IK_baseClaw_JNT** (see figure 5.39).
4. Rename it **leg_IK**. Rename also the end effector found at the end of the IK joint chain to **leg_EFF**.

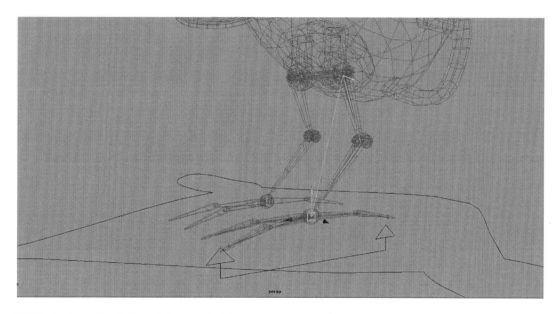

FIGURE 5.39 **Connecting the IK handle between the joints**

Right now, if you move the IK handle up on the Y-axis, you'll notice the foot is rotating off at an angle (see figure 5.40). This would happen even if you parented it to the **foot_CTRL**. We need to offer the option to the animator as to when to rotate it, as well as keeping the foot flat on the ground when the upper body is moving. To do that, we will add an additional IK handle that will "plant" the foot on the ground.

1. Create a new joint and place it between the two front claws.
2. Rename this joint **IK_frontHold_JNT** and parent it to the **IK_clawBase_JNT**.
3. Create a new IK handle (Single Chain Solver) between those two joints. Rename it **frontHold_IK** and its solver **frontHold_EFF**.
4. Parent **frontHold_IK** to **leg_IK**, and in turn parent it to the **foot_CTRL** (see figure 5.41).

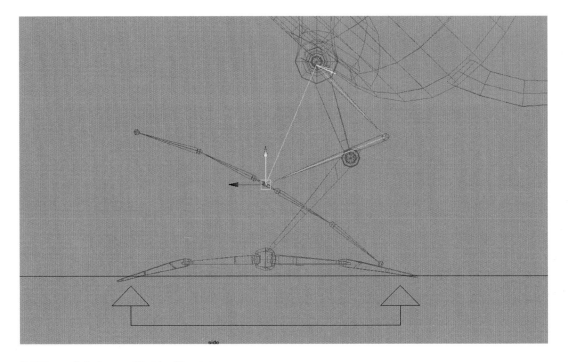

FIGURE 5.40 Default move of the L Leg IK control

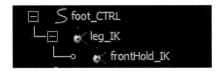

FIGURE 5.41 Parent IKs to each other and then to foot_CTRL

Now, if you move the **foot_CTRL**, the foot stays flat as you translate it around. Next, we will focus on creating a controller to emulate our "fake" knee.

Knee Controls

Knee and elbow controls typically use the **Rotate Plane IK** handle in combination with a pole vector constraint to keep the IK pointed in a set direction. An important point to remember—as mentioned in Chapter 3—is that for pole vectors to properly work, the joint chain and IK handles must be on a flat plane. If they're not, you will get rotation on the joints as they try to align themselves to the pole vector. In this particular example, Meep's legs are on a perfect flat plane, so there shouldn't be any issues.

1. Create an empty group and name it *pvAim_GRP*.
2. Snap position it on top of **IK_legTop_JNT** and **point constrain** to that joint.
3. Create a polygon sphere with a radius of 0.5. Rename it *pv_CTRL*.
5. Group it twice to itself. Rename the topmost group *pvPos_GRP*, and the second group *pvCtrl_GRP* (see figure 5.42).
4. Select **pvPos_GRP** and snap position it on top of **IK_legTop_JNT**. Freeze transformations and **parent constrain** it to the **pvAim_GRP**.
5. Select in this order: **IK_legTop_JNT**, **leg_IK** and **pvCTRL_GRP** and **point constraint**.
6. Select the **pv_CTRL** sphere and translate it 15 units in the negative Z-axis. Freeze transformations.
7. With the **pv_CTRL** still selected, select **leg_IK** and **Constrain > Pole Vector**.

FIGURE 5.42 **Knee hierarchy setup**

So far we've created a pretty standard knee pole vector setup. OK, so a slightly more convoluted way than simply throwing a locator behind the knee and setting a pole vector constraint. These setups typically will "flip" the knee if the IK handle moves above the rotate plane position. Based on the character design of Meep, the chances that the leg will ever have to move into that position is relatively small, but why take chances, right? The trick now is to prevent the knee from flipping. There are various ways of achieving this, including an efficient method of using the twist attribute in the IK handle itself and offsetting it through custom channel attributes. We will take a slightly different approach and use an aim constraint that will point at our IK handle, along with the constraints we used in the setup above, and add a couple of minor bells and whistles. These next couple of steps are the secret ingredient to the prevention of the flip.

1. Select the **leg_IK** first, followed by the **pvAim_GRP**.
2. Open the Aim Constraint attributes (**Constrain > Aim > □**) and change the *Aim Vector* to **-1** in the Y-axis. Under *Constraint axes*, uncheck "All" and select only the **X** and **Z**-axes (see figure 5.43).

If you move the **foot_CTRL** around, you'll notice the leg does not flip and remains quite manageable. You can tweak the position of the knee by translating the **pv_CTRL**. Now, depending on the style of your animator's needs, you might wish to leave the controls as is. We will take it one step

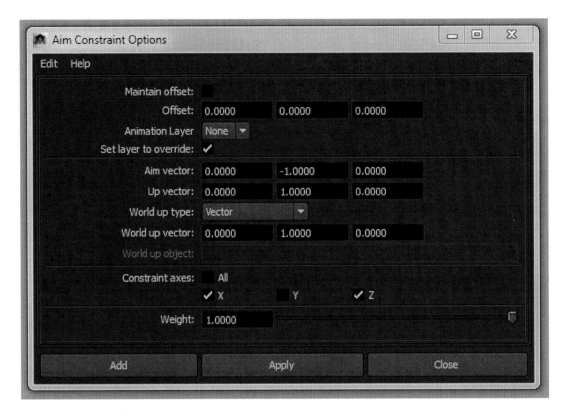

FIGURE 5.43 **Knee aim constraint options**

further and offer a way to do general movements via rotations and specific tweaks via translations.

1. Select the **foot_CTRL** and add the following three custom attributes:
    a. *Name*: _____; *Make Attribute*: Displayable; *Enum*; *OPTIONS*
    b. *Name*: kneeRotate; *Float*; *Default*=0
    c. *Name*: kneeVis; *Enum*; On, Off
2. Open the **Node Editor** and add the **foot_CTRL** and **pvCtrl_GRP** into it.
3. Connect **foot_CTRL > kneeRotate** to the **pvCtrl_GRP > Rotate Y** (see figure 5.44).
4. Create a **Reverse** node and rename it *kneeVis_RVN*. Expand the nodes options.
5. Connect **foot_CTRL > kneeVis** to **kneeVis_RVN > Input X**.
6. Connect **kneeVis_RVN > ouput X** to **pvCtrl_GRP > Visibility** (see figure 5.45).
7. Lock and hide the rotation, scale and visibility channels of the**pv_CTRL**.

Excellent! Now we can manipulate the rotation of the knee through the **foot_ CTRL** *kneeRotate* attribute, but if we need additional tweaks, we can unhide

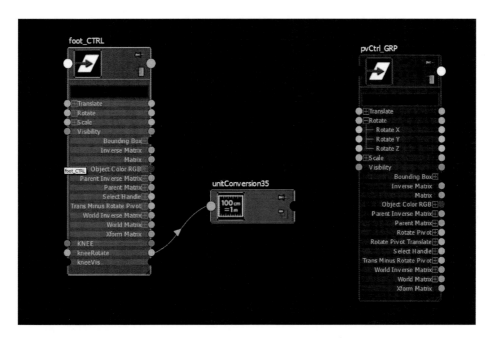

FIGURE 5.44 **Knee rotate connection**

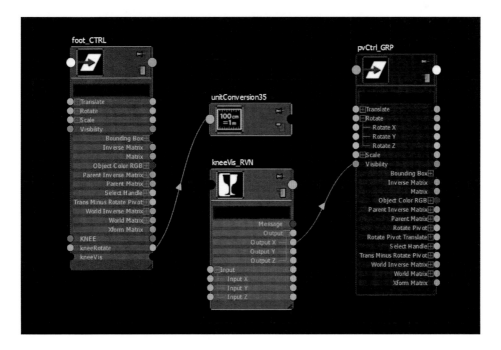

FIGURE 5.45 **Knee visibility connection**

and translate the **pv_CTRL** for fine-tuning using the *kneeVis* attribute. A last thing for the **pv_CTRL** is to make sure that it does not render mistakenly or visually affect in any way.

1. With the **pv_CTRL** selected, open the Attribute Editor.
2. Expand the **Render Stats** menu and uncheck all of the options (see figure 5.46).
3. Open the **Hypershade** and create a blue **Surface Shader** material. Rename it *left_MAT*.
4. Assign it to the **pv_CTRL** (see figure 5.47).

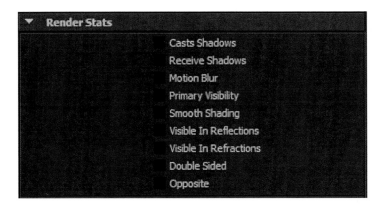

FIGURE 5.46 **Turn off render stats attributes for pv_CTRL**

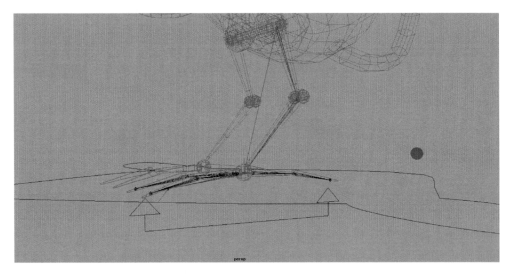

FIGURE 5.47 **Blue shader pvCtrl**

Stretchy IK Joints

For the stretchy IK setup, we will have to use a different approach than the one used for the FK joints. Rather than stretching each joint individually, we have to look at the IK chain as a whole in order to stretch it properly. The concept for the IK stretch is to first figure out the length of the IK chain at its default full extent. Once that length is known, we set a condition that states that if that length has not been met, do not stretch the joints (i.e., flexing the IK handle)—otherwise, stretch away. Again, there are different ways to achieve this. Using expressions is a common technique, along with scaling the joints along their primary axis. We will continue with our use of utility nodes and translating the joints. Feel free to experiment with different methods and see which ones work best with your setup.

We are going to set it up manually first, so you can see the actual process. Once that's done, automating this with a Python script should be relatively straightforward. It all boils down to a healthy sense of logic.

Start by creating 3 locators and name them **topJnt_LOC**, **midJnt_LOC** and **endJnt_LOC**. These locators will provide us with the various distance variables we will use for the stretch.

Set the following **point constraints** on these locators:

1. **topJnt_LOC** to **IK_legTop_JNT**
2. **midJnt_LOC** to **IK_legBend_JNT**
3. **endJnt_LOC** to **leg_IK** (the handle, not a joint)

We'll now make some measurements. Let's get our virtual measuring tapes in the form of distance nodes. Open the **Node Editor** and create 3 *distanceBetween* nodes. Name them **topJnt_DBN**, **endJnt_DBN** and **atRest_DBN**. Add the three locators from before into the Node Editor and connect them as follows (see figure 5.48):

1. **topJnt_LOC > RotatePivotTranslate** to **topJnt_DBN > Point1**
2. **topJnt_LOC > RotatePivotTranslate** to **atRest_DBN > Point1**
3. **topJnt_LOC > World Matrix [0]** to **atRest_DBN > InMatrix1**
4. **midJnt_LOC > RotatePivotTranslate** to **topJnt_DBN > Point2**
5. **midJnt_LOC RotatePivotTranslate** to **endJnt_DBN > Point1**
6. **endJnt_LOC > World Matrix [0]** to **atRest_DBN > InMatrix2**
7. **endJnt_LOC > RotatePivotTranslate** to **atRest_DBN > Point2**
8. **endJnt _LOC > RotatePivotTranslate** to **endJnt_DBN > Point2**

The **atRest_DBN** node will give us the distance of the chain when it's bent, while the other two distance nodes will provide us with the length of each joint. To find the total length of our chain, we are going to add the **topJnt_DBN** distance to the **endJnt_DBn**. We will use a *PlusMinusAverage* node to do so. Create one in the Node Editor and name it **totalJntLength_PMA**.

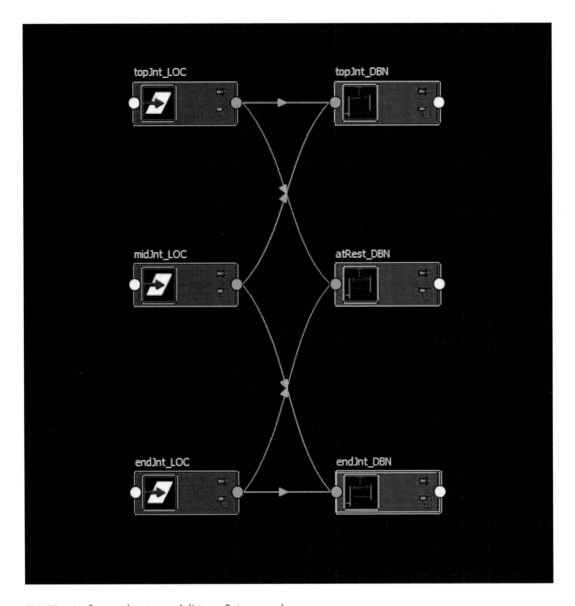

FIGURE 5.48 Connect locators and *distance Between* nodes

1. Connect **topJnt_DBN > distance** to **totalJntLength_PMA > Input 1D >
   Input 1D [0]**.
2. Connect **endJnt_DBN > distance** to **totalJntLength_PMA > Input 1D >
   Input 1D [1]**.
3. Make sure the **totalJntLength_PMA** operation is set to *Sum* (see
   figure 5.49).

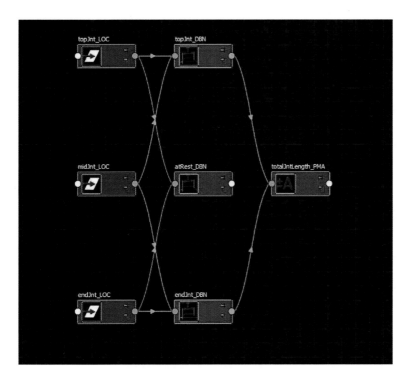

FIGURE 5.49 PlusMinusAverage joint length sum

Thinking a couple of steps ahead, we will want to have the option to turn on or off the stretch ability on the IK joints. Select the **foot_CTRL** and add an attribute called *stretch*. Make it an Enum data type and change the default values to *On* and *Off*. Add the **foot_CTRL** to the Node Editor and create a *Reverse* node named **stretchSwitch_RVN**. Connect the **foot_CTRL > stretch** to **stretchSwitch_RVN > Input > Input X** (see figure 5.50).

The Condition Node

OK, here comes the fun part. We will create our condition as stated a couple of pages back using the very useful *Condition* node (see figure 5.51). This node works as a typical If-Else statement in programming. Maya's help narrows it down to the following:

```
IF (First Term OPERATION Second Term) THEN
     Out Color = Color If True
ELSE
     Out Color = Color If False
```

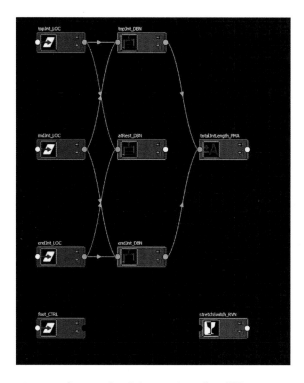

FIGURE 5.50 *Reverse* node switch connection to foot_CTRL

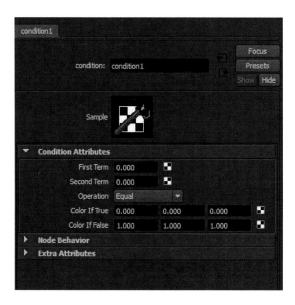

FIGURE 5.51 *Condition* node breakdown

In other words, if the value of the **First Term** is (**Equal, Not Equal, Greater Than, Less Than, etc.**) than the **Second Term**, then whatever value is in **Color If True** will happen. Otherwise, the value in **Color If False** will take precedence.

So in our case, this is the logic we would apply to our condition:

```
IF the value from the totalJntLength_PMA is less than or equal to atRest_DBN value
totalJntLength_PMA value takes precedence (basically don't stretch the joints because
totalJntLength_PMA will always be greater than atRest_DBN)
ELSE
atRest_DBN value takes over
```

We are setting, in effect, a false condition. You can do the same with *Greater Than*, except that you'll have to switch the condition parameters around and use the **totalJntLength_PMA** in our next math node. But before conditioning. . .

Remember the *stretch* switch? We are going to incorporate it now in our setup as we get ready for our **Condition** node. Create a **multiplyDivide** node, name it **switch_MDN**, set it to *multiply* and connect the following nodes (see figure 5.52):

1. **stretchSwitch_RVN > Output > OutputX to switch_MDN > Input > Input 1X**
2. **atRest_DBN > Distance to switch_MDN > Input > Input 2X**

Try now toggling on and off the *stretch* attribute from the **foot_CTRL**. When set to *On*, a value of 1 shows up in the **switch_MDN > Input 1X**, and 0 when set to *Off*. And we all know what happens when you multiply a number by zero! Zilch, nada, nil, null, the Great Void of Emptiness. Ok, you get the idea. So when our **atRest_DBN** value is set to zero, the condition will compare itself against that and based on our parameters will default to no-stretch.

Create the **condition** node and rename it **stretch_CDN**. Set the operation to "Less or Equal" and attach as shown below (see figure 5.53):

1. **totalJntLength_PMA > Output 1D to stretch_CDN > First Term** *and* **Color If True > Color If True R**
2. **switch_MDN > Output > Output X to stretch_CDN > Second Term**
3. **atRest_DBN > Distance to stretch_CDN > Color If False > Color If False R**

Almost there! We need now to figure out our stretch factor. Create a **multiplyDivide** node which you shall name **stretch_MDN**. I know, not very

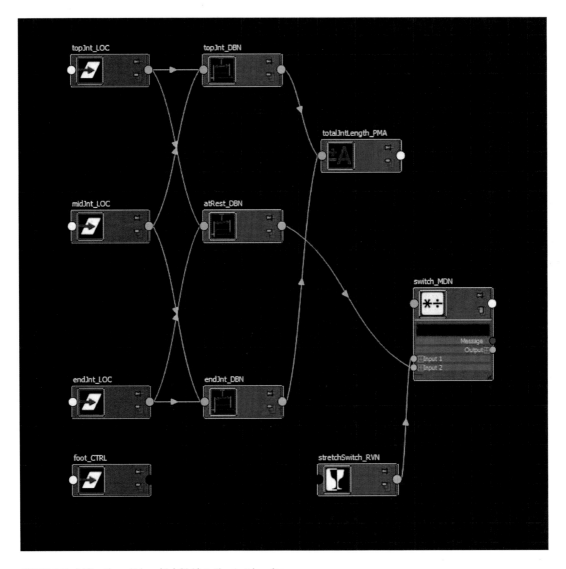

FIGURE 5.52 Adding the switch *multiplyDivide* to the stretch nodes

original, but it works for our purposes. Set the operation to *Divide* and connect (see figure 5.54):

1. **stretch_CDN > Out Color > Out Color R** to **stretch_MDN > Input 2 > Input 2X**
2. **atRest_DBN > Distance** to **stretch_MDN > Input 1 > Input 1X**

The last step left is to apply the stretch factor to our joints. We need to compare that with our current joint lengths and attach them to the Translate X channel.

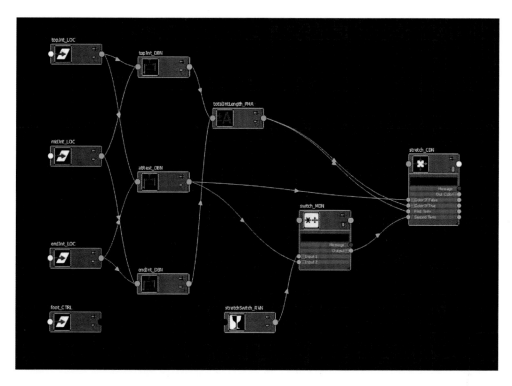

FIGURE 5.53 **Connecting the IK stretch condition**

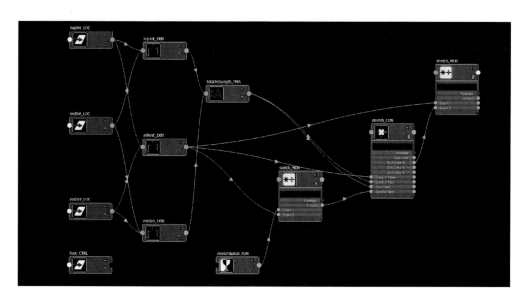

FIGURE 5.54 **Piping the output connections into the Stretch** *multiplyDivide*

Select **IK_legBend_JNT** and **IK_clawBase_JNT** and add them to the Node Editor. Create two additional *multiplyDivide* nodes and name them **IK_legBend_MDN** and **IK_clawBase_MDN** (see figure 5.55). Verify that the operation is set to *Multiply*.

1. **topJnt_DBN >Distance to IK_legBend_MDN > Input 1 > Input 1X**
2. **stretch_MDN >Output > Ouput X to IK_legBend_MDN > Input 2 > Input 2X**
3. **endJnt_DBN >Distance to IK_clawBase_MDN > Input 1 > Input 1X**
4. **stretch_MDN >Output > Ouput X to IK_clawBase_MDN > Input 2 > Input 2X**
5. **IK_legBend_MDN > Output > Output X to IK_legBend_JNT > Translate > Translate X**
6. **IK_clawBase_MDN > Output > Output X to IK_clawBase_JNT > Translate > Translate X**

And that's a wrap—at least for the stretch IK for this one leg.

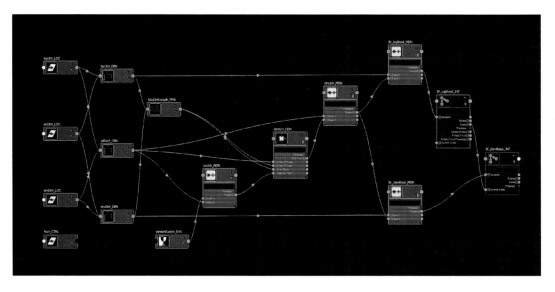

FIGURE 5.55 Stretch IK node complete setup

Going the Distance

As you've noticed, getting information back from our rig is important for the overall rigging process. Case in point—getting the length of the joints for the IK stretch, as we just did above.

We've used the *distanceBetween* node in Chapter 4 as part of our script, and now in the Node Editor as well. As you probably know, in order to get some visual feedback on the screen, we use the Distance Tool. We will make one for this next example and then explore more robust ways of getting that information in an upcoming script (*make sure the stretch value is off on the **foot_CTRL!***).

1. Create a Distance Tool (**Create > Measure Tools > Distance Tool**) and snap the first locator to the **IK_legTop_JNT** and the second locator to **leg_IK**.
2. Parent the first locator under **IK_legTop_JNT** and the second locator to **leg_IK** (see figure 5.56).
3. You should see a distance value of **10.187505** between the two locators (if you're using the file provided) (see figure 5.57).
4. Select the **foot_CTRL** and translate it in the Y-axis until the **leg_IK** is straight. You should have a value of about **11.75** or so (see figure 5.58).

You can obviously see the issues with this method. First, it takes too long and too many mouse clicks. Second, it works only if you manually drag the handles, which is not conducive to automation. Thirdly, it's not precise.

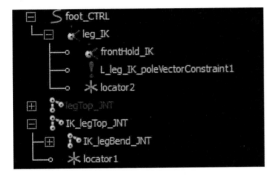

FIGURE 5.56 Using distance locators to measure length

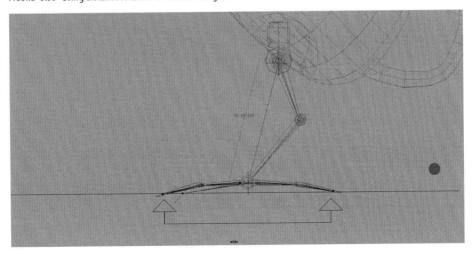

FIGURE 5.57 Getting the distance tool value

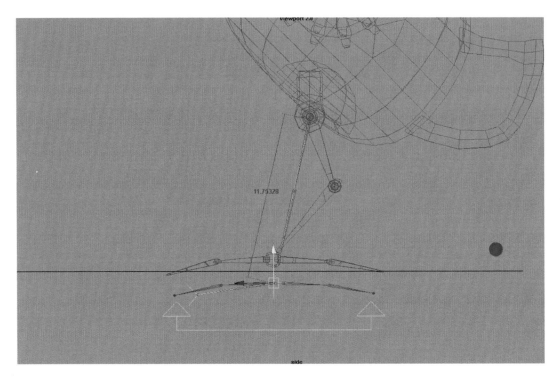

FIGURE 5.58 **Manually move foot control to straighten leg joints**

We are going to write a short script that will give us the length of our joint chain. There are two variants to this script. The first will return the length of selected joints. Later, we will modify it slightly to return the total length of a complete joint chain by selecting the root joint. We are going to introduce also the Maya API (Application Programming Interface). The API is based on C++ and allows access to Maya's internal libraries. Programmers can create new tools and plugins for Maya (not just scripts). It also evaluates much faster than MEL or Python. The advantage of Python is that it can access the API directly, as opposed to MEL. We are not going to delve too deeply with this topic but will focus on the relevant functions that will help us get the results we need.

Type the following in the Script Editor and save it as ***tgpGetSelLength.py***.

```
# RETURNS SELECTED JOINT LENGTH
import maya.api.OpenMaya as om
import maya.cmds as mc
```

```
def tgpGetSelLength():
    # define selected joints
    sel=[]
    sel=mc.ls(sl=True)
    length=0
    totalLength=lengthSelJoints(sel)

    print ("total length is {0}".format(totalLength))

def lengthSelJoints(sel):
    length=0
    # loop through selected joints until end of chain is reached
    for i in range(len(sel)):
        try:
            total=jointDistance(sel[i],sel[i+1])
            length+=total
        except:
            pass
    return length

def jointDistance (objA, objB):
    # get the worldSpace translation coordinates of the parent joint
    parentJnt=mc.xform(objA,q=1,t=1,ws=1)

    # get the worldSpace translation coordinates of the child joint
    childJnt=mc.xform(objB,q=1,t=1,ws=1)

    # find the vector of the parent joint
    vP=om.MVector(parentJnt[0],parentJnt[1],parentJnt[2])

    # find the vector of the child joint
    vC=om.MVector(childJnt[0],childJnt[1],childJnt[2])

    # find the distance between the vectors by using
    # the MVector.length() function
    # (This is the same as the distance equation in
    # we used in Chapter 04)
    length=om.MVector(vC-vP).length()

    return length
```

To test the script, select the **IK_legTop_JNT**, **IK_legBend_JNT** and **IK_clawBase_JNT,** then run the script `tgpGetSelLength()`. You should get the following result:

```
Total length of joint chain is 11.7535428688
```

The outcome is an effective and precise result without guesswork and unnecessary objects in your scene. And now you can use this in any future rigging setup where you need to find the length of selected joints in a chain. Another great advantage to this method is that it is not dependent on the primary axis of the chain and having to figure out the proper translation values based on that information.

To find the length of a complete chain by selecting only the root joint, change the following:

In *def tgpGetSelLength():*

```
totalLength=lengthSelJoints(sel,length)
```

In *def lengthSelJointsSel():*

```
def lengthSelJoints(sel,length):

    if not mc.listRelatives(sel,children=1):
      return length
    else:
        child=mc.listRelatives(sel,children=1,type='transform')[0]
        length=length+jointDistance(sel,child)
        return lengthSelJoints(child,length)
```

> **NOTE:** This last option won't work on Meep's legs because there are multiple joint branches extending from the **IK_baseClaw_JNT**. But if you try it on a single, continuous joint chain, you'll get the correct result. Also note that there are no error checks at this stage, so if the selections are not properly entered, you might get an error.

Once again, this is a perfect example of where scripting a little tool to automate this process becomes infinitely handy. The importance of going through the steps manually and working out any potential glitches becomes apparent once you start planning out the workings of your script.

Setting Up the Wings

Meep's wings are not what we would exactly call aerodynamic. There's no way a construction like this would even lift a millimeter should it be engineered and built. But thanks to the amazing powers of imagination, we are going to make Meep soar on his clunky flight limbs.

Back to more concrete issues, we have to figure out how to rig the wing for animation. Going back to the section where we analyzed the rig's behavior, we have to make the wing flap up and down, while connecting it to a system that will move the wing setup along the spherical shape of Meep's body.

The setup is not complicated per se. Rather—it's like figuring out a puzzle with cause and effect pieces.

Starting with the wing flap, we want to achieve something similar to figure 5.59. The key is to make the piston on the underside slide back and forth as the wing rotates up and down. As usual, there are multiple ways of achieving this. The most obvious is to use a driven key to control the flap attribute of the wing. That will work perfectly, but I'd like to explore yet another useful utility node called *remapValue*. This node is part of the remap nodes that Maya has, which are commonly used for material shading purposes. As with most utility nodes, it can be also used for our rigging purposes. The key advantage this node has is that it does not add additional animation curves to your joints. All the control is localized within the node itself.

Open **02_Meep_wing_setup.ma** and take a closer look at the left wing, regardless of your current political affiliations (see figure 5.60). The BND joints are point-constrained to the CTL joints, so they'll nicely follow along.

Let's take a moment and clean up a bit after us. Not only will this make our Outliner neater looking, but it will help also with containing everything in the proper hierarchies and make the overall manipulation of the characters easier to control.

Start by creating empty groups and name them as follows:

- MEEP
- GEO
- JOINTS
- CONTROLS
- __UTILITIES_DO_NOT_USE_

Parent all these groups under the MEEP group (see figure 5.61). Create another group and call it **ctrls_GRP**. Parent the **foot_CTRL** and **FK_legTop_GRP** under it. Take a look at figure 5.62 (see figure 5.62) and organize your

FIGURE 5.59 Illustration of wing flap range

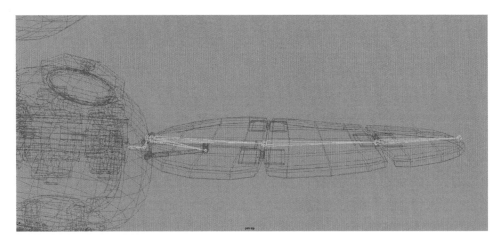

FIGURE 5.60 Position of the wing joints

Outliner accordingly. We will return and add to these groups later on, as we continue with Meep's rigging process, but this will be a good starting point.

FIGURE 5.61 **Hierarchy of group setup**

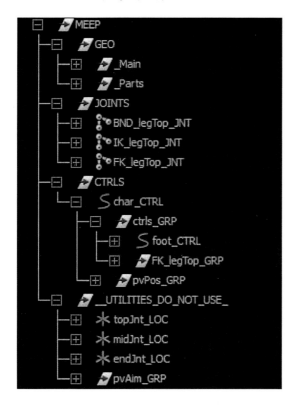

FIGURE 5.62 **Detailed hierarchy of group setup**

We are going to use the **tgpMechanix** script we wrote earlier to build the piston connecting the bottom of the wing to Meep's body. Run the script and create a piston similar to figure 5.63 (see figure 5.63A, B, C, D), using the Front and Top views for reference. You can delete the piston geometries (**topRod_geo_#** and **botRod_geo_#**) since we will replace them with Meep's geometry in due course.

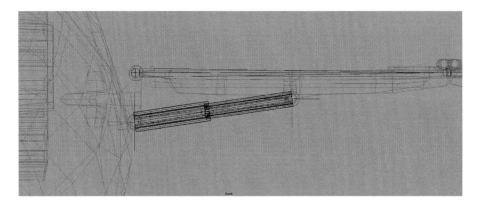

FIGURE 5.63A Position of the piston in all 4 views as created by tgpMechanix

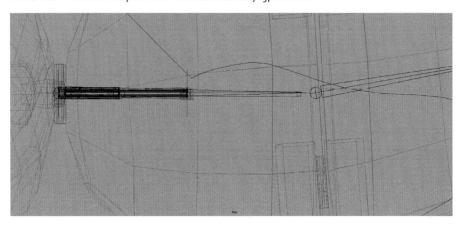

FIGURE 5.63B Position of the piston in all 4 views as created by tgpMechanix

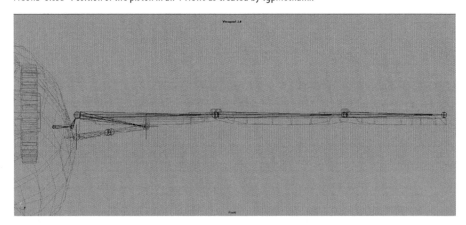

FIGURE 5.63C Position of the piston in all 4 views as created by tgpMechanix

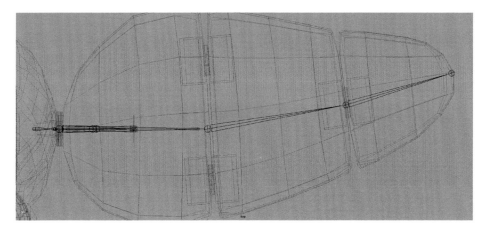

FIGURE 5.63D Position of the piston in all 4 views as created by tgpMechanix

Create a controller for the wing and rename it **wing_CTRL**. Group it to itself and name the group **wing_GRP**. Now move the group from the origin to **CTL_wingBase_JNT** and freeze transformations. For easier access to the controller, go into component mode and move it slightly above the wing (see figure 5.64).

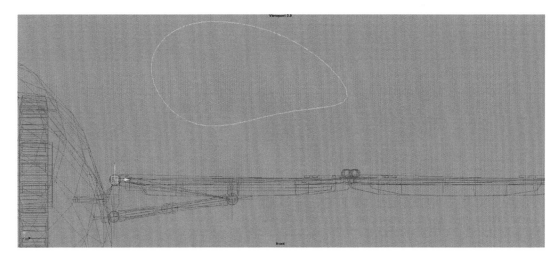

FIGURE 5.64 Create the wing controller

Establish a Single-Chain IK handle between **CTL_wingBase_JNT** and **CTL_wingMid_JNT**. Name the IK handle **flap_IK** and the effector **flap_EFF**. Create an empty group, rename it **flap_GRP** and snap it in position to **CTL_wingBase_JNT**. Freeze transformations on the group, and then make **flap_IK** its child (see figure 5.65).

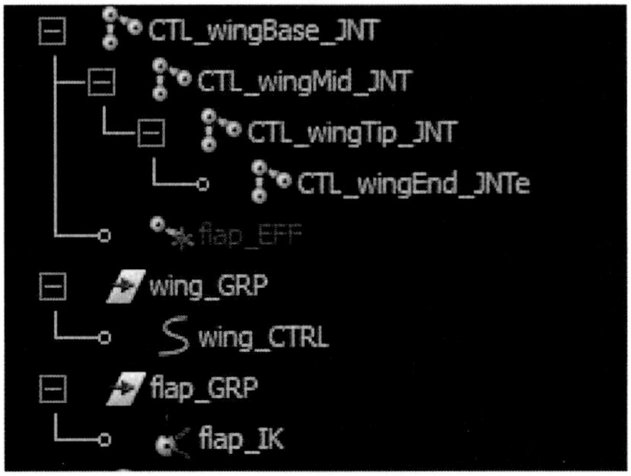

FIGURE 5.65 Connect the flapIK to flap_GRP

Create a new attribute named **flap** for the **wing_CTRL** with a *minimum* of **−30**, *maximum* of **50** and a *default* set to **0**. We will use to—you guessed it!—flap Meep's wings up and down. We want the controller to move with the wing as it animates so we'll create a direct connection between all the components. Direct connections are sometimes overlooked for their fancier counterparts like constraints and expressions, but they are very effective if you want simple, hassle-free links between objects.

Load **wing_CTRL** and **flap_GRP** into the Node Editor.

1. Create a *remapValue* node, and name it **flap_RMV**.
2. Connect **wing_CTRL > flap** to **flap_RMV > Input Value**.
3. Enter the following values in *the Input and Output Ranges* rolldown menu: *Input Min and Output Min* = **-50**; *Input Max and Output Max* = **50**.
4. **Flap_RMV > Out Value** to **flap_GRP > Rotate > Rotate Z** (see figure 5.66).

The wing is presently a-flappin'!

> **NOTE:** This setup works on the left wing. For the right wing, simply switch the values from positive to negative and vice versa.

Now, to set the slide, we have to figure out how much the actual wing slider geometry is going to move. Create a locator and bestow upon it the name **CTL_sliderLoc**. Group it to itself and name the group **CTL_sliderPos_GRP**. Snap the group to **topLoc_piston_#**. While you're at it, create a new group called **CTL_wing_GRP**, snap to **CTL_wingBase_JNT**, freeze transformations and parent **CTL_wingBase_JNT** and **flap_GRP**. Parent **CTL_sliderPos_GRP** to **CTL_wingBase_JNT** and freeze transformations (see figure 5.67).

wing_CTRL
flap
Message
swing
twist
flap_RMV
Message
Out Value
Input Value
unitConversion36
100cm =1m
flap_GRP
Rotate
Rotate X
Rotate Y
Rotate Z
Message

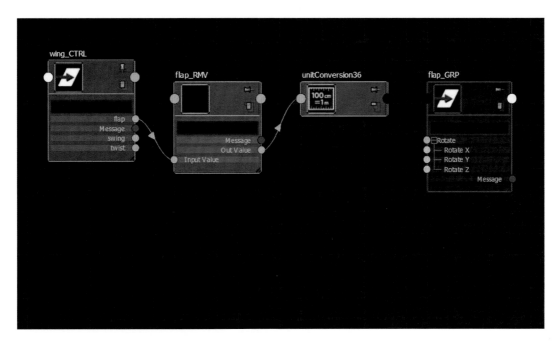

FIGURE 5.66 Connect wing_CTRL to flap_RMV

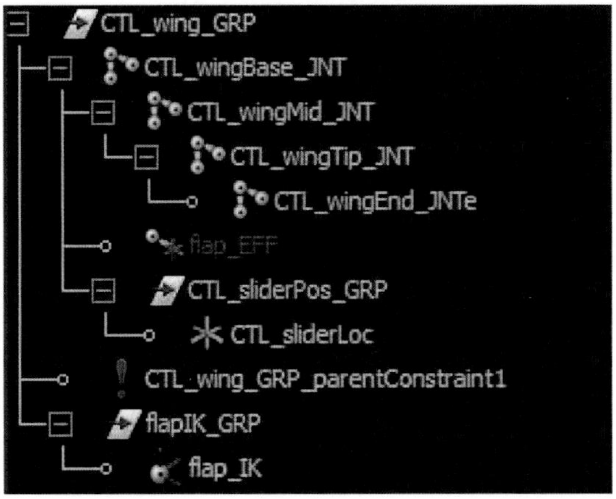

CTL_wing_GRP
CTL_wingBase_JNT
CTL_wingMid_JNT
CTL_wingTip_JNT
CTL_wingEnd_JNTe
flap_EFF
CTL_sliderPos_GRP
CTL_sliderLoc
CTL_wing_GRP_parentConstraint1
flapIK_GRP
flap_IK

FIGURE 5.67 Wing slider setup

If you translate the **CTL_sliderLoc** on the X-axis, you'll notice that a range between 4 and -4 will position it solidly along the **wingBar** geo. We will use those values for this example. To add another layer of boundaries, open the Attribute Editor for **CTL_sliderLoc** and under *Limit Information*, set the **Translate Limit X** to *Min* -4 and *Max* 4 (see figure 5.68).

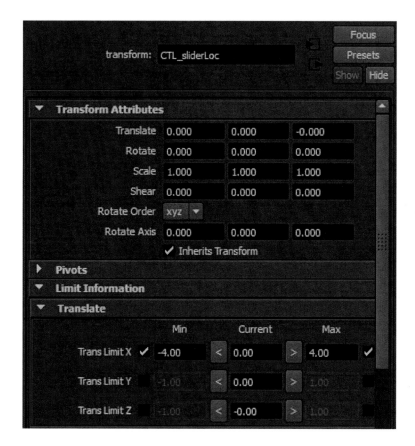

FIGURE 5.68 Setting the wing slider limits

Add the prefix "*wing_*" to the hierarchy of the **piston_GRP_#** that you created earlier (see figures 5.69 and 5.70). Create an empty group, snap it to the position of **wing_baseLoc_piston_#**, freeze transformations and name it **CTL_wingPiston_GRP**. Now select **CTL_sliderPos_GRP**, shift-select **wing_topLoc_piston_#** and point constrain, making sure that *Maintain Offset* is *enabled* (there might be a slight shift due to the positioning of the geometry, so this should prevent it from happening).

Load **wing_CTRL** and **CTL_sliderPos_GRP** into the Node Editor (see figure 5.71).

1. Create another *remapValue* node named **slider_RMV**.
2. Connect **wing_CTRL > flap** to **slider_RMV > Input Value**.
3. Enter the following values in *the Input and Output Ranges: Input Min* = **-100**; *Input Max* = **100**; *Output Min* = **-4**; *Output Max* = **4**.
4. **Slider_RMV > Out Value** to **CTL_sliderPos_GRP > Translate > Translate X**

220

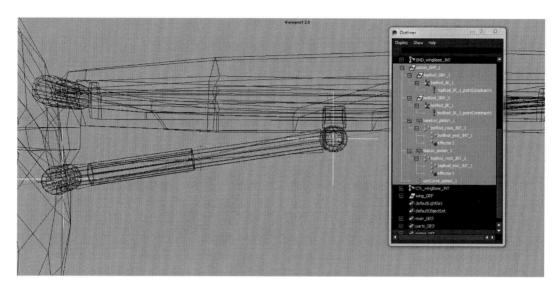

FIGURE 5.69 Piston group prior to adding the prefix

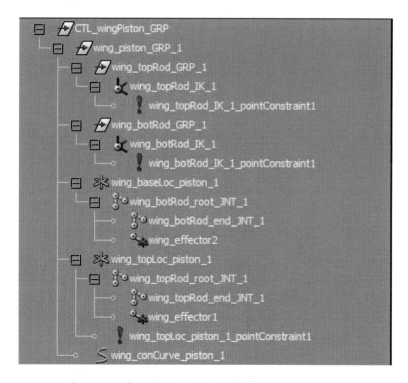

FIGURE 5.70 Piston group after adding the "wing" prefix

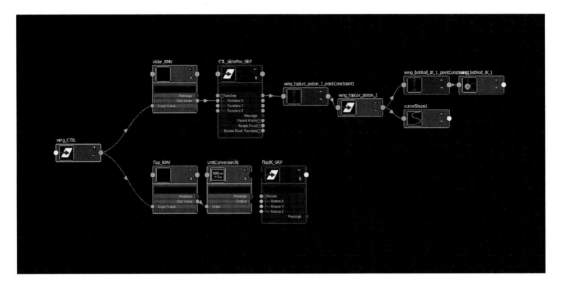

FIGURE 5.71 **Setting up the wing_CTRL**

Since we've been focusing on the control rig, we need also link it to the bind rig so that the geometry will have something to attach to. Point constraint **BND_wingBase_JNT** to **CTL_wingBase_JNT**.

Scrubbing the flap attribute, you'll see the wing moving up and down, as the joints set for the pistons expand and contract.

Open **03_Meep_wing_rotator_setup.ma** for the next part of the wing rig.

The **CTL_rotator_GRP** is made up of 4 locators, each with their own role in the scope of Meep's magical flight ability. Let's begin with a few connections. Start by parent constraining **CTL_wingPiston_GRP**, **CTL_wing_GRP** and **wing_GRP** to **CTL_wingConnector_LOC**.

You can do it manually or you can use this handy little bit of code (select **CTL_wingConnector_LOC** first followed by the other groups!):

```
objs=mc.ls(sl=True)
for i in range(1, len(objs)):
    mc.parentConstraint(objs[0],objs[i],mo=True)
```

Next, parent constraint **BND_rotator_GRP** to **CTL_wingSwingTip_LOC**. The connections between the joints and controllers is now ready. OK, almost. One additional little one: **CTL_wingBase_JNT > Rotate Z** to **wing_CTRL > Rotate > Rotate Z**

NOTE: This is to have the **wing_CTRL** rotate with the *flap* attribute. When you do the right side later on, you might need to insert a *multiplyDivide* node between the two, with a value of **-1** in **input2X** to reverse the rotation. Repeat for any additional controls that move in the opposite way than expected.

Select the **wing_CTRL** and add a couple more attributes to it named *twist* (*Minimum* = **-50** & *Maximum* = **50**) and *swing* (*Minimum* = **-30** & *Maximum* = **2**). I know I should be making a rock and roll comment right about now, but I'll spare you.

The way Meep was designed, we want the wing rotator geo to move in an arced motion inside the body but also have the ability to turn the wing so the flapping motion can be adjusted. To get this to work, we are going to cheat a bit.

NOTE: If you want to have visual feedback on what we are currently doing, select *L_wingRotator* from the *GEO>_Parts* group, duplicate it and parent it to **BND_rotatorBase_JNT**. Don't forget to delete it once you're done.

Select **CTL_rotator_GRP** and rotate the X-axis to *-50*. This will turn our wing to a slightly awkward angle, but there's a method to the madness, so read on.

Load into the Node Editor the **wing_CTRL, CTL_wingSwing_LOC** and **CTL_wingTwist_LOC:**

1. Connect **wing_CTRL > swing** to **CTL_wingSwing_Loc > Rotate > Rotate Y**.
2. Create a *plusMinusAverage* node and rename it **wingTwist_PMA**.
3. Connect **wing_CTRL > twist** to **wingTwist_PMA > Input 1D > Input 1D[0]**.
4. Since Maya doesn't offer the option to create additional 1D inputs intuitively, type the following in the Script Editor:
   `mc.setAttr("wingTwist_PMA.input1D[1]", 50)`.
5. Connect **wingTwist_PMA > Ouput 1D** to **CTL_wingTwist_LOC > Rotate > X** (see figure 5.72).

And for the grand finale for the wing rig (see, told you it wouldn't be too complicated. . .):

1. Select **CTL_wingMid_JNT** and **CTL_wingTip_JNT**.
2. Run the *tgpCtrlOrient.py* script.
3. Set the axis to Z; Radius = **1.75**; check both boxes and click on *Create*.

Two Controllers should appear on top of the selected joints. Make **CTL_wingMid_GRP** a child of **wing_CTRL** (see figure 5.73).

Meep is now ready to soar.

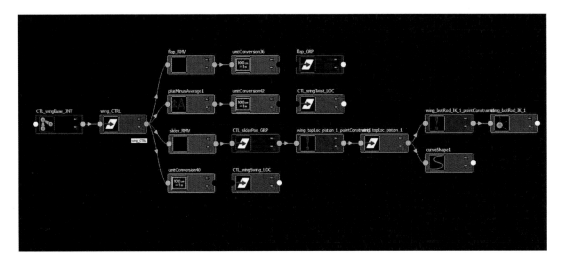

FIGURE 5.72 **Complete wing CTRL nodes**

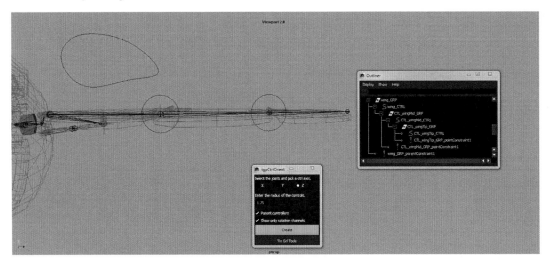

FIGURE 5.73 **Adding individual wing controls**

Neck

The neck is an interesting challenge. It's designed as a spring, so we will expect it to stretch up and down. In addition, we are going to give it a bobblehead motion and added flexibility along its length. There are a few methods to consider in order to achieve this setup:

1. **"Bendy" controls**—this is typically rigged using a spline IK setup, and manipulating the control curve that drives the spline IK with the use of clusters.

2. **Ribbon rig**—this setup usually involves the use of dynamic hair curves. It's very flexible but somewhat involved in its setup.

For this setup, we are going to use a variation of the FK leg setup, with a slight modification. Instead of controlling the stretchiness with a custom attribute, we will make it a bit more interactive and use a controller. Open **04_Meep_ neck_setup.ma** (see figure 5.74).

FIGURE 5.74 Default neck setup file

We will use the *tgpFKstretch.py* (see figure 5.75) script to accomplish this. The script combines elements from our *tgpMechanix.py* script, *tgpCtrlOrient.py* and a sprinkling of custom connections. Take a look at the code of the script to see its inner workings.

Change to a side view and position the locators as seen in figure 5.76. Change the number of spans to **10**, the control radius to **2** and check "Show only rotation channels". Press *Create*. You should have something similar to figure 5.77 (see figure 5.77). If you select the neck controls (2 to 10) and rotate them on the Z-axis, you'll get a fluid bending of the joints backward and forward (see figure 5.78). If you also select the top locator and translate it away from its original location, you'll notice the joints stretch accordingly (see figure 5.79).

Let's organize the Outliner a bit. Select **BND_FKstretch_JNT_GRP_1** and rename it **BND_neck_JNT_GRP**. Move it under the JOINTS folder. Rename **FKstretch_GRP_1** to **CTL_ neckStretch_GRP** and move it under **CTRLS > char_CTRL>ctrls_GRP** (see figure 5.80).

Let's move on now to the next setup—Meep's head.

FIGURE 5.75 **tgpFKstretch script**

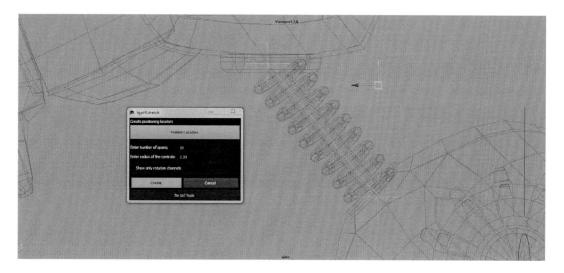

FIGURE 5.76 Setting up the tgpFKstretch locators on along the neck

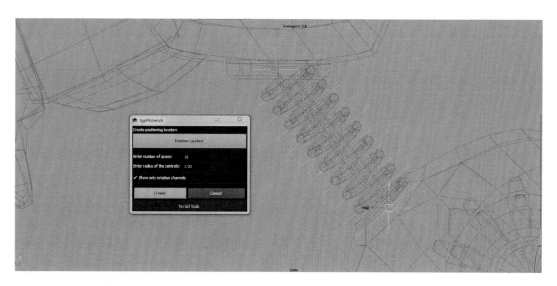

FIGURE 5.77 Creating the neck joints and controllers

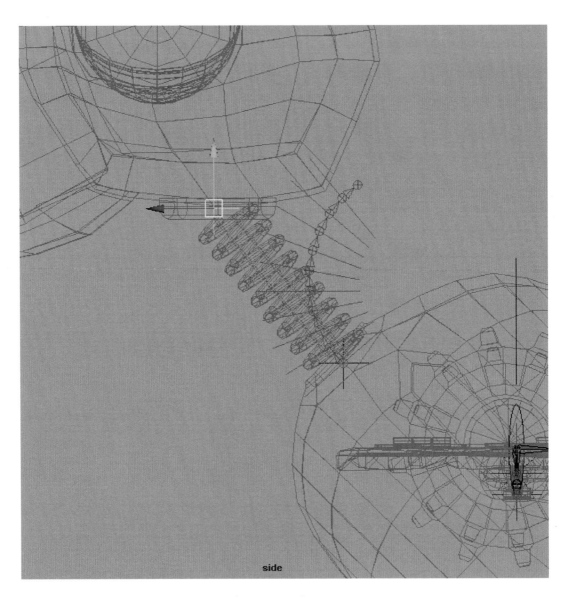

side

FIGURE 5.78 Rotating the neck joints by selecting all of the neck controllers

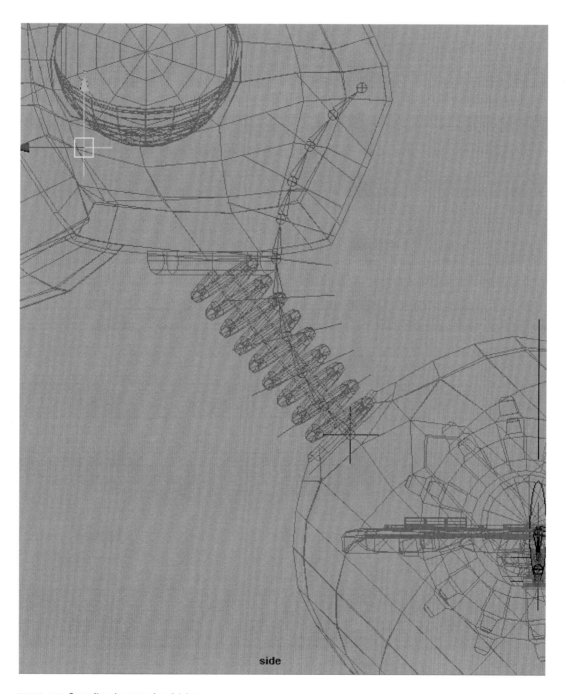

side

FIGURE 5.79 Extending the rotated neck joints

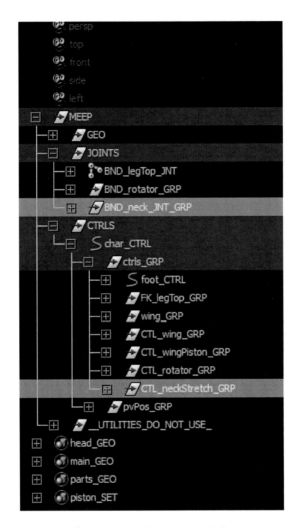

FIGURE 5.80 Organizing the neck groups in the Outliner

Building the Head

The head is relatively straightforward. There are not many moving parts in Meep's head design. The eyes, to keep true to the physiology of birds, don't move but rather the head points in the direction the eye will look at. This can give the animator a lot of freedom to create animated antics with the overall neck and head motions.

The main moving parts in this setup include the head itself, the eyelids (top and bottom on each side) and the lower beak. The range of motion can be effectively achieved through FK rotations and we will—once again—make use of our ***tgpCtrlOrient.py*** script to setup the relevant controllers.

Start by loading **05_Meep_head_setup.ma** (see figure 5.81). The main bind joints are already in place. We'll begin with the lower beak. Open ***tgpCtrlOrient***, check "Show only rotation channels", and select **BND_ jawBase_JNT**. Press the *Create* button, and *voila* . . . a moving beak (see figure 5.82).

We will repeat the same procedure for the eyelid joints (see figure 5.83). Don't worry too much about the controllers themselves, since we will link them to the **head_CTRL** once we're done.

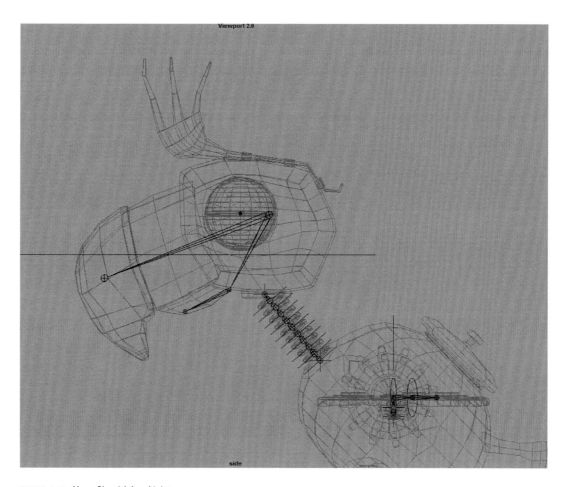

FIGURE 5.81 **Meep file with head joints**

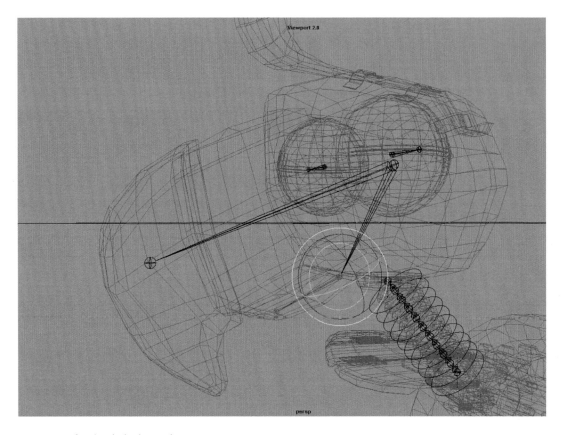

FIGURE 5.82 **Creating the beak control**

Select the **head_CTRL** and add the following attributes:

- *Beak* (*min **0**, max **75**, **0***)
- *L_topEyelid* & *R_topEyelid* (*min **0**, max **75**, default **0***)
- *L_bottomEyelid* & *R_bottomEyelid* (*min-**75**, max **0**, default **0***)

Connect the attributes to the relevant controls in the rotate-Z channels (see figure 5.84). I've added a *multiplyDivide* node to the beak, where ***input2X*** is set to *-1* so the beak rotation is positive instead of negative. This is optional.

Parent the eyelid rotation controls to BND groups, making them siblings to the eyelidBase controls. Freeze their transformations and in the Node Editor connect the ***rotateX*** output of the **eyelid_CTRL** to the ***rotateX*** input of the **eyelidBase_CTRL** (see figure 5.85). Now lock and hide all of the channels except for the rotate X of the eyelid_CTRLs. The eyelidBase and beak controls have also been hidden.

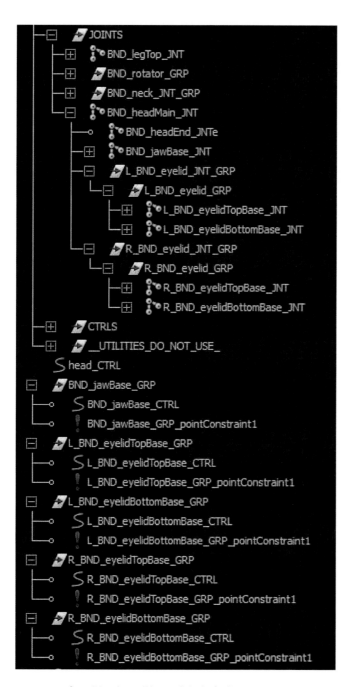

FIGURE 5.83 Organizing the eyelid controls in the Outliner

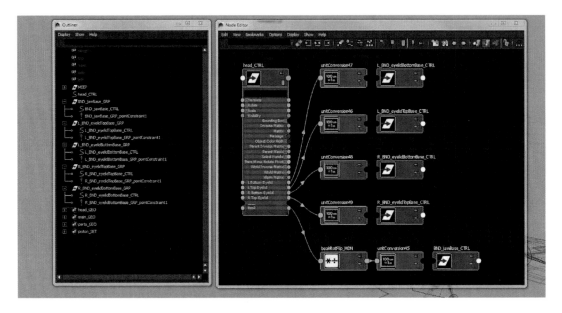

FIGURE 5.84 Connections from head_CTRL to eyelid controls

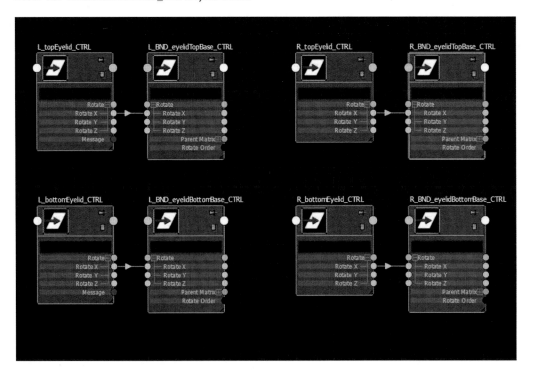

FIGURE 5.85 Connections between eyelid controls to BND joint controls

234

For the next phase, we are going to play one of my favorite games—rigging Tetris™ (this said with a healthy dose of sarcasm)—with the joints and controls we've setup so far.

1. Create an empty group called **head_CTRL_GRP**. Snap the pivot to **BND_headMain_JNT**.
2. Parent the **head_CTRL** under it (see figure 5.86).
3. Parent **BND_headMain_JNT** to it, and group it to itself. Rename the group **BND_headMain_GRP** (see figure 5.87).
4. Parent **head_CTRL_GRP** under the **neckStretch_CTRL**, then parent-constrain it to the last neck control (**BND_FKstretch_CTRL_10**). Parent **neckStretch_CTRL** to the **ctrls_GRP** (see figure 5.88).
5. Select **topLoc_FKstretch_1** and parent-constrain it to **neckStretch_CTRL**.
6. Select the **head_CTRL** and lock and hide the translate, scale and visibility channels. Change the Rotate Order to ZXY.

If you managed to follow all of this (while humming the Tetris™ soundtrack . . . bonus points) you should be able to move and rotate the head control and the eye and beak joints will follow, as well as extending the neck joints. If you select the neck controls (all except for the bottom one—we want to keep that one locked to the body) and rotate them in the Z-axis, the neck joints will curve and the head will follow along. Just in case, you can see the end result by opening the file *06_Meep_head_completed.ma*.

To simplify the neck control's selection process, you can create a quick selection set and add it to a shelf (**Create > Sets > Quick Select Set. . .**). Handy and helps with the war against carpal tunnel syndrome!

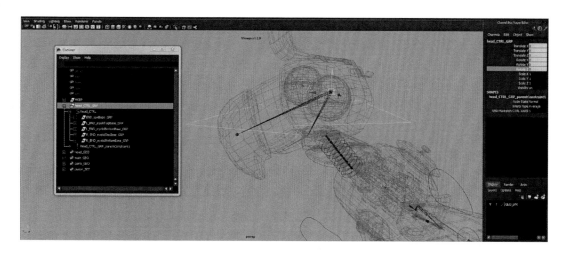

FIGURE 5.86 **head_CTRL_GRP** in position

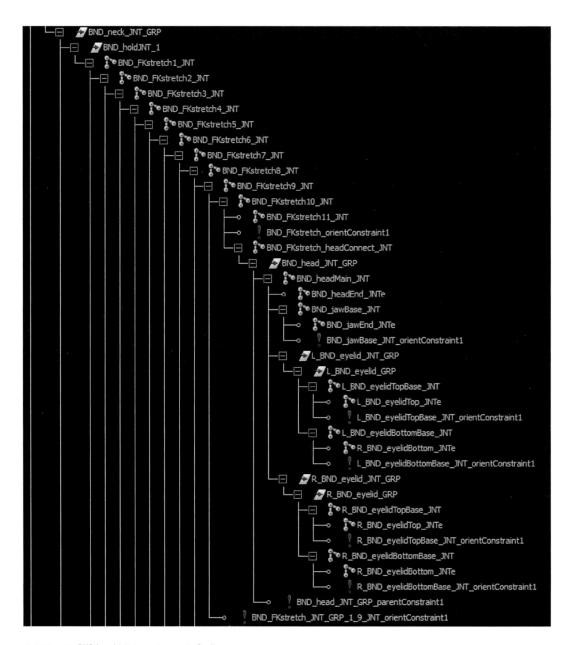

FIGURE 5.87 **BND head joint group setup in Outliner**

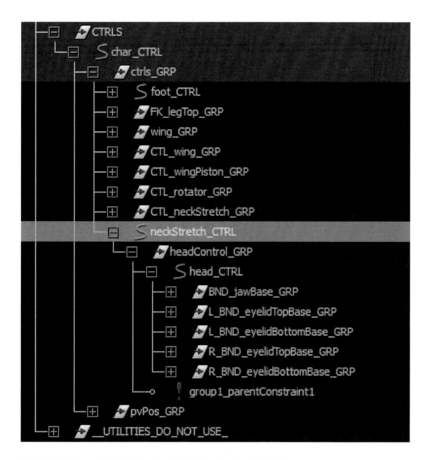

FIGURE 5.88 Connecting the headControl_GRP under the ctrls_GRP

Putting Together the Body

The last stretch! Now that we have the individual parts of Meep in place, it's time to put them all together. Load **07_Meep_body_setup.ma** into Maya. The leg and wing setups have been applied to the right side. You'll notice also that each side is properly prefixed with a "L_" or "R_" to identify them properly.

Due to Meep's simplistic body structure—hey, a rigid teapot for a body . . . who wouldn't want that? No lower backaches, direct access to the inner workings thanks to a removable lid, the occasional buff at the machine shop for a shiny new look . . . but I digress—we are not going to need to worry about heavy deformations when it comes to painting weights. All the main body elements can be weighted to one single joint, which will translate beautifully into the game engine of choice.

Create a single joint in the side view and place it somewhere within Meep's body. Rename it **BND_root_JNT** and parent it to the **JOINTS** group

Create a new controller called **body_CTRL**. I used a NURBS circle and scaled the CV's in the front to give it a point. Snap and freeze transformations of the **body_CTRL** on top of the **BND_root_JNT** you created earlier. Parent-constraint **BND_root_JNT** to **body_CTRL**, and in turn parent the **body_CTRL** to the **ctrls_GRP** (see figure 5.89).

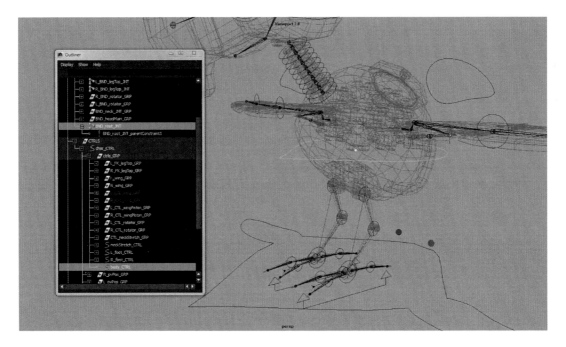

FIGURE 5.89 **Setting up the BND_root_JNT position**

The role of the **body_CTRL** is to take care of all of the rig motion above the legs—except when the legs are in FK-mode. Typically, the legs are in IK-mode, thus planting them firmly on a surface, so when the **body_CTRL** is activated, the rest of the rig moves while grounded. To allow the IK legs to be independent, create a new locator named **legHold_LOC** and place it above the leg joints (see figure 5.90). Parent it to the **body_CTRL**, along with the rest of the groups and controls, except for the Left and Right foot controls (see figure 5.91).

To connect the IK legs, navigate to the **_UTILITIES_DO_NOT_USE_** group and under the **IK_legs_GRP**, select **the L_IK_legTop_JNT** and parent-constraint it to the **legHold_LOC**. Repeat with **R_IK_legTop_JNT**.

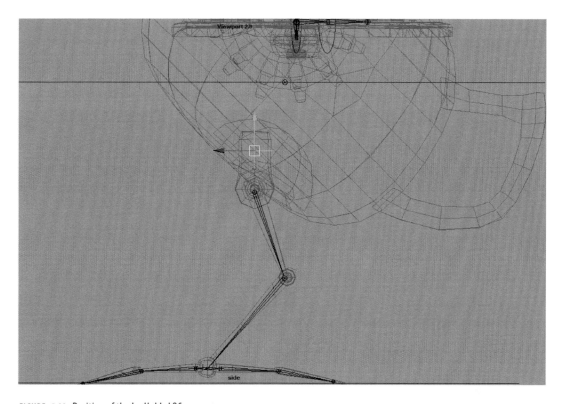

FIGURE 5.90 **Position of the legHold_LOC**

While we're there, parent-constrain the **FK_legs_GRP** to the **body_CTRL**.
So far we've dealt with the control joints. We need now to connect the BND
joints. Create two empty groups and name them **L_BND_leg_JNT_GRP** and
R_BND_leg_JNT_GRP. Parent them under the *JOINTS* group, and then place
under them the relevant BND joints. Parent-constraint the new groups to the
body_CTRL (see figure 5.92).

All this juggling will properly set the hierarchy for the legs to move with the
body. Now, if you set the legs to IK-mode and try to move the **body_CTRL**
up, you'll notice a double transformation happening on the BND joints (see
figure 5.93).

The cause is the parent-constraint of the BND joints. When it's in IK-mode,
the double transformations happen, but if you change it to FK-mode (via the
char_CTRL), you'll notice the joints behave properly. In order for us to fix that,
we'll need to create a switch to enable and disable the constraint to affect
the joints, depending on the mode we choose. We will do that using—you
guessed it—utility nodes once again! We will start with the left leg first.

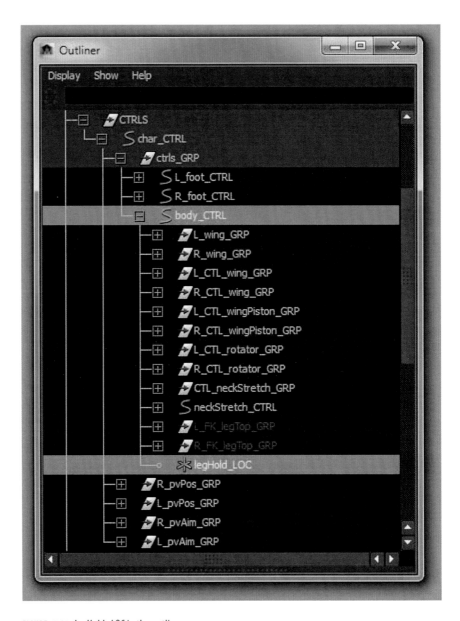

FIGURE 5.91 **legHold_LOC in the outliner**

FIGURE 5.92 Connecting the BND groups to the body_CTRL

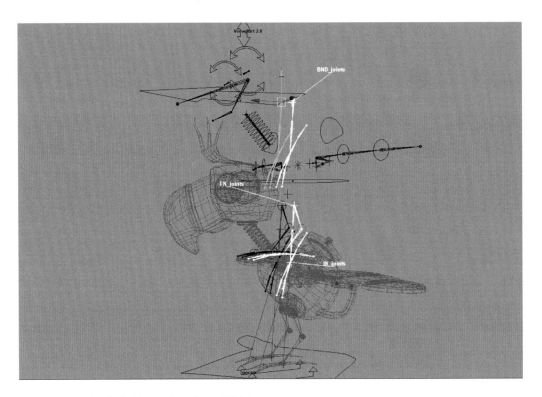

FIGURE 5.93 Results of a double transformation on BND joints

1. Load **char_CTRL**, **body_CTRL** and **L_BND_leg_JNT_GRP** into the Node Editor (see figure 5.94).
2. Create a *condition* node and name it **L_IKFK_legWeight_CDN**. Leave the default values as is.
3. Connect **char_CTRL** > **L_leg_IKFK** to **L_IKFK_legWeight_CDN** > **First Term** (see figure 5.95).
4. Connect **L_IKFK_legWeight_CDN** > **Out Color R** to **L_BND_leg_JNT_GRP_parentConstraint1** > **Body CTRLW0** (see figure 5.96).

The double transformations are taken care of for the leg now. One more thing to do in order to keep this organized and flowing is to turn on and off the visibility of the controllers. Again, we could use driven keys, but since the Node Editor is open and we have our nodes present, might as well use them.

1. Add to the currently open scene the **L_foot_CTRL** and **L_FK_legTop_GRP**.
2. Create a new *condition* node and name it **L_legVis_CDN**.
3. Change the **Color If True** > **R** to **1** and **Color If False** > **R** to **0**.
4. Connect **char_CTRL** > **L_leg_IKFK** to **L_legVis_CDN** > **First Term** (see figure 5.97).
5. Connect **L_legVis_CDN** > **Out Color R** to **L_foot_CTRL** > **Visibility**.

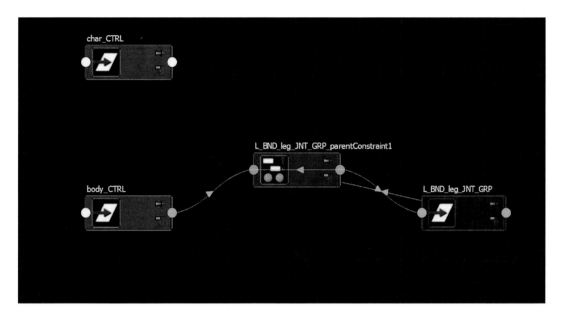

FIGURE 5.94 **Load nodes to begin correcting double transformations issue**

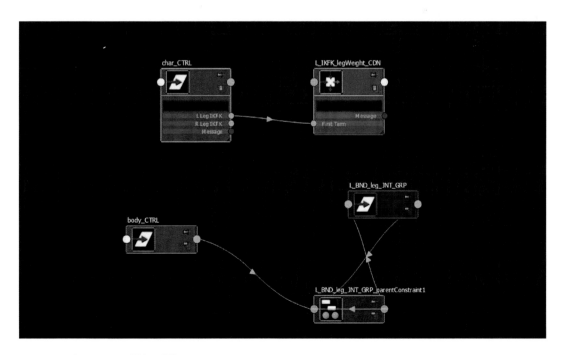

FIGURE 5.95 **Connect char_CTRL to CDN node**

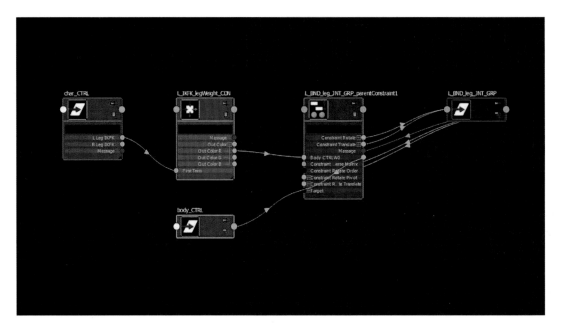

FIGURE 5.96 Finish connections for double-transform problem

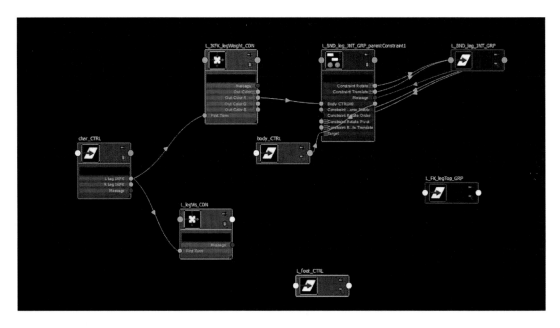

FIGURE 5.97 Creating the L_legVis_CDN connection

Great! The IK setup is now properly "hiding" when we switch from FK to IK via the char_CTRL. And now for the FK. . .

1. Create a *reverse* node and name it **L_IK_vis_RVN**.
2. Connect **L_legVis_CDN** > **Out Color R** to **L_IK_vis_RVN** > **Input X**.
3. Finally, connect **L_IK_vis_RVN** > **Output X** to **L_FK_legTop_GRP** > **Visibility**.

Repeat to the right side and the legs are now ready.

Finishing Touches

You can load the weighted version of Meep from the file directory—**08_Meep_weighted.ma**—and see how everything was put together. The geometry is bound to the joints using a straightforward smooth bind to selected joints with a max influence between 1 or 2 joints (for the stretchy legs). The only difference is the neck, where the max joint influence is set to the number of joints, so we can get a decent deformation.

The controls are color coded now. I'm using standard coloration (yellow for center, red for right and blue for left). Typically, if you select the top node in a hierarchy and override its colors (**Attribute Editor > Display > Drawing Overrides > Enable Overrides**) it will affect all of its children nodes.

Here's a little script that will create the color overrides, but on the shape node This way, even if you mistakenly change the transform node, it won't affect it. To use it, select the curves for which you want to change the colors and run the script.

```
# Change color overrides

# get shape nodes
sel=mc.listRelatives(mc.ls(sl=True),shapes=True)

# Default color index: 6=blue, 13=red, 17=yellow

for i in range(len(sel)):
    mc.setAttr(sel[i]+".overrideEnabled", True)
    mc.setAttr(set[i]+".overrideColor", 6)
```

Move the controllers around and get a feeling for Meep's movement range. Feel free to change things around to get Meep to move the way you want.

Global Scale

One major addition is the functionality of the global scale to the rig, which you probably saw in the **char_CTRL** attributes. In general, scaling a rig is one of those things that—when they don't work as you expect, which is, unfortunately, often—cause you to go and learn a new language so you can swear floridly at the screen and take more-than-average coffee breaks just to calm yourself. Yet there will be times during production that you'll need to scale your character's rig and you'll want to make sure that it behaves the way you expect.

We will cover a way that will prevent this from happening on Meep, which you can then apply to your rigs.

First, to see what exactly we're dealing with—select the **char_CTRL** and scale it on all 3-axes. Not a pretty sight (see figure 5.98). This is the result of double transformations on the geometry and the controls that manipulate it. As we've discussed earlier in this book, one of the core basics of rigging is to understand the logic of how the different components interact and relate to one another, as connections are made between them. Remember, Maya is a node-based program, so every object (node) has an input and an output connection. What usually happens in double-transformations is that there is more than one influencing node on an object, and it causes that object to transform in 3D space at a different rate than its input node.

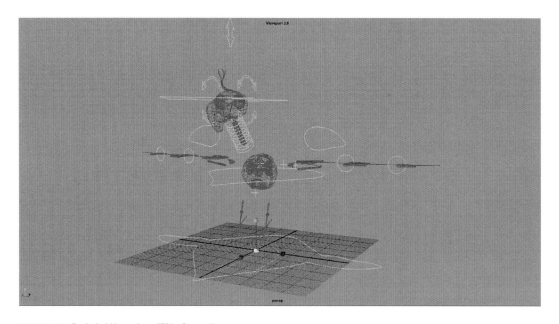

FIGURE 5.98 **Exploded Meep char_CTRL after scaling**

Now, if you were to take a closer look at the hierarchy of Meep in the Outliner, you will notice that we have two levels of parents sitting above our **char_ CTRL**. Let's try something else: Make sure to undo any scaling changes you made and select the topmost group (**MEEP**). Scale it on all 3 axes and notice the changes this time (see figure 5.99). The rig doesn't explode as *badly* as before, but the geometry still doesn't scale in the same rate as the joints. The reason is that the **MEEP** group is transforming (scaling in this case) all of its children nodes. Those nodes include the mesh *and* the controls and joints that also affect the mesh through constraints, direct connections and skinning. We have to figure out a way to separate which connection will influence the transformations of the mesh. There is an actual easy way to do so.

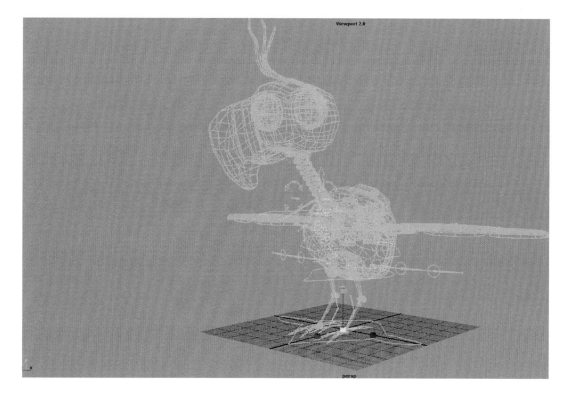

FIGURE 5.99 Scaled Meep using the topmost MEEP node

Select the **GEO** group and open its transform attributes in the Attribute Editor (see figure 5.100). Notice that checkbox beside *Inherits Transform*? Uncheck it.

Surprise! The mesh just scaled down to the size you set with the **MEEP** group (see figure 5.101).

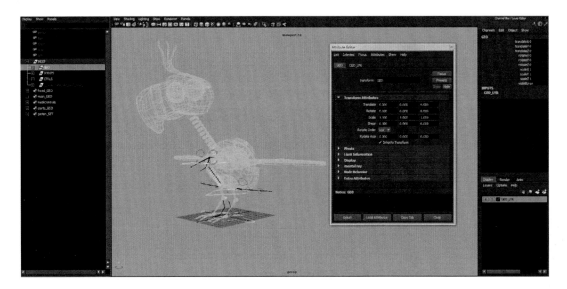

FIGURE 5.100 **GEO group Attribute Editor**

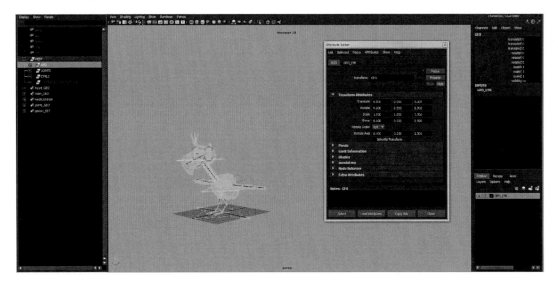

FIGURE 5.101 **Uncheck the Inherits Transform from GEO group**

What *Inherits Transform* does is allow or prevent that object to take on the transformation of its parent or not. Since Meep's mesh is already being manipulated through the bind joints, which in turn are manipulated by the controllers and so on, leaving *Inherit Transform* enabled causes the geometry to scale disproportionately.

Good. We are on the right track here. Now, rather than having to dig through the hierarchy and select our top node to scale our mesh, let's make it a bit more friendly to the animator.

Select the **char_CTRL** and add a new attribute called *globalScale*. Give it a *Minimum* value of 0.1, leave *Maximum* blank and *Default* value of 1.

Rename the current **MEEP** group to **GLOBAL_SCALE**. Group it to itself and rename this new group **MEEP** (see figure 5.102).

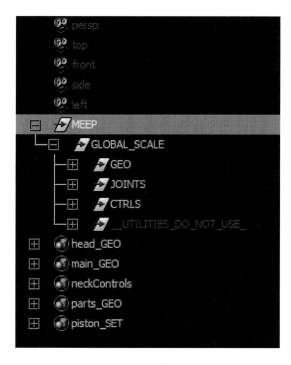

FIGURE 5.102 Rename MEEP and GLOBAL SCALE groups

In the Node Editor, hook up **the char_CTRL > globalScale** attribute to all 3 scale attributes of the **GLOBAL_SCALE** group (see figure 5.103). Now we'll be able to scale Meep directly from the viewport.

On a first pass, things seem to be working well, but on a closer look we'll notice a few small glitches (see figure 5.104):

1. The neck joints are disproportionally stretched.
2. If you enable the *stretch* attribute on the IK foot controls, you'll see the joints scale at an extreme angle.

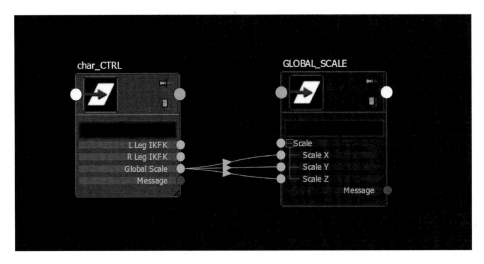

FIGURE 5.103 Connect char_CTRL to GLOBAL_SCALE

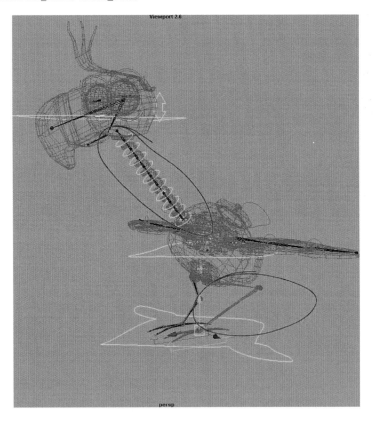

FIGURE 5.104 Neck and IK glitches during scaling

We'll take care of the neck first. Load the **char_CTRL** and **FKstretch_mult_MDN1** (you might have to dig up a bit to get it. It's connected to the top and base locators) (see figure 5.105).

1. Create a new *multiplyDivide* node and name it **neck_globalScale_MDN**. Set the operation to ***divide***.
2. Connect **FKstretch_mult_MDN1 > Ouput X** to **neck_globalScale_MDN > Input 1X**.
3. Connect **char_CTRL > globalScale** to **neck_globalScale_MDN > Input 2X** (see figure 5.106).

The role of the **neck_globalScale_MDN** node is to help us maintain the same ratio of the joint length as it's getting scaled. Right now, the BND_FK stretch joints are being double transformed. By dividing their stretched value by the global scale, it will help us maintain the same ratio, regardless of the character's global scale.

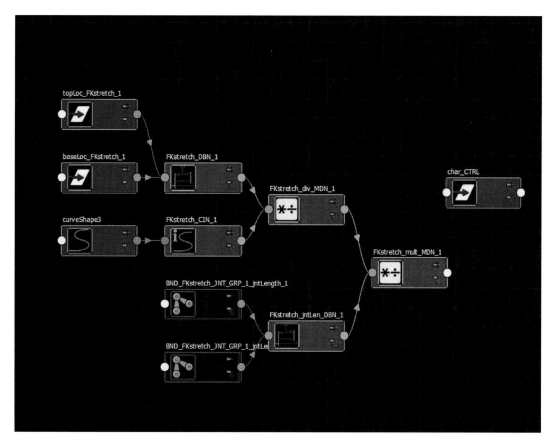

FIGURE 5.105 Neck global scale setup

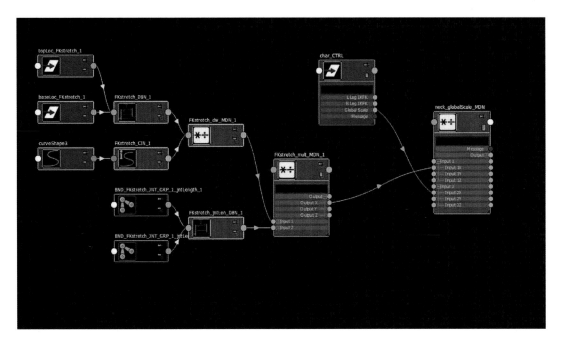

FIGURE 5.106 **Neck global scale connections**

The next step is to connect the output value of **_neck_globalScale_MDN_** to the translate X of all of the joints in question. Select from the *second* joint to the last in the chain (see figure 5.107). Do not select the first! Do the connections manually? Sure you can, but why would you? Time is precious!

Here's a bit of code that will do that for us:

```
sel=mc.ls(sl=True)
for i in range(len(sel)):
    mc.connecAttr("neck_globalScale_MDN.outputX", sel[i]+".translateX",f=1)
```

The length of the neck joints should now be at their proper distance.

Excellent! Now let's take care of the IK legs and wrap this up. We'll use a similar technique, but with a few minor changes.

Remember when we setup the stretch IK leg, we created 3 locators to help us measure the distance between the joints? One of the major advantages of using these locators was to give us a dynamic value, rather than locking in a set number for the distance. We'll start with the left leg:

1. Load into the Node Editor the output connections of **L_topJnt_LOC**, **L_midJnt_LOC** and **L_endJnt_LOC** (see figure 5.108).

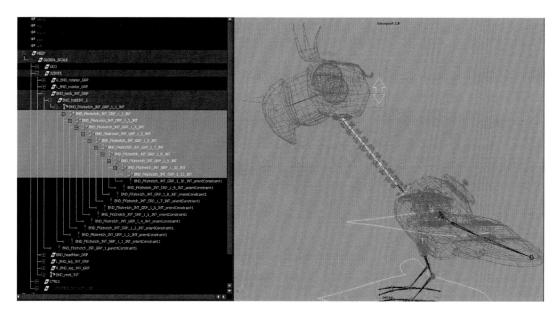

FIGURE 5.107 Selection of the neck joints prior to fixing the scaling glitch

2. Add the **char_CTRL** to the Node Editor.
3. Create a *multiplyDivide* node called **L_leg_globalScale_MDN** (see figure 5.109) and set to *multiply*.
4. Connect **L_totalJntLength_PMA > Output 1D** to **L_leg_globalScale_ MDN > Input 1X**.
5. Connect **char_CTRL > globalScale** to **L_leg_globalScale_MDN > Input 2X**.
6. Update the following connection**: L_leg_globalScale_MDN > Output X** to **L_stretch_CDN > Color If True R** *and* **First Term** (see figure 5.110).

If you scale Meep's global scale and enable the **L_leg_CTRL** stretch option, you'll see that it doesn't go all wonky. Redo the above steps for the right leg.

You can check out the final rigged version of Meep by loading **09_Meep_ FINAL.ma**.

We've covered quite a bit of stuff in this chapter. By now, you should have a much better idea of how to approach the rigging process of a character. Even though Meep is a relatively simple mechanical character, many of the steps we covered can be easily applied to more complex and organic characters. I hope that by now you are much more comfortable in writing your own scripts that will help you out with automating many of the rigging steps.

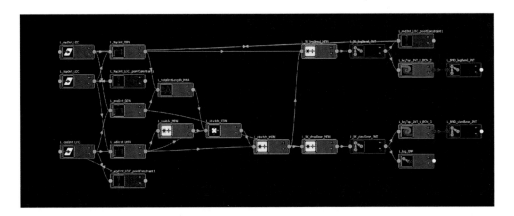

FIGURE 5.108 Leg globalScale nodes loaded into the node editor

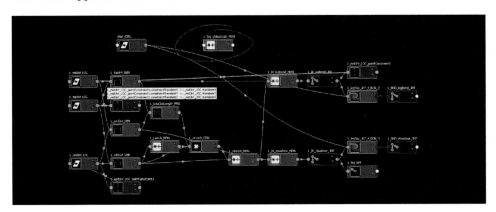

FIGURE 5.109 Creating the leg globalScale MDN node and setting it to Multiply

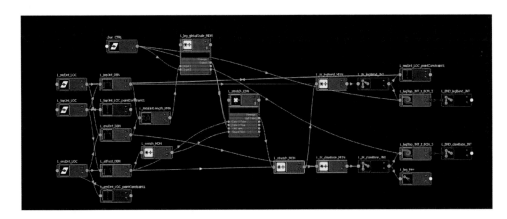

FIGURE 5.110 Leg globalScale completed

Chapter 6
Rigging Humanoids

Rigging Leaf

In the next couple of chapters we are going to use everything we've covered so far and apply it to the heroine of our game, Leaf. Rigging bipedal/humanoid characters is probably going to comprise the majority of a character rigger's work, and having a good toolkit to help the process along is invaluable. Also, before jumping in and beginning Leaf's rig, we will revisit some of the core concepts we covered in Chapter 5 and expand on them with advanced functionality.

Beyond the rigging pre-flight that we covered last chapter, an important concept to keep in mind is to make the rigs as modular as possible so they can be fitted and adapted to a variety of creatures/characters with a minimum amount of modification. For example, humanoid characters typically have two arms, two legs, a torso and a head. Now, if you are creating a variant for a humanoid—say an alien creature for your latest FPS game that has, beyond the typical humanoid template, an extra set of arms, 3 fingers and a tail—you'll want to make sure that your rigging tools have the ability to answer to those requirements. On the other hand, creating rigs for very specific creature types—octopuses (not octopi!) as an example—will call for custom rigs. Although, mind you, a lot of the core concepts of a biped rig will apply to the majority of your rigging needs. Think of rigging as a collection of small modules that fit in with specific functionality, and then neatly tied together in a holistic and streamlined package, ready to be used by a—hopefully—grateful animator. After all, the animator will be your main audience, be it yourself or somebody else.

Analyzing the Bind Skeleton

Oftentimes, you will find that the animation rig and the binding joints are one and the same. This can work well for complex, cinematic rigs. But since we are working with a rig that has to go into a game engine—and due to the limitations of said engines—the control rig will have to be separate from the bind rig itself. Game engines like their rigs to be as simple and straightforward as possible, without any fancy bells and whistles. In other words, IK systems, deformers and other advanced features that are found in 3D software do not cross over easily—or at all—into contemporary game engines. Maybe as these engines evolve things will change, but in the meantime we will follow the old adage of separating Church and State and keeping our rigs separated yet linked through various methods we will discuss shortly. In the next few chapters, we will examine the workflow of creating the bind skeleton, creating the control rig and finally bring the animation from our control rigs to Unity.

There are many ways of doing this next part. One is the tried and true draw-the-joints lovingly on your character and repeat as often as you need for each creature in your 3D production line. In a small project that might work, but if you are involved in a situation where multiple—and different—characters are needed, a short deadline or any other production woes, then a more effective system has to be found.

Members of the 3D community have been incredibly generous and offered over the years very useful tools to help speed up this process. A simple Google search will easily provide links to tens of autorigging solutions that will allow the user to place joints and with a few clicks of a mouse, and even have an animation-ready rig.

Maya, too, offers one such solution within its expansive toolset, called HumanIK (HiK). It is a full-body inverse kinematics (IK) solution and allows for a quick rigging method—albeit not foolproof and with some issues that hopefully will be addressed in later updates. We will use the Skeleton Generator that is part of the HiK system to generate our base skeleton and then customize it to our purposes. We will *not* use it as part of our rigging system.

> **NOTE:** Prior to Maya 2012, HiK used Full Body IK (FBIK). That technology has been evolved to the current HiK system, with includes updated functionality. It is also available in the latest incarnations of Maya LT—a version of Maya that is geared toward indie game developers. You can check it out on Steam as well (www.steampowered.com).

To T-Pose or not to T-Pose?

This question will come up very often during the rigging process of a bipedal character: which pose to use when setting up the rig? Should you use the traditional, albeit rigid T-pose with straight legs and arms out, or the more relaxed A-pose with arms bent halfway between shoulder and hip?

You will find endless reasons for one over the other. Both have their advantages and disadvantages. Also, one of the (current) limitations of HiK is that it works only with the T-pose, and forces us to use that setup.

As we discussed briefly in chapter 2, it's important to plan ahead of time the construction of the 3D model. If you're doing the modeling and rigging, it's much easier to resolve issues as they come about. But if you are part of a team and are working with a modeler, getting early versions of the model to test out the rig setup is a good strategy to prevent unnecessary hold-ups later in the production.

Getting back to the T-pose question, the main part of a bipedal rig that will be affected by the pose chosen is the upper torso, specifically the shoulders, arms and neck. The legs, midsection and head won't be greatly affected by being in either a T- or A-pose (see figure 6.1). One of the more glaring issues is the space between the shoulders and neck. As soon as you start lifting your arms from your sides upward, once you go over 45 degrees or so the clavicles are engaged and start to raise your shoulders higher. That motion will stretch the pectoralis major muscle (the chest muscle) and the trapezius muscle on the shoulder. You might notice some rigs that are set at the T-pose, but with shoulders are at in a relaxed state. If you're working with cartoony, soft characters then it might not be an issue. Yet if you are trying to rig somewhat realistic characters, it looks odd. Another issue is dealing with rigid geometry on the shoulders (shoulder pads, shoulder armor, etc.). To give them a realistic range of motion, they'll have to be modeled already flexed or raised, rather than as per a neutral pose. Another issue is the amount of "stretch" you'll get in the armpit/upper chest area. It can be resolved with complex rigging setups, especially if you're working with a cinematic rig with no set limits on the amounts of joints that you can use in the bind skeleton. Then again, if you're creating a rig for a game, where joint limitations are a concern, you'll have to find some creative ways to get around this.

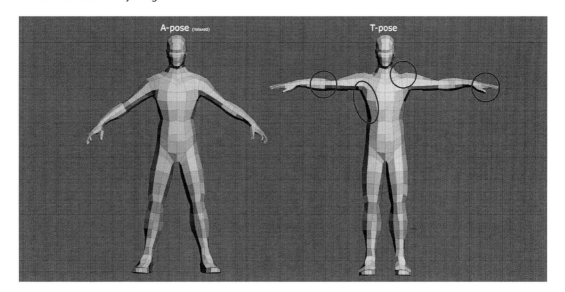

FIGURE 6.1 **A- and T-pose comparison**

Having said all of that about the T-pose, it does have its advantages: it fits a generic and standardized pose, which can be adapted to almost all bipedal creatures. Coming up with a standardized relaxed pose will be a lot more complicated, because of the immense variety in character designs. Another reason to rig in the

T-pose is that most game engines (and current mocap setups) still use that setup. A key advantage is getting the controls in place, especially along orthogonal planes. For IKs to work properly, the joints that are being solved have to be on a flat plane, otherwise orientation problems and "jumping" joints will occur.

We will explore this further and use the best of both worlds for our workflow. It's obviously easier to rig in the T-pose but it's preferable to bind the geometry in the relaxed A-pose.

Human IK Overview

Let's first familiarize ourselves with the HiK system. If you already know your way around it, feel free to skip to the next section.

Start a new scene in Maya, and in the Animation module, select **Skeleton > Human IK. . .** (see figure 6.2).

> **NOTE:** Depending on your version of Maya, your HiK menu might look slightly different than the one shown in these examples. In case it's not loaded, you can load it manually by selecting the mayaHIK plug-in using the Plug-in Manager (**Window > Settings/Preferences > Plug-in Manager**).

FIGURE 6.2 **Loading the HiK menu**

The HiK menu is divided into 4 main sections (see figure 6.3). Click on the **Skeleton** button under the *Create* section. A generic skeleton named "Character1" will appear on your viewport, as well as a UI with options to modify the skeleton setup (see figure 6.4).

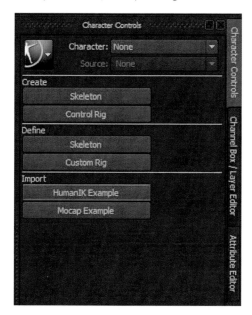

FIGURE 6.3 **Details of the HiK menu**

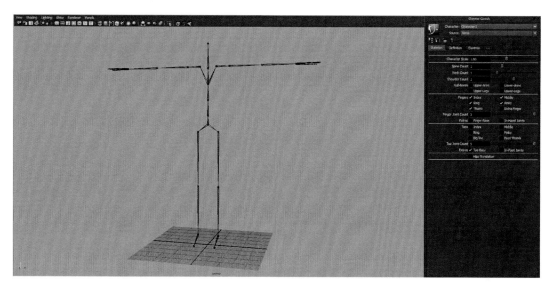

FIGURE 6.4 **Default HiK skeleton**

Here's a list of things to keep in mind as we set up our base HiK binding skeleton:

1. The joint orientation is set to World. You'll have to re-orient the joints as you tweak the skeleton.
2. Save any edits you make as you work (from HiK menu: **Edit > Skeleton> Save Edits**). Earlier versions of HiK would sometimes reset the skeleton if you would undo or mistakenly switch out windows (it seems to have been fixed with current versions of Maya).
3. When working with a symmetrical character, work only the left side to make the joint tweaks. You can then mirror to the right side, but not vice versa. From the HiK Menu select **Edit > Skeleton> Mirror Left> Right**. Mirroring works only with translations, so joint re-orientation will have to be taken into account on both sides. . .unless you delete one side and use Maya's mirror joints function.
4. You might get a common error—especially with the arms—stating "The (left/right) arm doesn't seem to be parallel to the X axis". You can ignore that since we will be using a custom control rig.
5. Once you finish setting the proper joint tweaks, lock the ***Skeleton Definition*** to prevent any accidental changes.
6. In certain cases, you want to make sure that the ***Automatically Orient Joints*** checkmark (Move Tool settings) is checked off (for example, at the root joint, or wrist joint) before re-orienting the joints.
7. To rename your skeleton to something a bit more descriptive, go to **Edit > Definition > Rename**.
8. Remember to only translate the joints into position, not rotate. For any joints that will utilize IK, make sure to keep the joint chains on a flat plane to prevent any potential glitches later on.
9. You probably already know this, but just as a quick reminder—to move a joint by itself without affecting any child joints attached to it, press and hold the D key to go to pivot-mode.

The general skeleton setup is self-explanatory. You can modify and change the number of joints per body section, and add additional extra joints for refined control. Remember, this is the bind skeleton that will be bound and exported to the game engine. The goal is keep it as light as possible, but offer the right amount of deformation capabilities.

> **NOTE:** Maya's Help offers more in-depth information on HiK. Search for "Character Controls menu button" for all of the options available when first loading HiK, as well as "HumanIK character structure" for joint setup explanations.

Creating the Bind Skeleton

Open **01_Leaf_skelPrep.ma**. No, Leaf is not the avatar of a Hindu goddess. Rather, I duplicated her arms and rotated them in order to straighten them so they fit into the HiK generated T-pose (see figure 6.5). This will greatly help as a reference with the placement of the arm joints.

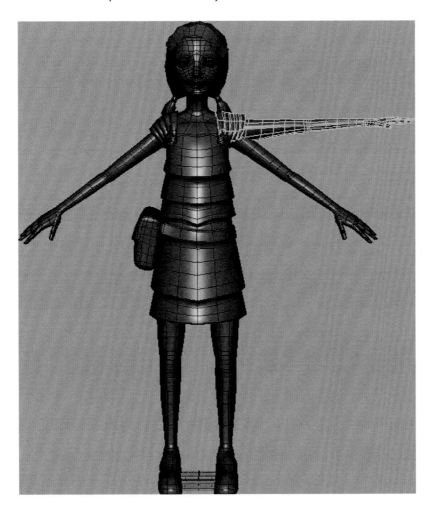

FIGURE 6.5 **Setting Leaf's arms in a T-pose**

These are the steps I took to get it properly set up with the HiK Skeleton Generator:

1. Adjust the skeleton to the mesh, making sure the joint spaces are properly positioned in the areas of flex (knees, shoulders, elbows, wrists, neck and

torso) using the straight arm as reference. The skeleton generator was used to modify the number of bones (see figure 6.6).

2. Once the skeleton fit the right dimensions, the HiK nodes were deleted from the Outliner (make sure to uncheck *DAG Objects Only* to see them) (see figure 6.7).
3. The right side was then deleted (see figure 6.8).
4. The joints were properly oriented using the default orientation settings (see figure 6.9).
5. The joints were rotated into the relaxed arm positions and checked to make sure they fit properly. I also made note of the joint rotation values used (see figure 6.10).
6. Once the joints were in place, they were mirrored to the right side and renamed (see figure 6.11).

Depending on your character setup, you might want to add additional joints to help you with the weighting of the mesh. Sometimes the default base skeleton is not enough to properly deform the mesh, so adding additional bind joints can help greatly with this setup.

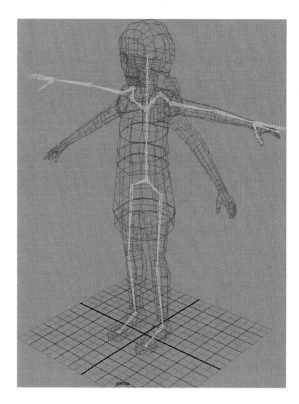

FIGURE 6.6 Leaf's initial joint placement

FIGURE 6.7 Deleting HiK nodes after setting up the skeleton

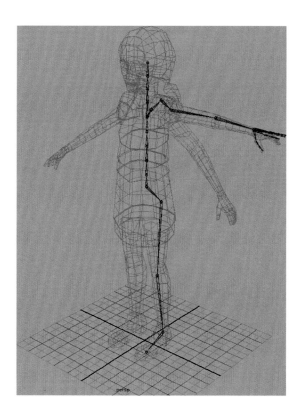

FIGURE 6.8 Deleting the skeleton's right side, prior to mirroring

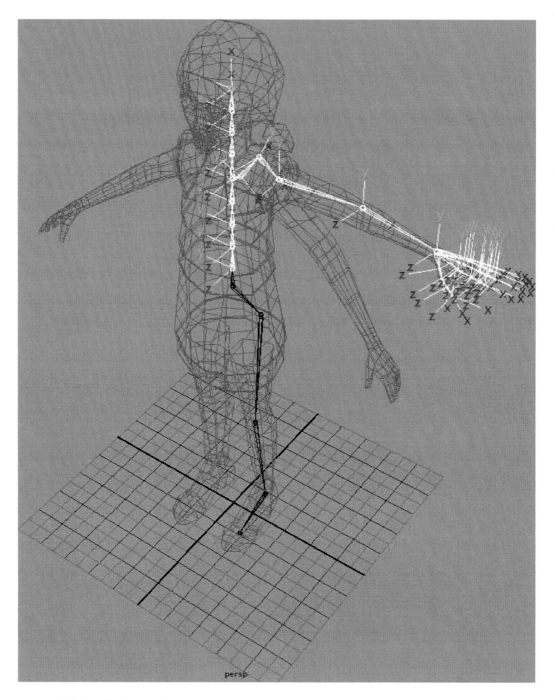

FIGURE 6.9 Orienting the joints properly

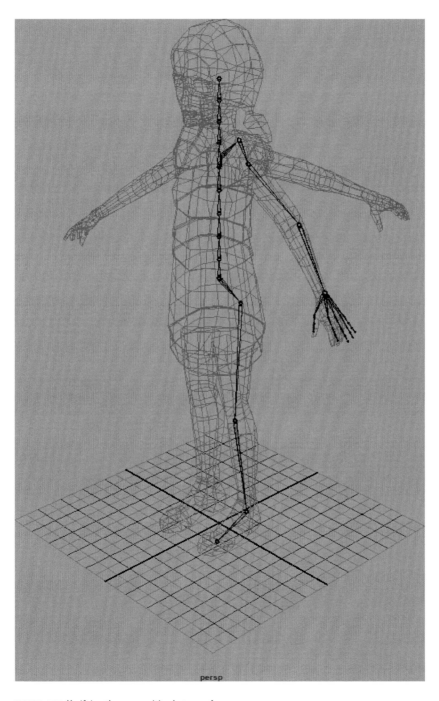

persp

FIGURE 6.10 Verifying the arm position between A

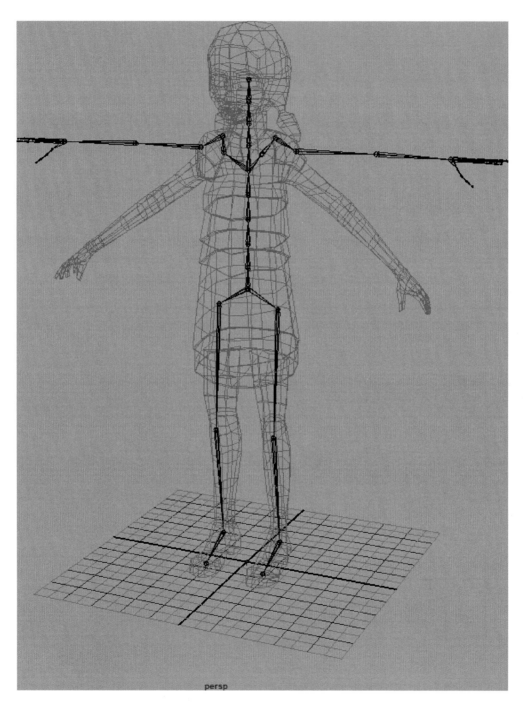

FIGURE 6.11 Completed bind skeleton

There are other methods of deforming the mesh alongside the joints. For example, using **influence objects**, which are geometry meshes (polygons or NURBS) that act similarly to joint deformers. They affect the weighting of vertices just like a regular joint would, and their main advantage is that they can be shaped and molded to fit specific areas in your main mesh to provide you with more precise control. Think of them as basic muscle systems that go under your mesh's skin. **Corrective blendshapes** are also a very common method of tweaking a bound mesh. Sometimes simple weighting of vertices to joint does not provide the proper deformation you're looking for, and can even warp the mesh in undesirable ways. You can create a sculpted (ergo modeled) blendshape in the shape you wish your mesh to take after it reaches the desired pose. You then create an animated setup that updates whenever your character reaches that particular pose and switches to the corrective blendshape. Other deformers such as the wire tool, or some of the non-linear deformers can also help greatly with this.

For cinematic rigging and animation, the use of these deformation methods is a non-issue. Current 3D game engines, on the other hand, are a bit sensitive to when it comes to the use of custom deformers other than joints, and the options mentioned above might not work. Check the documentation of your game engine of choice to see if these methods are supported. As well, it depends if you're using different software other than Maya for your 3D rigging. There might be slight differences in the way each software approaches mesh deformers.

Rotate Order

A step that oftentimes gets overlooked is the setting of the Rotate Order of the joints. It seems like a negligible step, but it can prevent a lot of potential pitfalls during the animation phase. It can prevent animation curves from behaving erratically and prevent the occasional joint pop, gimbal lock and other nasty animation gremlins.

In a nutshell, the Rotate Order of an object is the order in which objects revolve around their axes. Straightforward and to the point, right? Well, maybe it's a bit more involved than this. When you look at the Rotate Order of an object, you are offered a dropdown of the three axes in different configurations, with XYZ as the default. The way Maya evaluates Rotate Order is by working backwards from the last axis toward the first.

In other words, with the default Rotate Order of XYZ, the Z-axis affects both the Y- and X-axes when it is being rotated. Next, the Y-axis affects the X-axis but not the Z-axis. Finally, rotating on the X-axis will only rotate around itself, without affecting the other two axes.

If you were to create a parent/child hierarchy of rotations to illustrate the default XYZ Rotate Order, the Z-axis is the parent of the Y-axis, and the Y-axis, in turn, is the parent of the X-axis (see figure 6.12).

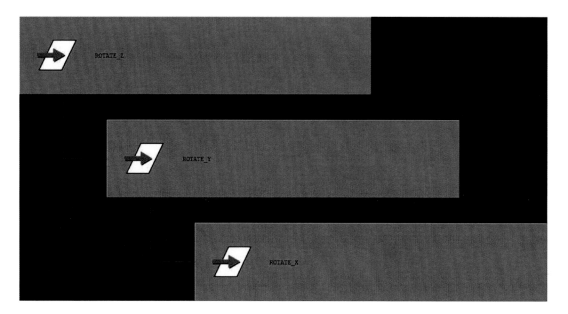

FIGURE 6.12 **Default rotate order hierarchy**

To establish the Rotate Order of joints during rigging, you first have to figure out what are the common rotations your rigged character/object will undertake, and what is their order of importance. Take the spine, for example: The most common action we do with our spine is twisting from side to side (Y-axis), especially along the upper chest part. The next common is leaning forward and back (X-axis), and finally swaying side to side (Z-axis). In this case, our spine joint's Rotate Order will be ZXY.

Scripting tgpRotateOrder

FIGURE 6.13 **tgpRotateOrderscript**

We will need to change the Rotate Order of the joints for our needs. We will write our own little Rotate Order script to help out and automate that process (see figure 6.13).

```
import maya.cmds as mc
from tgpBaseUI import BaseUI as UI
'''
Create a button using the following in the Script Editor
import tgpRotOrder as ro
reload(ro)
ro.tgpRotOrder()
'''
class tgpRotOrder(UI):
   def __init__(self):
      self.window="roWindow"
      self.title="tgpRotateOrder"
      self.winSize=(350,120)
      self.createUI()
   def createCustom(self,*args):
      mc.optionMenuGrp ("rotOrdersOpt", label="Change Rotate Order To: ")
      mc.menuItem (label="XYZ") #0
      mc.menuItem (label="YZX") #1
      mc.menuItem (label="ZXY") #2
      mc.menuItem (label="XZY") #3
      mc.menuItem (label="YXZ") #4
      mc.menuItem (label="ZYX") #5
      mc.separator(st="in")

      mc.showWindow(self.window)

   def createButtonCmd(self, *args):
      self.changeOp()

   def changeOp(self,*args):
      selObj=mc.ls(sl=True)
      if (len(selObj)<1):
         mc.warning("Please select one or more objects!")
      else:
         getRotOrder = mc.optionMenuGrp ("rotOrdersOpt", query=True, value=True)

         for obj in selObj:
            if (getRotOrder == "XYZ"):
               mc.setAttr(obj +".rotateOrder", 0)
```

```
    elif (getRotOrder == "YZX"):
       mc.setAttr(obj +".rotateOrder", 1)
    elif (getRotOrder == "ZXY"):
       mc.setAttr(obj +".rotateOrder", 2)
    elif (getRotOrder == "XZY"):
       mc.setAttr(obj +".rotateOrder", 3)
    elif (getRotOrder == "YXZ"):
       mc.setAttr(obj +".rotateOrder", 4)
    elif (getRotOrder == "ZYX"):
       mc.setAttr(obj +".rotateOrder", 5)
print "Changed Rotate Order to " + getRotOrder
```

Analyzing the script, we let the BaseUI class take care of the interface. The user is then asked to choose the proper rotation order which is then applied to the selected objects. The command that enables the dropdown is the optionMenuGrp. The options are then specified within the menuItem commands. You can make that list as long as you need. Note that the values specified in the label flag are those that are queried in the *if-else* section at the end of the script, so make sure that you spell them properly.

This is another one of the small utility scripts that you can add to your rigging toolkit that makes things a tad easier and more automated.

> **NOTE:** Now that we did it the long way, here's another way to change the Rotate Order of multiple objects directly, using the xform command. Select the objects you want to affect, and type the following:
>
> mc.xform(preserve=True, rotateOrder="xyz")
>
> *between the quotes you can put any of the rotate order variations*
>
> As my aikido sensei always says, "Shortcuts make for hard falls". There's a lesson in there somewhere.

Below you'll find a table with the suggested Rotate Orders for the main bind skeleton joints (remember, we're using the default joint orientation, with X-axis as the primary joint axis):

Joint Name	Rotate Order
BND_Neck(0/2)_JNT	ZYX
BND_R/L_Shoulder_JNT	XZY
BND_R/L_UpArm_JNT	XZY
BND_R/L_Elbow_JNT	ZXY

Joint Name	Rotate Order
BND_R/L_Wrist_JNT	YZX
Finger joints	XYZ
BND_Spine(0/4)_JNT	ZYX
BND_Hips_JNT	ZYX
BND_Root_JNT	ZYX
BND_R/L_UpLeg_JNT	ZYX
BND_R/L_Knee_JNT	YXZ
BND_R/L_Ankle_JNT	XZY
BND_L_BOF_JNT	XYZ

NOTE: Feel free to experiment with the Rotate Order axes to make it fit your animation requirements.

Binding Leaf's Mesh to the Skeleton

The art of binding the mesh to the joints is one of patience and occasional frustration, but it's one of those necessary steps in the pipeline. Maya has been improving the skinning tools from version to version, and their latest iteration (as of Maya 2015, including LT) is the geodesic voxel bind method. This method greatly improves the binding of the mesh to the skeleton and gets us most of the way there. It will be one of the methods we will explore to bind our mesh to the joints.

NOTE: For geodesic voxel binding to properly work, the joints *must* be within the boundaries of the mesh itself. Contrary to some of the other binding methods where joint influence can occur even if the joints are outside the boundaries of the mesh, this will not generate the expected results with this particular binding method. Another requirement is that the mesh normals have to face outward.

In a nutshell, when a mesh is bound to a skeleton, the vertices of the mesh are being influenced by the joints in their vicinity. As the joints move, they deform/move the vertices based on the weight values assigned to them. This can lead to a range of motion of the mesh starting from the very subtle to the totally rigid. We will use the **Smooth Bind** option for this.

NOTE: As noted in an earlier chapter, rigid binding has been removed in the current version of Maya (2015). You can achieve the same result by setting the Max Influence to 1.

Before the actual binding though, we're going to use a very simple trick to help us get the best of both worlds—the posing and the rigging. Select the shoulder and upArm bind joints on both sides, and on frame 1, key their rotation channels in the T-pose. This way we ensure that their rotations are zeroed out at this stage.

Move the time slider to frame 2 and rotate the bind joints so they fit into the relaxed pose position of the character. For our purposes, the bind shoulder joints were both rotated on the Z-axis. The upArm bind joints were rotated on the Z-axis and Y-axis. Once in place, key the rotation values in the relaxed pose (see figure 6.14).

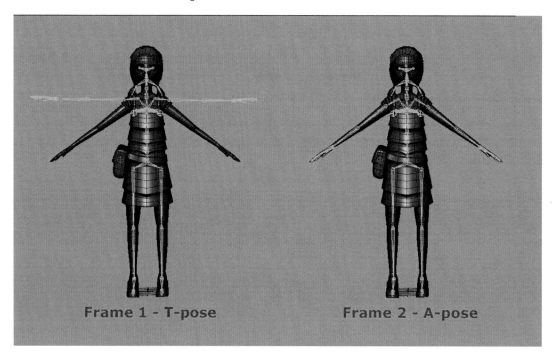

Frame 1 - T-pose   Frame 2 - A-pose

FIGURE 6.14 **Keyed A- and T-poses**

By putting the above method in place, we can now first bind the mesh to the bind skeleton in the relaxed pose and work out any weighting kinks we might encounter. Then by switching back to frame 1, we can start building our control rig based on the position of the joints in their T-pose. This trick adds a couple of extra steps to the process, but I found it helps with the shoulder deformation issues.

Since Leaf's bind skeleton has a few additional custom joints attached to it, we are going to individually select the joints we want to influence the binding. Some of the end joints, for example, will not affect the binding process, so we can safely ignore them.

NOTE: You've probably noticed Leaf's mesh slightly changed between the examples. She is going through a design evolution, so to speak, until she reaches the final look. This is very common in production, where changes happen constantly to meet the design requirements, as well as to resolve potential issues that crop up during game mechanics or cinematic shots. It feels like a dance sometimes, as in one step forward, two steps back. And this is where automation saves the day.

Open **02_Leaf_skelPrebind.ma**. The animation on the bind joints between T-pose and relaxed pose is in place (frames 1 and 2). We first have to figure out first how we want Leaf's mesh to be connected to the joints. Currently, Leaf's model is a single mesh made up of a combination of multiple individual meshes for the sake of simplicity and game engine optimization.

- **Body**—we will use the geodesic voxel binding method for this. This is the most "organic" part of the model—as organic as a character made of metal can be—and will have the most amount of deformations
- **Eyes and eyelids**—will have minimal deformation
- **Hair**—ponytails have separate joints

Smooth Bind Overview

FIGURE 6.15 **Smooth binding options menu**

Let's open the **Smooth Bind** menu options (**Animation > Skin > Smooth Bind > □**) (see figure 6.15). First, a few words from your sponsors about the options: this is one of those Maya windows that I found users often place blind faith in the **Bind Skin** button at the bottom of the interface to do the work properly, while silently praying to the rigger's celestial pantheon for the bind to pull through with decent results. On alternating Tuesdays, when Mars is aligned just so with the Medusa nebula it might work, but why leave things to chance, right?

1. **Bind To**—by default it is set to **Joint hierarchy**. This works well if you want to bind the whole joint chain starting at the root (regardless if the root or another joint was selected) to the entire mesh. Good for straightforward, seamless meshes. The second option is **Selected joints**. This offers you control over which joints in the chain will influence the mesh. More work to setup, but offers greater flexibility. The last option, **Object hierarchy** allows the binding of the mesh to transform nodes, and not only to joints. Not commonly used but very useful if you want components to manipulate your mesh (clusters, CVs, etc.).
2. **Bind Method**—the meat and potatoes of the binding setup, so to speak. **Closest distance** will bind the vertices closest to the joints, ignoring any hierarchies. This could cause problems by having unrelated joins affect vertices that aren't supposed to be connected to them. **Closest hierarchy** follows the joint hierarchy and influences the vertices in that order. The **Heat map** option assigns each joint as a heat source, and its influence cools off as the vertices move away from it. The joints must be within the mesh for it to work, otherwise influence will move up the chain to a parent joint that *is* within the mesh. The final option is the **Geodesic voxel** method, which we discussed earlier.
3. **Skinning Method**—Maya offers two types of skinning methods and a third option that allows blending between them. The first, **Classic linear**, deforms the mesh and does not maintain the volume during the deformation (i.e., bow tie effect). The second option, **Dual quaternion** tries to maintain the mesh's volume as much as possible and typically yields better results than the classic linear. The **Weight blended** option allows you to blend between the two skinning methods during the weight painting options (a value of 0 for classic linear and 1 for dual quaternion).
4. **Normalize Weights**—The three options offered are **Interactive**, **None** and **Post**. The default **Interactive** mode will normalize the weights by adding or removing them as you paint them on the mesh, always making sure that the total weight equals 1. This happens with every brush stroke and is constantly updated. The **None** option won't keep track of the weights, which can cause your vertices to have bigger or smaller values than 1 and cause unwanted results if not properly tracked. With **Post**, the normalization of the weights happens during the deformation of the

274

mesh, as opposed to during the weight painting stage. In this case, you might also see values greater or smaller than 1 as you're painting the weights, but they will be normalized as the mesh deforms.

5. **Weight distribution**—available only for the *Interactive* normalize option. *Distance* gives higher weight values to joints closer to the influenced vertices, while **Neighbors** balances the vertex weights among the surrounding influencing joints.

6. **Allow multiple bind poses**—A good option if you have different meshes bound to the same joints. It allows setting more than one default bind pose per mesh. I personally uncheck that option.

7. **Max influence objects**—A very important option to pay attention to. This limits the numbers of joints that can influence the deformation of your mesh. The default settings of 5 joints seems a bit high, but test it with your meshes to see how they deform after the bind. Usually, a value of 3 works well, but again, that depends on each individual case. Also, depending on the bind method, you can adjust the falloff/dropoff rate to fit your needs, found at the bottom slider.

8. **Maintain max influences**—when this option is checked, your vertices cannot have a greater number of joints influencing them as set in the max influence slider.

9. **Remove unused influences**—vertices that would receive zero-influence from the joints will not be included in the bind process. Helps optimize the scene and keep things lighter.

10. **Colorize skeleton**—self-explanatory.

11. **Resolution (only available for geodesic voxel)**—sets the voxel precision used to calculate the bind volume. As always, the higher the number, the better (usually) the quality but also the longer the time needed. Start at low levels and evaluate as needed.

You can find additional information on this process in Autodesk's knowledge network (knowledge.autodesk.com). Well worth a stop for expanding your overall Maya know-how.

So now that we know what we're getting ourselves into, go ahead and take some time to experiment with the mesh and skeleton provided. Explore all of the above-mentioned options, testing out the various binding combinations. This will give you a better understanding of how Maya evaluates this process. As well, make note of the various results you get. This is one of those instances where no matter how much you read about, you can't beat hands-on experience.

The initial binding of Leaf's mesh was set to the following values, while in the relaxed pose (frame 2). The bind joints have been pre-selected and placed in the **bodyJoints_SEL** set:

Bind to: *Selected joints*
Bind method: *Geodesic voxel*

Skinning method: *Dual quaternion*
Allow multiple bind poses: *off*
Max influences: *3*
Falloff: *0.50*
Resolution: *1024*

Weight Assignment and Painting

This is probably one of the absolutely least favorite parts of the character binding process, yet a hugely critical step in the rigging process. Not that it is hard, per se, but rather time consuming, and this is where most of the frustration will manifest itself. It's often seen as a chore but thankfully with a little of pre-planning (see, we always come back to that) and some great little tools available from the community, it makes the process more manageable. One of those tools is the *ngSkinTools* plugin (www.ngskintools.com) which uses layers to separate the weights of the mesh and then blend them back together. This plugin is definitely worth a look and a try. It's still in beta at the time of writing this, but it streamlines the weight painting process immensely. Just the mirroring weights option is worth its weight in virtual gold.

There are a few steps you can take to minimize that frustration of weight painting:

1. **A good and efficient mesh**—this is the key and foundation to a good, solid rig that will provide the anticipated animation results. Placing the right amount of loops in the correct places on the mesh will greatly help with preventing unwanted deformations.
2. **Proper positioning of the joints**—a talent that comes only with experience and more than that. . .an almost tangible sense of knowing how the mesh will deform. Expect a lot of trial and error with this particular phase. Repetition and experimentation will lead to that experience, so keep at it.
3. **Know your tools**—understanding the various tools and options available within Maya, as well as exploring third-party options geared toward mesh skinning and weight painting can vastly improve your workflow. Press every button, check those checkboxes, and read the manual!
4. **Have a good soundtrack**—to paraphrase, music tames the savage beast, and frustration is definitely one heck of a beast. Earphones on, and paint those weights away.

The other main method of managing the skinned weights is through the **Paint Skin Weights Tool** found in the newly organized *Skin* dropdown. As an aside, I'm glad Autodesk reorganized the menus and cleaned them up. It's much easier to find things now without having to dig through submenu after submenu.

The options are too many to discuss within these pages, but the documentation for each of tools is explained in great detail in Autodesk's Knowledge Network.

In Leaf's case, I carefully painted the weights, making sure to test every so often the deformations by rotating the bind joints and fixing any errant weight. The geodesic voxel did a pretty good job of doing most of the heavy lifting. What really remained was tweaking the weights along the various joints.

Make use of the various tools such as **Hammer Skin Weights**, **Prune Small Weights**, and occasionally the **Smooth Skin Weights** tool. Find your rhythm, and happy weight painting.

You can find the bound version of Leaf by opening **03_Leaf_skelBound_default.ma** (see figure 6.16).

This brings us to the next step in the rigging process, which is setting up the control rig. Keep calm, caffeinate and onward ho!

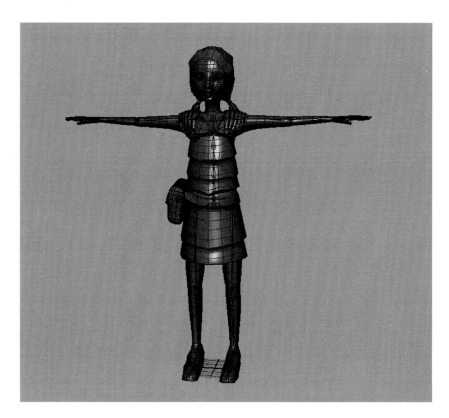

FIGURE 6.16 **Leaf's smooth bound skeleton**

Chapter 7
The Control Rig

The Control Rig

So here we finally are. Time to put all of the tidbits we've covered in the past chapters into action.

As with Meep, we are going to start working our way from the ground up, starting with the leg setup. Figure out the features you'll want to incorporate in your rig and list them in order. We will go over the steps of actually building the rig bit by bit to understand the process first, and then see how to apply that as code. Here are the things we want to see in our leg rig:

1. Both IK and FK systems
2. Stretchy joints
3. Multiple foot pivot points (heel, ball of foot, toe)
4. Knee control

If you have done any humanoid rigging in the last decade or so, you are probably familiar with the IK reverse foot setup. A quick recap: a typical leg includes a hip, knee, ankle, ball-of-foot and toe joints (see figure 7.1). The reverse foot creates a control setup (either another set of joints, locators or groups) starting at the heel of the foot, connecting the toe, toe base and finally ankle, in that order (see figure 7.2). The leg IK handle connects between the up leg joint and the ankle joint. Two more IK handles are then created, one connecting the ankle joint to the ball-of-foot joint, and the other connecting the ball-of-foot joint to the toe joint. The functionality comes by the parenting setup of the IK handles, the joints and additional groups (or locators) to the reverse foot rig, which creates a hierarchical structure conducive to the manipulation of the foot rig. The ability to roll the foot has typically been done using Maya's driven keys, allowing channels to drive the various positions of the foot.

We will explore a similar method, but instead of using driven keys, we will use the **_remapValue_** utility node, with a similar approach as we did earlier with Meep's wings. Anoop Ak, a technical director at Dreamworks, came up with a unique and creative take on the traditional reverse foot setup. You can find his original tutorial on www.creativecrash.com or on his personal website, www.codecg.com. The rig we will discuss below is based on this setup and will enable us to control the various pivoting and rolling positions of the foot. Again, the emphasis will be on creating flexible controls, but without adding

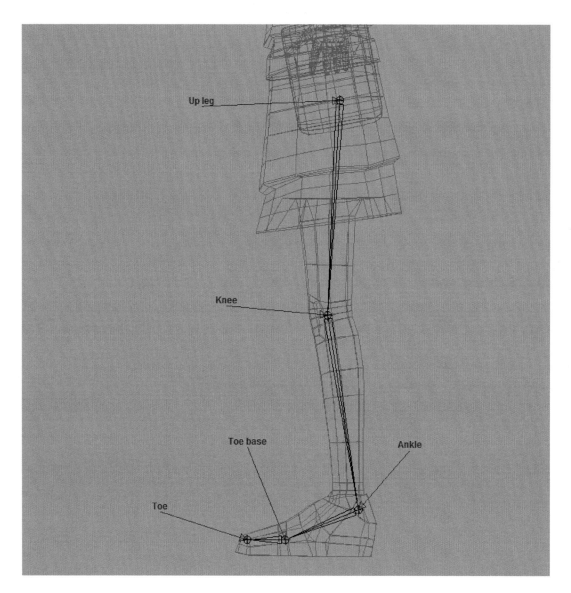

FIGURE 7.1 Basic leg joint setup

keyframes on the control channels. Not to say that driven keys aren't very useful. On the contrary, they offer very precise control over your rig. But it's always nice to see different ways of achieving similar results. We will explore driven keys later in the chapter.

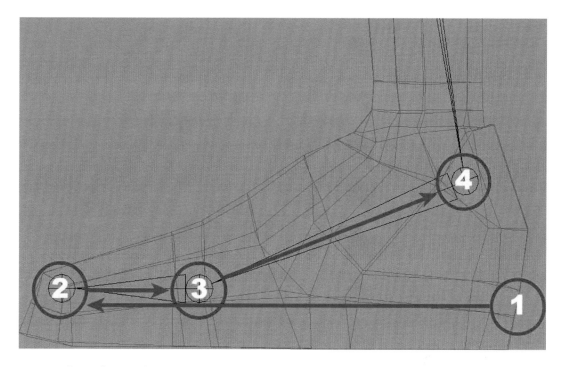

FIGURE 7.2 Reverse foot control setup, starting at the heel, going to the toe, toe base and finally ankle

snapAB Script

Before we start, here is a useful little script that can help with the very common snapping of one object to another, along with some additional options. We are using the xform command to query the position of the source object and saving it in an array. We then use those values to move the target object to that same position. xform is an extremely versatile command and I recommend you take the time to go over the various flags available:

```
def snapAB(srcObj,tgtObj,option):
    '''

    option:
    0 - don't freeze transformations
    1 - freeze transformations
    2 - point constraint target object to source object
    '''

    posSrc=mc.xform(srcObj,q=True,ws=True,t=True)
```

```
mc.move(posSrc [0], posSrc [1], posSrc [2],tgtObj,
    absolute=True, ws=True)

if (option==1):
  mc.makeIdentity(tgtObj,apply=True, t=1, r=1, s=1)

if (option==2):
  mc.pointConstraint(srcObj,tgtObj)
```

You can add additional flags and options if you wish to customize the script further. Use it as a standalone script or as a utility as part of a larger script suite.

Building the IK Leg

Let's begin by loading **01_Leaf_Leg_Start.ma** into Maya. We have a basic, standard bind leg joint setup (see figure 7.3). This might seem like a step backwards, but I'd like to go over the mechanics of building the leg first without any additional distractions, so to speak. Once this is covered, we can apply it to our previously bound character, either manually or using the better way—via script.

1. Duplicate the BND chain twice, renaming each duplicated chain with either the **IK** or **FK** prefix.
2. Group each new chain under a new named group (**IK_L_Leg_GRP** and **FK_L_Leg_GRP**).
3. Place the newly created groups under the **_UTILITIES_DO_NOT_USE_** group in the Outliner (see figure 7.4).

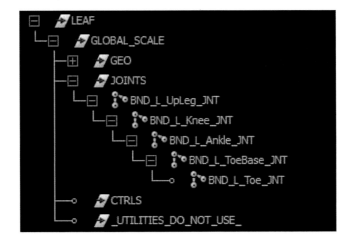

FIGURE 7.3 BND leg joint setup in Outliner

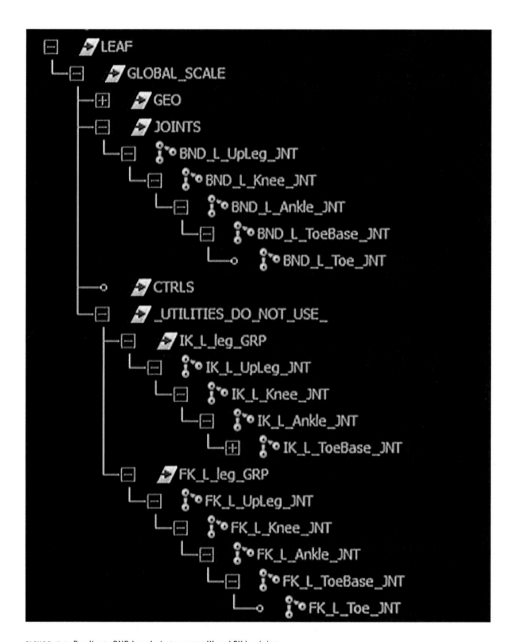

FIGURE 7.4 Duplicate BND leg chain to create IK and FK leg joints

Starting with the left leg IK setup:

1. Create an IK handle with a rotate-plane solver between **IK_L_UpLeg_JNT**
   and **IK_L_Ankle_JNT**.

2. Rename it **IKankle_L_Leg_Handle**.
3. Create two additional IK handles—single-chain solvers this time. The first between **IK_L_Ankle_JNT** and **IK_L_BOF_JNT** and the second between **IK_L_BOF_JNT** and **IK_L_Toe_JNT**.
4. Name them **IKbof_L_Leg_Handle** and **IKtoe_L_Leg_Handle** respectively.
5. Create 3 locators and name them **L_heelRig_LOC**, **L_bofRig_LOC** and **L_toeRig_LOC**.
6. Snap both the **L_heelRig_LOC** and **L_bofRig_LOC** to the **IK_L_BOF_JNT**.
7. Do the same to **the L_toeRig_LOC** with the **IK_L_Toe_JNT**.
8. Move the **L_heelRig_LOC** on the Z- and Y-axes so it's placed at the heel of the mesh (see figure 7.5).
9. Freeze transformations on each of the rig locators.
10. Create two empty groups, named **L_bofPivot_GRP** and **L_toeTap_GRP**.
11. Snap these two groups to the **IK_L_BOF_JNT** position. Freeze transformations.

This next part is the logic, if you will, that allows the creation of the reverse foot. The key is the hierarchical structure of the locators and groups that provide additional pivot points for the IK handles. Set the groups, locators and IK handles as illustrated in figure 7.6.

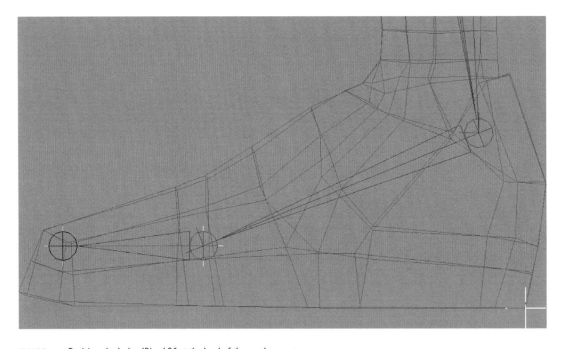

FIGURE 7.5 Position the L_heelRig_LOC at the heel of the mesh

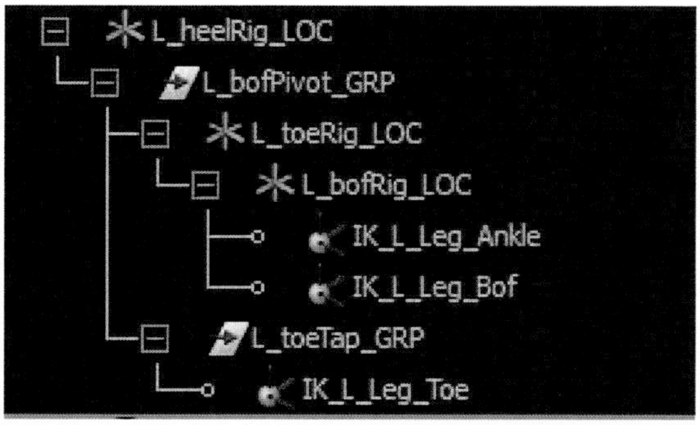

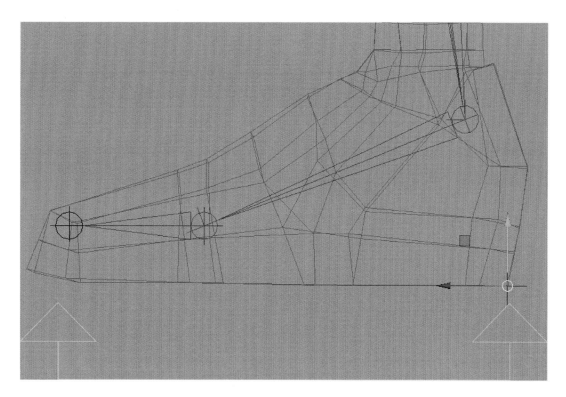

FIGURE 7.6 Arranging the reverse foot hierarchy

Create a controller for the leg and name it **IK_L_Leg_CTRL**. Make sure the pivot point of the control is positioned on top of the **L_heelRig_LOC**, and freeze transformations. This will enable us to rotate the foot on the heel (see figure 7.7).

FIGURE 7.7 Creation and positioning of foot control and pivot

Make the **L_heelRig_LOC** a child **of IK_L_Leg_CTRL**. The initial foot control structure is now in place. In the **Attribute Editor**, change the Rotate Order of the foot control to **ZXY**.

We need now to add the control channels to our **IK_L_Leg_CTRL**. Create them based on the following table (see figure 7.8):

Attribute Name	Type	Minimum	Maximum	Default
kneeTwist	Float			
roll	Float	0	20	0
rollValue	Float	0	100	50.0
toeBendValue	Float	0	1	0.5
Pivot	Float			
toeRoll	Float			
toePivot	Float			
toeTap	Float			
Stretch	Enum	On	Off	← use Enum Names

NOTE: I added a couple of locked channels to act as separators between the KNEE and FOOT channels.

For the foot roll setup, we'll start by creating the *remapValue* nodes. Open the **Node Editor**:

1. Create two *remapValue* nodes, and name them **bofRoll_L_Leg_RMV** and **toeRoll_L_Leg_RMV** respectively.
2. Select **bofRoll_L_Leg_RMV** and open its attributes.
3. Click on the value graph and move the rightmost point towards the center. Add a new point at the right end of the curve. Change the middle point **Selected Position** to **0.5** and the **Selected Value** to **1.0**.
4. Select the rightmost point on the graph and change its **Selected Value** to **0**.
5. Change the **Input Max** value to **20** (see figure 7.9).
6. Select **toeRoll_L_Leg_RMV** and, as above, move the rightmost point towards the center. Change the **Selected Position** to **0.5** and **Selected Value** to **0**.
7. Change the **Input Max** value to **20** (see figure 7.10).
8. Connect the following attributes from **IK_L_Leg_CTRL** to **bofRoll_L_Leg_RMV**:
   Roll > Input Value

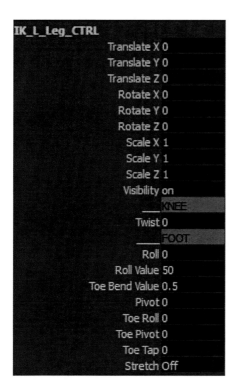

IK_L_Leg_CTRL
Translate X 0
Translate Y 0
Translate Z 0
Rotate X 0
Rotate Y 0
Rotate Z 0
Scale X 1
Scale Y 1
Scale Z 1
Visibility on
KNEE
Twist 0
FOOT
Roll 0
Roll Value 50
Toe Bend Value 0.5
Pivot 0
Toe Roll 0
Toe Pivot 0
Toe Tap 0
Stretch Off

FIGURE 7.8 Foot control attributes

Roll Value > Ouput Max
Toe Bend Value > Value / Value[1] / Value_Position (see figure 7.11).
9. Connect the following attributes from **IK_L_Leg_CTRL** to **toeRoll_L_Leg_RMV**:
Roll > Input Value
Roll Value > Ouput Max
Toe Bend Value > Value / Value[1] / Value_Position (see figure 7.12).
10. Connect **bofRoll_L_Leg_RMV > OutValue** to **L_bofRig_LOC > Rotate X**.
11. Create an **addDoubleLinear** node and rename it **toeRoll_L_Leg_ADL**.
12. Connect **toeRoll_L_Leg_RMV > OutValue** to **toeRoll_L_Leg_ADL > Input 1**.
13. Connect **IK_L_Leg_CTRL > toeRoll** to **toeRoll_L_Leg_ADL > Input 2** (see figure 7.13).

NOTE: Make sure that the points added on the *remapValue* node graph are added *after* the original two. Otherwise, the above setup won't work properly.

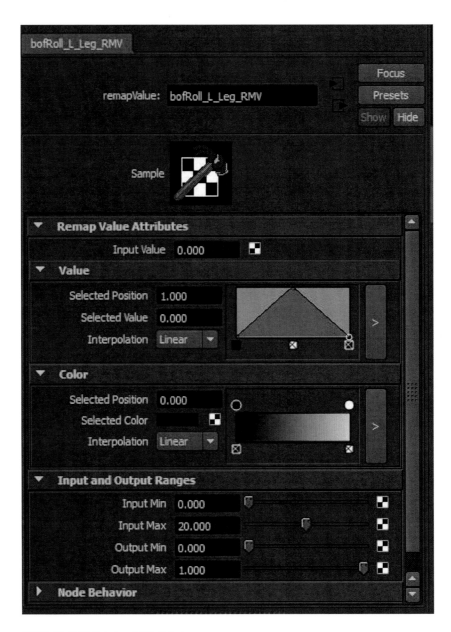

FIGURE 7.9 BofRoll_L_Leg_RMV attributes

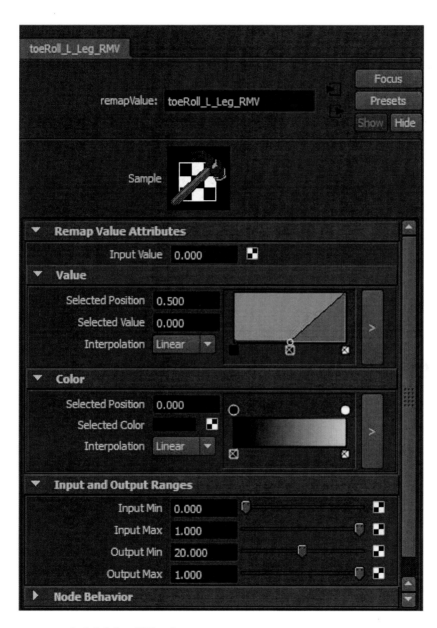

FIGURE 7.10 ToeRoll_L_Leg_RMV attributes

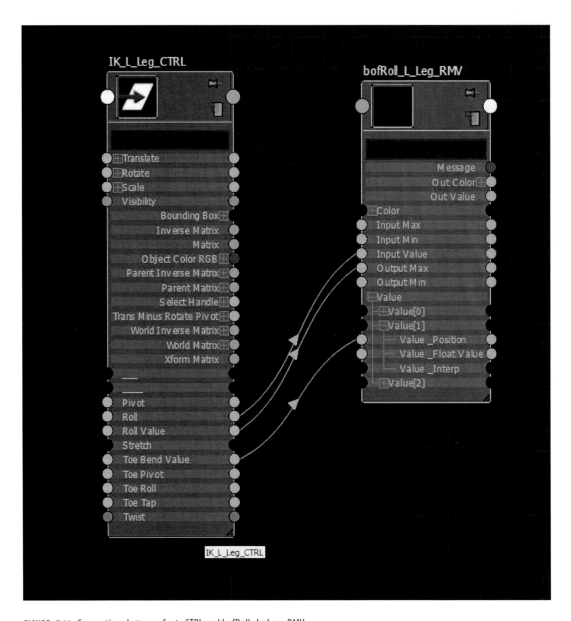

FIGURE 7.11 Connections between foot_CTRL and bofRoll_L_Leg_RMV

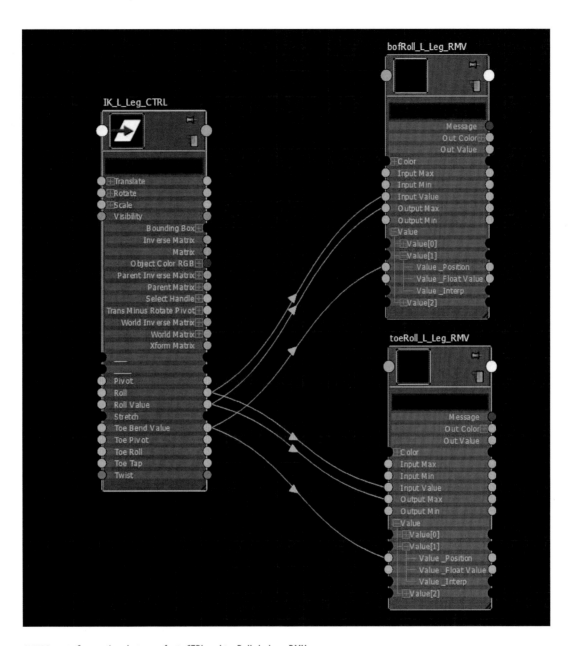

FIGURE 7.12 Connections between foot_CTRL and toeRoll_L_Leg_RMV

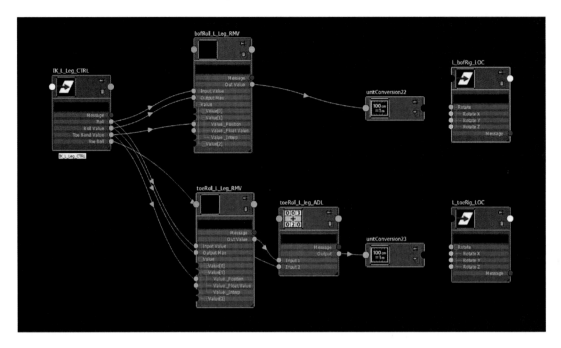

FIGURE 7.13 Completing the foot roll connections

If you scrub the roll channel, you'll notice the foot rolling on the ball-of-foot and then lift to roll on the toe. As the toe lift occurs, the ball-of-foot straightens back. You can also tweak (and key) how much and when during the animation the ball roll will occur by modifying the **Roll Value** and **Toe Bend Values**.

1. For the Pivot channel, connect the Connect **IK_L_Leg_CTRL > Pivot** to **L_bofPivotGrp > Rotate Y**.
2. For the Toe Tap channel, connect the Connect **IK_L_Leg_CTRL > Toe Tap** to **L_toeTapGrp > Rotate X**.
3. For the Toe Pivot, connect the Connect **IK_L_Leg_CTRL > Toe Pivot** to **L_toeRig_LOC > Rotate Y** (see figure 7.14).

Our foot is now ready for most of the motions you'll need for a game character. To add the stretch, knee pole vector and FK functionality, the setup is identical to what we used for Meep in Chapter 5. Please revisit that chapter if you need a refresher. You can find the completed IK leg setup by opening the file **02_Leaf_Legs_Done.ma**. Take a look at the Outliner to see how the various controllers, rig joints and helper nodes have been organized (see figure 7.15).

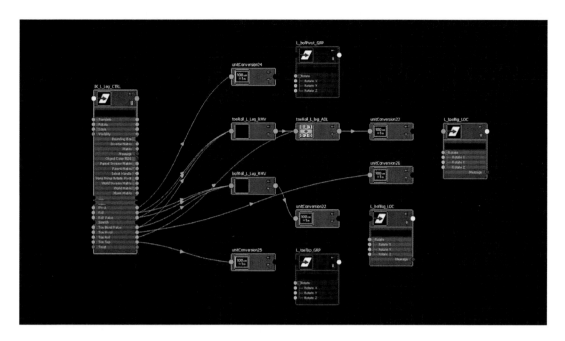

FIGURE 7.14 Adding the additional foot pivot point controls

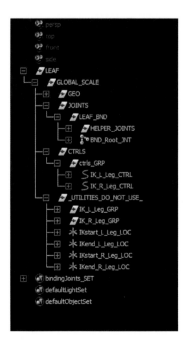

FIGURE 7.15 Complete leg setup outline

Automating the Limb Creation—the Limb Class

Looking at the leg setup, a thought might have crossed your mind that "hey, this is similar to what an arm setup would do!"—minus, of course, the foot bits. A typical arm and leg rig are similar to each other in terms of their overall mechanics, having 3 main pivots (shoulder, elbow, wrist and hip, knee, ankle). Where they begin to differ is at the extremities (hands, feet) where custom controls have to be adapted. To take care of the shared elements, we can create a unique limb class in Python that will deal with these common features based on user input, and then focus on the extremities on a case-by-case basis.

Since we now have a bind skeleton, our control rig script will be based on the naming convention we gave it and query it directly. We will also make use of our tabbed UI class as discussed in Chapter 4 to build our interface.

> **NOTE:** It's up to you how you want to approach this part of the control rig creation. If you want to write a script that will work with any type of naming/joint convention, offer the user an option to select the relevant joints and take it from there. On the other hand, you could also create your own skeleton generator, thus having full control over the initial joint placement and naming conventions. For our purposes, since we already know the names of the bind joints, we will use that to move things along. Strive to make your scripts as open-ended as possible (*when* possible).

The main rigging script (***tgpRigger.py***) will deal with the bulk of the automation, including the creation of the specific controls. The separate classes (tgpLimb, tgpSpine, etc.) will create the generic setup and pipe it back into tgpRigger. The script is too long to print in these pages, but you should open it up in your code editor and read through the comments.

Using a Dictionary

Let's take a closer look at the ***tgpLimb.py*** class found in the scripts folder. First, checks are made to see which conditions were sent from the tgpRigger script (IK, FK, and mirror—along with the name of the limb).

One of the first things to realize is that since this class will take care of all limbs (arms and legs), we have to find a way to separate and identify them. Using a list will work if we're dealing with, say, the legs only. But as soon as you introduce the arms, the list will grow to include the arm joints as well, and that could lead to some balancing headaches. This is where dictionaries again come to the rescue and help us maintain a clear separation between the control joints, regardless of the limb itself.

Let's take a simple example to illustrate the issue:

```
jntsDict={}
# create leg key and nested values
jntsDict["leg"]=[["L_upLeg_JNT","L_knee_JNT","L_ankle_JNT"],
     ["R_upLeg_JNT","R_knee_JNT","R_ankle_JNT"]]
# # create arm key and nested values
jntsDict["arm"]=[["L_upArm_JNT","L_elbow_JNT","L_wrist_JNT"],
     ["R_uparm_JNT","R_elbow_JNT","R_wrist_JNT"]]
print jntsDict
```

We first establish the dictionary jntsDict. Note the curly brackets. We follow by setting two sets of keys and values, one for the legs and one for the arms. The values, for the purpose of this example, are nested lists holding left and right joints (useful if you are going to mirror the joints of your rig).

Printing jntsDict will give us the following result (edited for legibility):

```
>>> full dictionary
{'arm': [['L_upArm_JNT', 'L_elbow_JNT', 'L_wrist_JNT'], ['R_uparm_JNT', 'R_elbow_JNT',
'R_wrist_JNT']], 'leg': [['L_upLeg_JNT', 'L_knee_JNT', 'L_ankle_JNT'], ['R_upLeg_JNT',
'R_knee_JNT', 'R_ankle_JNT']]}
```

Both keys and their respective values belong now to the *jntsDict* dictionary. The next bit of code will illustrate how we can start pulling information out of the dictionary, to be used for our rigging needs.

```
for keys,values in enumerate(jntsDict):
    print keys
    print jntsDict[values]
```

This will enumerate the keys i and print the dictionary values v as listed.

```
>>> enumerated keys and their values in dictionary
0
[['L_upArm_JNT', 'L_elbow_JNT', 'L_wrist_JNT'], ['R_uparm_JNT', 'R_elbow_JNT', 'R_
wrist_JNT']]
1
[['L_upLeg_JNT', 'L_knee_JNT', 'L_ankle_JNT'], ['R_upLeg_JNT', 'R_knee_JNT', 'R_ankle_
JNT']]
```

The enumerate command will iterate through each key, with the numbering starting at zero.

If we add now another for-loop to our code, we can extract the individual joints (i.e., values) from each key:

```
for keys,values in enumerate(jntsDict):
   print keys
   print jntsDict[values]
   for jntsList in range(len(jntsDict[values])):
     print jntsDict[values][jntsList]
     for items in range(len(jntsDict[values][jntsList])):
       print jntsDict[values][jntsList][items]
```

The result we get now separates each list individually—*x*, and then each item in the list—*y*.

```
>>> jntsList loop
['L_upLeg_JNT', 'L_knee_JNT', 'L_ankle_JNT']
>>> items loop
L_upLeg_JNT
L_knee_JNT
L_ankle_JNT
>>> repeat for second list
['R_upLeg_JNT', 'R_knee_JNT', 'R_ankle_JNT']
R_upLeg_JNT
R_knee_JNT
R_ankle_JNT
```

Another, more elegant way of accessing this information is to use Python's built-in dictionary functions. We can achieve the same result by using the *items()* operation.

```
jntsDict={}
jntsDict["leg"]=[["L_upLeg_JNT","L_knee_JNT","L_ankle_JNT"],
     ["R_upLeg_JNT","R_knee_JNT","R_ankle_JNT"]]
jntsDict["arm"]=[["L_upArm_JNT","L_elbow_JNT","L_wrist_JNT"],
     ["R_uparm_JNT","R_elbow_JNT","R_wrist_JNT"]]

for keys,values in jntsDict.items():
   print keys,values
   for value in values:
```

```
    print value
    for item in value:
        print item
```

Detailed examples of the various Python functions are to be found in the
official Python documentation at https://docs.python.org/.

NOTE: Sometimes, coming from scripting in MEL trying to adapt to
Python's logic takes a bit of adjustment. The first example with the
dictionary would follow a MEL-like process, while the latter example
follows a much more Pythonic way of thinking. In this case, Python rules!

Coding tgpLimb

Getting back to our script, we can now build a form of a dynamic dictionary,
whose values will be populated by our UI selections and identified by the
limb key.

```
import maya.cmds as mc
import maya.api.OpenMaya as om

class Limbs(object):
    def __init__(self):

        self.getAxis=""
        # dictionaries
        self.dHandles={}
        self.dIkjnts={}
        self.dFkjnts={}
        self.dPvPos={}

    def prepLimb(self,limbName,rigJoints,IK,FK,mirror):

        if mirror:
            #split the rigJoints list into separate sublists
            for i,mirroredJnts in enumerate(rigJoints):
                self.buildLimb(limbName,mirroredJnts, IK, FK)

        else:
            self.buildLimb(limbName,rigJoints, IK, FK)
```

The first part of the ***tgpLimb.py*** script checks if the joints are mirrored or not
as per the option set in the ***tgpRigger.py*** GUI. It then forwards the list of BND

joints to the main method that creates the IK and/or FK control joints. The core of the buildLimb method first duplicates the BND joints by invoking the dupJoints method. The idea here is to send any repetitive tasks to their own specific method, thus saving us on retyping the same code all over again. There are instances where, due to the nature of the rig, a general method can't take care of everything and similar code has to be re-entered. An example is the creation of the additional IK handles that deal with the reverse foot setup for the legs—which we will cover shortly.

After the control rig creation, the buildLimb method then checks to see which limb it's dealing with. Once the limb is established, it then checks if the IK and/or FK conditions are true, and creates the necessary functionality for the control joints.

```
def buildLimb(self,limbName,rigJoints,IK,FK):
    #duplicate the rigJoints (for IK and/or FK)

    self.getAxis=self.getPrimaryAxis(rigJoints)

    FKjoints=[]
    IKjoints=[]

    # pre-built group. Write message script?
    utilitiesGrp="_UTILITIES_DO_NOT_USE_"

    # ####################
    # LEG SETUP
    # ####################

    if (limbName=="Leg"):

      if IK:
        for i,joint in enumerate(rigJoints):
          self.dupJoints(i,joint, rigJoints,"IK_",IKjoints)

        startIkJnt=IKjoints[0]
        midIkJnt=IKjoints[1]
        connectIkJnt=IKjoints[2] #use for leg
        bofIkJnt=IKjoints[-2]
        endIkJnt=IKjoints[-1]

        mc.select(startIkJnt)
```

```
jntSide=self.getJntSide(startIkJnt)

IKgrp=mc.group(n="IK_{0}_{1}_GRP".format(jntSide,limbName))

mc.parent(IKgrp,utilitiesGrp)

# create the IK handle

mc.select(startIkJnt)
mc.makeIdentity(apply=True,rotate=True)

rigIkHandle=mc.ikHandle(sj=startIkJnt, ee=connectIkJnt,
                            sol="ikRPsolver",                >>>

        n ="IKankle_{0}_{1}_Handle".format(jntSide, limbName))[0]

rigEff=self.renameEff(rigIkHandle, jntSide, limbName)

# CREATE IK HANDLES FOR FOOT CONTROL

bofIkHandle=mc.ikHandle(sj=connectIkJnt, ee=bofIkJnt,
                            sol="ikSCsolver",                >>>
                    n="IKbof_[0]_[1]_Handle".format(jntSide,limbName))[0]

bofEff=self.renameEff(bofIkHandle, jntSide, limbName)

toeIkHandle=mc.ikHandle(sj=bofIkJnt, ee=endIkJnt,
                sol="ikSCsolver",                >>>
                n="IKtoe_[0]_[1]_Handle".format(jntSide,limbName))[0]

toeEff=self.renameEff(toeIkHandle, jntSide, limbName)

# get pv position
startVc=self.getVector(startIkJnt)
bendVc=self.getVector(midIkJnt)
endVc=self.getVector(connectIkJnt)

self.createPv(startVc,bendVc,endVc,limbName,jntSide,rigIkHandle)

allHandles=[rigIkHandle,bofIkHandle,toeIkHandle]
# hide handles
for h in range(len(allHandles)):
```

```
        mc.setAttr(allHandles[h]+".v",0)

    # update ikHandle dictionary

    self.dHandles.setdefault(limbName,[]).append(allHandles)

    allEffs=[rigEff,bofEff,toeEff]
    self.dEffs.setdefault(limbName,[]).append(allEffs)

    # update IK dictionary

    self.dIkjnts.setdefault(limbName,[]).append(IKjoints)

  if FK:

    for i,joint in enumerate(rigJoints):
      self.dupJoints(i,joint, rigJoints,"FK_",FKjoints)

    self.createMainFK(FKjoints, limbName, utilitiesGrp)

# ####################
# ARM SETUP
# ####################

if (limbName=="Arm"):

  if IK:
    for i,joint in enumerate(rigJoints):

      self.dupJoints(i,joint, rigJoints,"IK_",IKjoints)

    startIkJnt=IKjoints[0]
    midIkJnt=IKjoints[1]

    lastIkJnt=IKjoints[-1]

    mc.select(startIkJnt)

    jntSide=self.getJntSide(startIkJnt)

    IKgrp=mc.group(n="IK_[0]_[1]_GRP".format(jntSide,limbName))
```

```
        mc.parent(IKgrp,utilitiesGrp)

        # create the IK handle

        mc.select(startIkJnt)
        mc.makeIdentity(apply=True,rotate=True)

        rigIkHandle=mc.ikHandle(sj=startIkJnt, ee=lastIkJnt,
                                                sol="ikRPsolver",        >>>

                        n="IK_{0}_{1}_Handle".format(jntSide,limbName))[0]

        armEff=self.renameEff(rigIkHandle, jntSide, limbName)

        # get pv position
        startVc=self.getVector(startIkJnt)
        bendVc=self.getVector(midIkJnt)
        endVc=self.getVector(lastIkJnt)

        self.createPv(startVc,bendVc,endVc,limbName,jntSide,rigIkHandle)

        allHandles=[rigIkHandle]
        # hide handles
        for h in range(len(allHandles)):
          mc.setAttr(allHandles[h]+".v",0)

        # update ikHandle dictionary
        self.dHandles.setdefault(limbName,[]).append(allHandles)

        allEffs=[armEff]
        self.dEffs.setdefault(limbName,[]).append(allEffs)
        # update IK dictionary
        self.dIkjnts.setdefault(limbName,[]).append(IKjoints)

      if FK:

        for i,joint in enumerate(rigJoints):
          self.dupJoints(i,joint, rigJoints,"FK_",FKjoints)

        self.createMainFK(FKjoints, limbName, utilitiesGrp)

    return
```

> **NOTE:** As a way to update our dictionaries for the various control joints, we are using the Python `setdefault` function. It adds the relevant control joints to the proper key in the dictionary.

The rest of the class is made up of the smaller utility methods. The `dupJoints` method takes the enumerated list, the individual BND joint, the BND list, the kinematic-type name, and the kinematic-type joint list.

As each new control joint gets created, it gets appended to the kinematic-type joint list, which builds itself as the loop iterates through the BND joints.

```python
def dupJoints(self,num,joint,rigJoints,kName,kJnts):
    dupJnt=mc.duplicate(joint,renameChildren=True)[0]
    jntName=rigJoints[num].replace("BND_","")
    dupJnt=mc.rename(dupJnt,"[0][1]".format(kName,jntName))
    mc.setAttr(dupJnt+".radius",0.01)
    kJnts.append(dupJnt)
    self.delChldJnt(dupJnt)

    # skip the first joint when parenting
    if num>0:
      mc.parent(dupJnt,kJnts[num-1])
    return
```

The FK setup is the same for both arm and leg limbs, so we use the same method to create it, as seen below. It simply parents the FK control joints to a parent group node.

```python
def createMainFK(self,FKjoints,limbName,group):

    # organize FK rig control joints
    startFkJnt=FKjoints[0]
    mc.select(startFkJnt)

    jntSide=self.getJntSide(startFkJnt)
    FKgrp=mc.group(n="FK_{0}_{1}_GRP".format(jntSide,limbName))
    mc.parent(FKgrp,group)

    # freeze
    mc.select(startFkJnt)
    mc.makeIdentity(apply=True,rotate=True)
```

```
        # update FK dictionary
        self.dFkjnts.setdefault(limbName,[]).append(FKjoints)


        return
```

The next method creates the pole vector for the IK control joints. It uses vectors to calculate the placement of the pole vectors. We will discuss this in more depth a bit later on in the chapter.

```
def createPv(self,startVc,bendVc,endVc,limbName,jntSide,rigIkHandle):

        startBend= bendVc-startVc
        endBend = bendVc-endVc
        aimVc = endBend+startBend
        aimVc=aimVc.normal()
        aimVc*=30 #this can be any number you choose

        # position the aim vector
        poleVc= bendVc+aimVc

        tmpPvLoc=mc.spaceLocator(n="tmpPv_{0}_{1}_LOC".format(jntSide,limbName))[0]
        mc.xform(tmpPvLoc, translation=poleVc,ws=1)
        mc.setAttr(tmpPvLoc+".v",0) # hide tmp pole vector

        mc.poleVectorConstraint(tmpPvLoc,rigIkHandle)

        # update pole vector dictionary
        self.dPvPos.setdefault(limbName,[]).append(tmpPvLoc)

        return
```

And finally, to wrap up the tgpLimb class, we have a sprinkling of small utility methods. Typically, if you find that you use many of those utility methods in a variety of scripts that you write, a good idea is to create a utility class that you can point to as part of your larger suite of scripts. Think of it as your Swiss Army utility tool. You'll find that it becomes an indispensable part of your scripting toolkit.

NOTE: For illustration purposes, the next methods are part of the tgpLimb class, but they will be in their own utility class in the production version of the script.

```
# deletes child joints of selected
def delChldJnt(self,jntName):
   chldJnt=mc.listRelatives(jntName,children=True)
   if chldJnt:
     mc.delete(chldJnt)

 # extracts joint side based on the naming convention set
 def getJntSide(self,jntName):
   jntType,jntSide,jntName,jntSfx=jntName.split("_")
   return jntSide

 # return the vector of a joint
 def getVector(self,jntName):
   vc=om.MVector(mc.xform(jntName,q=1, translation=1, ws=1))
   return vc
# establishes primary axis of a joint chain based on vector values
 def getPrimaryAxis(self,jnts):
   primAxis=""
   startJnt=jnts[0]
   endJnt=jnts[len(jnts)-1]

   endJntWP=mc.xform(endJnt,q=True,t=True)
   endJntPos=om.MVector(endJntWP[0],endJntWP[1],endJntWP[2])
   # normalize the vector
   endJntNormal=endJntPos.normal()

   # get info from X,Y,Z axis
   for i in range(0,3):
     if endJntNormal[i]==1:
       if i==0:
         primAxis="x"
       elif i==1:
         primAxis="y"
       elif i==2:
         primAxis="z"
   return primAxis
```

Building the Spine

This part of the rig is one of those "hard to please" setups, since depending on how it is built, it might ease certain styles of animation, but complicate others. Unfortunately, there's not a single magic setup that will answer to all of the requirements, but with the concepts we explored so far, you will be able to create a spine rig that will fit your needs. For our example, we will build Leaf's spine using a simple yet flexible setup using a spline IK along with a stretch option thrown in there for good measure.

Hips, Shoulders . . .

Start by duplicating **BND_Root_JNT**, and delete the hip, shoulder and chest joints. In other words, everything but the spine and neck/head joints. Rename the duplicated root joint **ctrlRoot_JNT**, and the spine joints with an *IK* prefix, i.e., **IK_Spine0_JNT**, **IK_Spine1_JNT**, etc., and the joints from the neck upward with an *FK* prefix (see figure 7.16).

NOTE: Open **03_Leaf_Spine_Start.ma** to follow along with the duplicated spine joints already in place.

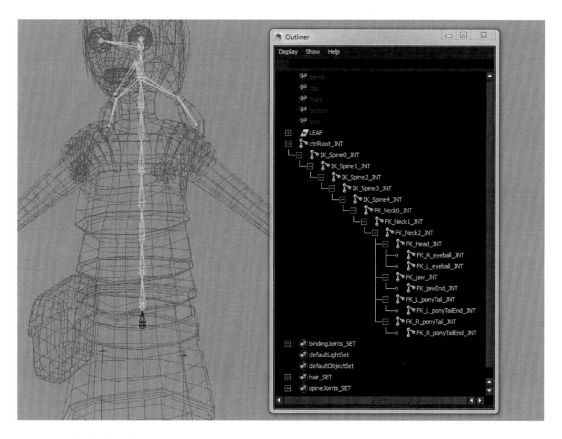

FIGURE 7.16 Starting the spine setup

In order to properly see the deformations of the control spine on the bind skeleton, we can do a direct connection between the Transform channels of the two sets of joints. Since we know the names of the joints, here's a simple little script to automate that process:

```
# Link Transform channels of BND joints to ctrl joints
ikobjs=["IK_Spine0_JNT","IK_Spine1_JNT","IK_Spine2_JNT",
    "IK_Spine3_JNT","IK_Spine4_JNT"]
bndobjs=["BND_Spine0_JNT","BND_Spine1_JNT",
    "BND_Spine2_JNT","BND_Spine3_JNT","BND_Spine4_JNT"]
# do a 1 to 1 connection
for i in range(len(ikobjs)):

    mc.connectAttr(ikobjs[i]+".translate",bndobjs[i]+".translate")
    mc.connectAttr(ikobjs[i]+".rotate",bndobjs[i]+".rotate")
    mc.connectAttr(ikobjs[i]+".scale",bndobjs[i]+".scale")
```

Open the IK Spline Handle Tool options and uncheck **Auto Parent Curve**. Change the number of spans to **2** (see figure 7.17). Connect the spline between **IK_Spine0_JNT** and **IK_Spine4_JNT**. Rename the IK handle to **spine_IK** and the curve to **spine_CRV**.

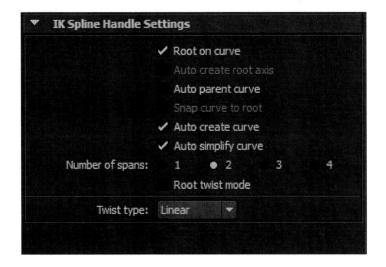

FIGURE 7.17 Spline IK options

The spline IK is controlled by the curve connected to it, which in turn moves the joints around. One way of manipulating the control vertices of the curve is by creating clusters on them. It's definitely an option, but that means that we will have to deal with additional nodes in our rig. Another way is to bind the curve to control joints and manipulate it through them. It's a cleaner way of achieving the same effect.

Duplicate the spine IK chain again and delete everything except for **IK_Spine0_ JNT** and **IK_Spine4_JNT**. Rename them **hip_CTRL_JNT** and **torso_CTRL_JNT** respectively. Change their joint radius to 7 in order to see them better. We will use these two joints as the drivers of the spline IK (see figure 7.18).

Select the two newly created control joints, followed by the **spine_CRV**. Open the **Smooth Bind** options and change *Bind To* to *Selected Joints* and the

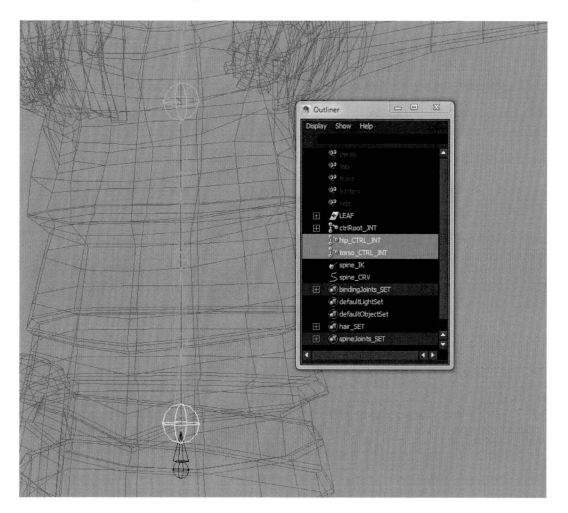

FIGURE 7.18 Create two control joints

Max Influences to **2**. If you rotate and translate the spine control joints, you'll see the spine flexing. Undo any transformations you made on the joints (you know you shouldn't be playing with raw joint rotations, right?)

You might have noticed that if you try rotating the control joints on the primary axis (X in this case) when it's at rest, nothing happens. To enable that function, we have to use the **Twist** function that is part of the spline IK. This attribute will allow for a gradual rotation of the IK handle, starting at the top of the joint, next to the handle. Now, there's a feature within the spline IK called **Advanced Twist Controls**. It offers the ability to tweak the twist function and add controls to it. It's commonly used with standard spine setups and works well in most cases. There is also another very useful attribute called **Roll**. This attribute rotates the IK handle on its axis, starting at the root of the IK. The biggest difference is that **Roll** rotates the complete chain, while **Twist** offers a gradual rotation to the chain.

We will look at a setup that will allow us to gradually rotate the chain from both the top and bottom of the joint chain, giving us further control over our spine. This setup can be adapted to work pretty much on any rig that requires twist functionality.

Start first by creating a couple of curve controllers for our joint controls. Snap them to the joints and name them **torso_CTRL** and **hip_CTRL**. Once they're in place, make sure to freeze transformations. Parent constrain the **hip_CTRL_JNT** to the **hip_CTRL**, and **torso_CTRL_JNT** to the **torso_CTRL** (see figure 7.19).

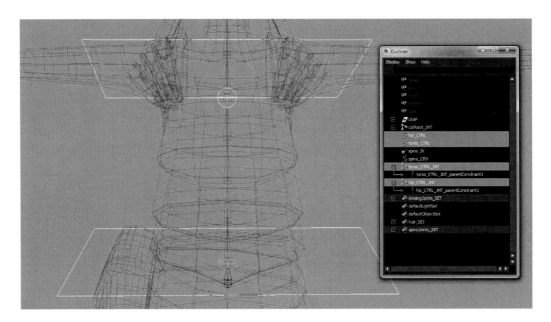

FIGURE 7.19 Creation and positioning of spine controls

Planning ahead, we will also modify the default rotate order of our IK spine joints, along with the various controllers. The default is XYZ, but after analyzing and ranking the order of rotations the spine has, we will change it to ZYX. Remember, Maya evaluates the rotation starting at the rightmost axis and moves to the left. Based on observation, the most common movement the spine makes is a twisting movement (i.e., along the X-axis) followed by the forward and back bending motion (Y-axis) and finally the sidebend (Z-axis).

> **NOTE:** The above rotation axes in this example are based on the default joint settings with X as the primary axis. If you wish to change that, make sure the primary axes are constant throughout the spine chain and adjust the Rotate Order accordingly.

Now to our twist and roll controls! Add a new attribute to the **hip_CTRL** called **rollEnable** with an Enum data type. Set the **Enum** names to **Off** and **On** (see figure 7.20).

In the Node Editor create three **multiplyDivide** nodes named **spineRollSwitch_MDN**, **spineRollValue_MDN** and **twistRollSumMult_MDN**.

1. Connect **hip_CTRL > Roll Enable** to **spineRollSwitch_MDN > Input 1X**.
2. Connect **hip_CTRL > Rotate Y** to **spineRollValue_MDN > Input 1X**.
3. Connect **spineRollSwitch_MDN > Output X** to **spineRollValue_MDN > Input 2X**.

This allows us to create the switch that will enable or disable the roll function on the **hip_CTRL**. Next, create a **reverse** node called **spineRollReverse_RVN**. Its purpose is to counter-rotate the values coming out the roll value as they get fed into the spline IK. Now connect **spineRollValue_MDN > Output X** to **spineRollReverse_RVN > Input X** (see figure 7.21).

Add the **torso_CTRL** and **spine_IK** nodes to the Node Editor. Create two **addDoubleLinear** nodes, named **twistRollSum_ADL** and **rollSumValues_ADL**.

1. Connect **torso_CTRL > Rotate Y** to **twistRollSum_ADL > Input 1**.
2. Connect **spineRollReverse_RVN > Output X** to **twistRollSum_ADL > Input 2**.
3. The **twistRollSum_ADL > Output** should connect to both **spine_IK > twist** and **twistRollSumMult_MDN > Input 1X**.
4. Set **twistRollSumMult_MDN > Input 2X** to **-1**.
5. Connect both **twistRollSumMult_MDN > Ouput X** and **torso_CTRL > Rotate Y** to **rollSumValues_ADL > Input 1** and **Input 2** respectively.
6. Finally, connect **rollSumValues_ADL > Output** to **spine_IK > Roll** (see figure 7.22).

FIGURE 7.20 Add roll attribute to hip_CTRL

And there you have it—a spline IK that twists from both ends! You have finer control than simply using the advanced twist controls options. With this setup, an FK control setup to fine-tune the position of the joints is not required—although feel free to create it if you wish.

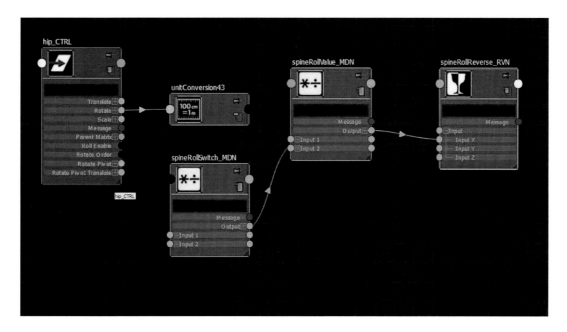

FIGURE 7.21 Connecting the roll attributes

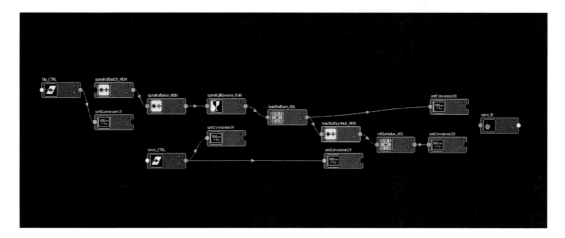

FIGURE 7.22 Connecting the twist and roll attributes to the spine_IK

Stretching the Spine

The next step is to create the ability to stretch the spine. For this particular example, we will use the scale attribute to control the stretch of the joints, but you can just as well use translations instead, as we did for the limbs. The main difference between the two methods is that for translation, it will require you to create *distanceBetween* nodes between each of the joints. Using the scale channels in this case is much faster—and also shows another a different approach to tackling the same issue.

As you know by now, for the stretch to work, we need to find the default length of the joint. Since we're using a curve with the spline IK, we can find the length of that curve via the *curveInfo* node.

Select the **torso_CTRL** and add a **Stretch** attribute using *Enum* as a data type with *Off/On* values:

1. Select the **spine_CRV** and **torso_CTRL** nodes and load it in the Node Editor.
2. Create a *curveInfo* node and rename it **spineCrvLength_CIN**.
3. Isolate the **spine_CRVShape** node and connect **spine_CRVShape > World Space[0]** to **spineCrvLength_CIN > Input Curve**.
4. If look at the Attribute Editor for the **spineCrvLength_CIN**, you'll see the length of the curve in the *Arc Length* channel. Make a note of that number.
5. Create a *multiplyDivide* node called **spineStretch_MDN**. Set the operation to *Divide* and enter the *Arc Length* value in the **Input 2X** channel.
6. Connect **spineCrvLength_CIN > Arc Length** to **spineStretch_MDN > Input 1X**.
7. Create a *condition* node and rename it *spineStretch_CDN*. Set *Second Term* to **0**, *Operation* to **Equal** and *Color if True R* to **1**.
8. Connect **torso_CTRL > Stretch** to **spineStretch_CDN > First Term**.
9. Connect **spineStretch_MDN > Output X** to **spineStretch_CDN > Color If False R**.
10. Bring **IK_Spine0_JNT** to **IK_Spine3_JNT** to the Node Editor.
11. Finally connect **spineStretch_CDN > OutColor R** to all of the **scale X** channels of the IK spine joints (see figure 7.23A).

By moving the **torso_CTRL** now, the spine will stretch with it. One of the aspects of stretching joints that we haven't discussed yet is the deformation of the mesh in terms of squashing and stretching. If this is something you wish your character to have, it's a very simple feature to add.

1. Create a new *multiplyDivide* node and call it **spineSquashStretch_MDN**.
2. Change the operation to *Power*.
3. Enter -**0.5** in the **Input 2X** channel. This is the equivalent of dividing 1 over the negative square root of the **scale X** value which will provide us with the proper squash/stretch scale values for the other 2 axes.
4. Connect **SpineStretch_CDN > OutColor R** to **spineSquashStretch_MDN > Input 1X**
5. Connect **spineSquashStretch_MDN > OutColor R** to all of the **scale Y** and **scale Z** channels of the above-mentioned IK spine joints (see figure 7.23B).

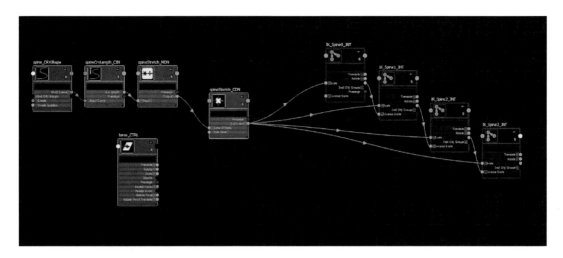

FIGURE 7.23A Connecting the stretch attribute to the joints

Do a quick cleanup of the Outliner by parenting the **torso_CTRL_JNT, hip_CTRL_JNT**, **spine_IK** and **spine_CRV** under the **ctrls_GRP**.

This setup works well for the requirements of Leaf's game motions and requires only one control rig to be connected to the BND chain.

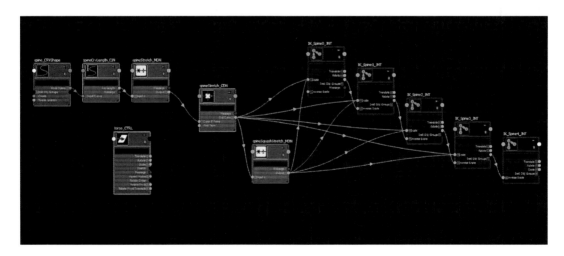

FIGURE 7.23B Creating the squash and stretch to the body

The Neck and Head

The head—and its subtle movements—can portray an incredibly wide array of emotions in a character. Looking at a silhouetted character and observing the motions of the head, you can tell that a slight tilt represents curiosity, or warns of incoming danger; a wide, slow arc tilted upwards shows amazement at a celestial body streaking through the skies; or a rapid bobbing of the neck up and down shows eagerness—among endless of other examples. And that's without showing facial expressions.

Our neck setup is going to be based on a mix of FK rotations and constraint goodness. First, we need to figure out what is the range of motion of the neck and head? There are 6 major motions that the head makes:

- Forward and backward nodding (flexion and extension)
- Looking side to side (lateral rotation)
- Ears-to-shoulders (lateral flexion)

There are two pivot points, one at the base of the neck and the other where the spine ends—the atlas vertebra—right under the cranium (occipital bone, to be precise). The flexion, extension and lateral rotations would, in a 3D rig, be controlled from the top pivot while the lateral flexion will involve the bottom neck pivot as well. Another point to take into consideration with the neck is the ability of the head to stay focused on one spot while the shoulders/torso moves. We will want to give the animators an option to have the head follow the rotation of the shoulders or disengage from them and keep the head locked in one position.

As before, connect the Transform attributes of the BND joints to the FK control joints. The one difference is the **BND_Neck2_JNT**. This joint will be *orient constrained* to the **FK_Neck2_JNT**, as you'll see shortly.

1. Select **FK_Neck2_JNT** and group it to itself.
2. Rename the group **headFollow_GRP**.
3. The new group, by default, will be positioned on the node above (**FK_Neck1_JNT**). Snap-move its pivot to **FK_Neck2_JNT**.
4. Create a new controller called **lookAt_CTRL**. I made mine look like goggles by scaling down a NURBS circle and modifying a few CVs. Snap position it to **FK_Neck2_Jnt**.
5. Group it to itself and name the group **lookAtFollow_GRP**. The group should be located at the Origin.
6. Translate **lookAt_CTRL** about an arm span in front of the head joints, and freeze transformations. This control will be our main head mover.
7. Add two attributes to **lookAt_CTRL**: *Shoulder Follow* and *Head Follow* with data type for both attributes is *Enum*, with *Off/On* values (see figure 7.24A).
8. Aim constraint **headFollow_GRP** to **lookAt_CTRL** using the following settings:
   Aim Vector to **0,0,1**
   Up Vector to **1,0,0**

9. As you move the **lookAt_CTRL**, the head follows its direction. This is due to the aim constraint we used on the **headFollow_GRP**. Since we don't have a similar node in our BND setup, the rotation values would not have been properly transferred over. That is why we orient constrained the **BND_Neck2_JNT** to its FK equivalent.

10. Select **lookAtFollow_GRP** and parent constrain it to the **torso_CTRL** using default values. This will enable us to lock the **lookAtFollow_GRP** to the shoulder's rotation or move independently from it.

11. To create the ear-to-shoulder motion (lateral flexion), hook **lookAt_CTRL > Rotate Z** to **FK_Neck2_JNT > Rotate Z**. Simple as that!

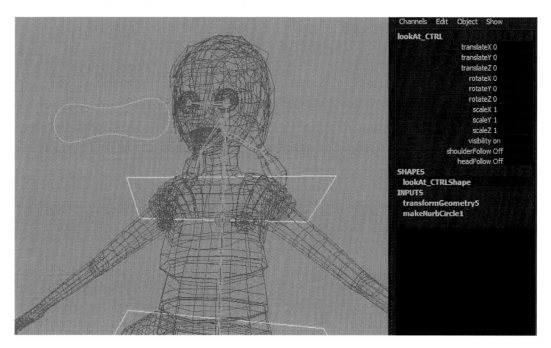

FIGURE 7.24A LookAt control

With these two constraints in place, we are going to create a switch that will enable us to override the head's motion to either follow the **lookAt_CTRL** or be rotated via the neck's FK joints. The **lookAt_CTRL** will remain the primary head mover, but sometimes you might need to pose it in a specific manner, and this setup will provide some of that ability.

Begin by creating two *condition* nodes called **shoulderFollow_CDN** and **headFollow_CDN** respectively in a clear instance of the Node Editor. Leave the settings as defaults (Operation is *Equal*). Load up the **lookAt_CTRL**, **lookAtFollow_GRP_parentConstraint1** and **headFollow_GRP_aimConstraint1**:

315

1. Connect **lookAt_CTRL > Shoulder Follow** to **shoulderFollow_CDN > First Term**.
2. Connect **lookAt_CTRL > Head Follow** to **headFollow_CDN > First Term**.
3. Connect **shoulderFollow_CDN > Out Color R** to **lookAtFollow_GRP_ parentConstraint1 > Shoulder ControlW0**.
4. Connect **headFollow_CDN > Out Color R** to **headFollow_GRP_ aimConstraint1 > Look At ControlW0** (see figure 7.24B).

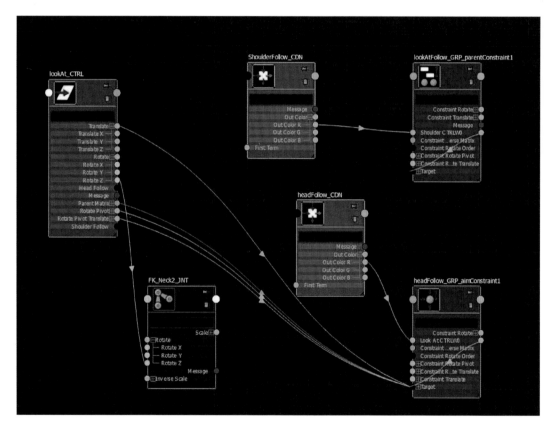

FIGURE 7.24B lookAt control node connections

Getting there. . .the last step with the neck setup is to enable a switch between the **lookAt_CTRL** (translation) to a rotation based FK control. Select **FK_Neck_JNT** and **FK_Neck1_JNT** and run the *tgpControlOrient* script once again (see figure 7.25). This will create a couple of FK controllers on our FK joints. Change the shape of the controller's CVs to make them more accessible, since they are located within the torso and neck meshes. I modified the shape **of FK_Neck1_CTRL** to surround the head, since it will act as the main FK head controller (see figure 7.26).

FIGURE 7.25 TgpControlOrient script

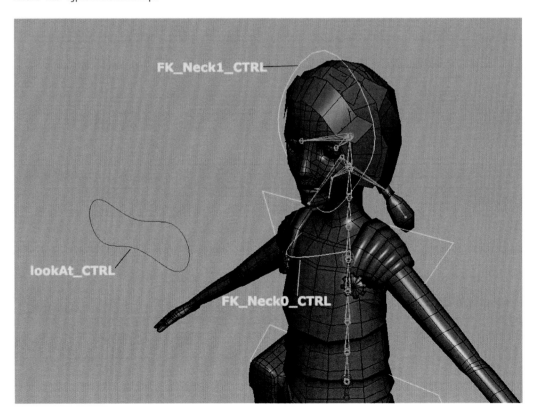

FIGURE 7.26 Head controls

1. Select the **lookAt_CTRL, FK_Neck1_CTRL** and **FK_Neck1_JNT_ orientConstraint1** and load them up in the Node Editor.
2. Create a condition node named **FKFollow_CDN**.
3. Set **FKFollow_CDN**'s *Color If True* to **1**, *Color If False* to **0**. Operation is "*Equal*".
4. Connect **lookAt _CTRL > headFollow** to FKFollow _CDN *First Term* input.
5. Connect **FKFollow _CDN > Out Color R** to **FK_Neck1_JNT_ orientConstraint1 > FK Neck1 CTRLW0**.
6. Connect **FKFollow _CDN > Out Color R** to **FK_Neck1_CTRL > visibility** (see figure 7.27).

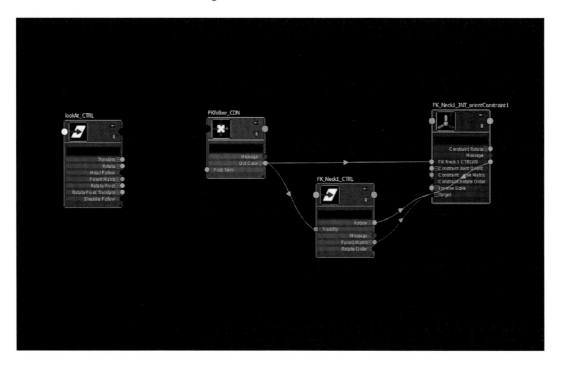

FIGURE 7.27 Neck control connections

Now, when the **lookAt_CTRL** attribute *headFollow* is set to **On**, Leaf's head will follow where the controller is pointed. When turning it **Off**, the **FK_Neck1_CTRL** appears and you can control the head via FK rotations. Again, you might not use it often—or at all—but the ability is there should you need it.

Additional motion to the neck can always be added, such as jutting the head forward. Based on the requirements of your project, you can provide that functionality by expanding the current setup or adding new controls to take care of those motions. Add the **lookAtFollow_GRP** to the **ctrls_GRP** to organize the Outliner.

Open **04_Leaf_Spine_Done.ma** to see the completed spine and neck/head setup.

Building the Arms

The arms for our rig follow a very similar setup as we did for the legs. It uses the same *tgpLimb.py* class. Some of the differences are the aim orientation for the elbow pole vector controls (to point in the Z-axis instead of the Y-axis), but that is established in the *tgpRigger.py* script. Also, instead of using *blendColor* nodes to connect the bind joints to the control ones, we are now using point and orient constraints. The reason is to add more flexibility with the hands and shoulders by using the constraint weights.

Looking at **05_Leaf_Shoulders_Start.ma**, you'll find the arm controls have been already placed in the rig, using the *tgpRigger.py* script. Currently they are set as IK only controls to simplify the next step, which will be setting up the shoulders.

Shoulders have always been notorious for being problematic. There are so many subtle variations in position from seemingly endless arm/torso combinations, that creating a solid rig that will manage to account for all of the motion is a challenge in character setup. Maybe that is one of the main reasons many of the game characters have shoulder pads to cover that area.

We haven't yet discussed Maya's driven keys in detail, but I think it's about time we start making use of their abilities. What makes the driven keys very useful is that we can control exactly *and* limit the amount of motion a certain object will have, as well as *when* that motion takes place. In other words, time and distance—just like those physics classes in high school—all controlled with animation keys.

Setting Up the Clavicles

We'll first start by analyzing what we'll need for this to work properly: the clavicles get engaged as soon as the elbows are about shoulder height and start lifting upward toward the ears. We'll create a rig solution that will enable a semi-automatic shoulder lift and roll depending on the position of the arm. As well, if our character needs to be able to shrug or simply roll the shoulders while keeping the arms down, we'll create a switch to give the animator control over each of the shoulders independently.

1. Create a shoulder controller, aptly named **L_Shoulder_CTRL**. Group it to itself and name the group **L_Shoulder_GRP**. Snap the group to the

BND_L_Shoulder_JNT. Freeze transformations to ensure that the pivot point remains on the bind joint position (see figure 7.28).

2. Create a 2-joint chain from the **BND_L_Shoulder_JNT** to the **BND_L_UpArm_JNT** and rename them **IK_L_Clavicle_JNT** and **IK_L_ClavicleEnd_JNT** respectively.

3. Parent them under a new group called **IK_L_Clavicle_GRP**. Make sure to move the pivot point of this group to the **BND_L_Shoulder_JNT** position

4. Create a single-chain IK between the clavicle joints and name it **IK_L_Clavicle_Handle**. Group it to itself and rename it **IK_L_Clavicle_Handle_GRP**. Parent this new group under **IK_L_Clavicle_GRP**.

5. For the auto-clavicle setup, we'll use a locator to drive the shoulder motion. Create a locator with the grand sounding name of **L_autoClavicle_LOC** and snap it as well to the **BND_L_Shoulder_JNT** (looks like there's a party happening at that location. . .).

6. As before, group it to itself, name the group **L_autoClavicle_GRP** and ensure its pivot is snapped to the party address (**BND_L_Shoulder_JNT**).

7. Parent the **L_autoClavicle_GRP** to the **IK_L_Clavicle_GRP** (see figure 7.29).

8. Parent the **L_Shoulder_GRP** to the **torso_CTRL**.

9. Parent the **IK_L_Arm_GRP** to the **IK_L_ClavicleEnd_JNT**.

10. Parent the **IK_L_Clavicle_GRP** to **IK_Spine4_JNT**. We've just linked the clavicle to the control spine, which will enable us overall control of the arm down the line.

11. Select in this order**: L_autoClavicle_LOC**, **L_Shoulder_CTRL** and **BND_L_Shoulder_JNT**, and then parent constraint using the default settings

12. Again, select in this order**: L_autoClavicle_LOC**, **L_Shoulder_CTRL** and **IK_L_Clavicle_Handle_GRP**, and then parent constraint using the default settings.

So far, we have all of the elements in place. Next, we'll create the switch between the two control states.

1. Add an **Off/On** enum attribute called **AutoClavicle** to the **L_Shoulder_CTRL**.

2. Load **L_Shoulder_CTRL, BND_L_Shoulder_JNT_parentConstraint1** and **IK_L_Clavicle_Handle_GRP_parentConstraint1** to the Node Editor.

3. Create a new *Condition* node called **L_autoClav_CDN** with default settings.

4. Set **Color If True R** to **0**; **Color If True G** to **1**.

5. Set **Color If False R** to **1**; **Color if False G** to **0**.

6. Connect **L_Shoulder_CTRL > Auto Clavicle** to **L_autoClav_CDN > First Term**.

7. Connect **L_autoClav_CDN > Out Color R** to **BND_L_Shoulder_JNT_parentConstraint1 > L_autoClavicle_LOCW0**.

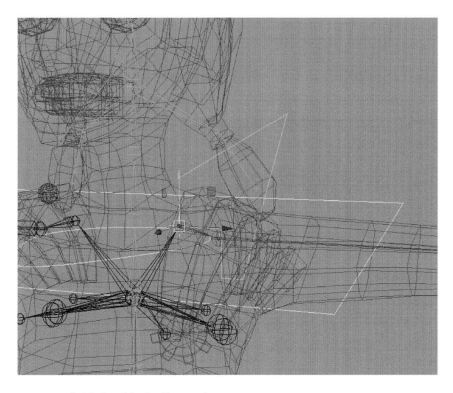

FIGURE 7.28 Positioning of the shoulder control

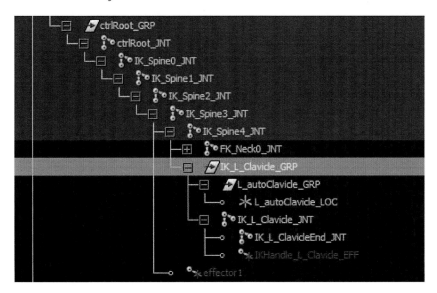

FIGURE 7.29 Clavicle setup

8. Connect **L_autoClav_CDN > Out Color G** to **BND_L_Shoulder_JNT_ parentConstraint1 > L_Shoulder_CTRLW1**.

9. Repeat the same **Out Color** connections as above from **L_autoClave_ CDN** to the **IK_L_Clavicle_Handle_GRP_parentConstraint1** (see figure 7.30).

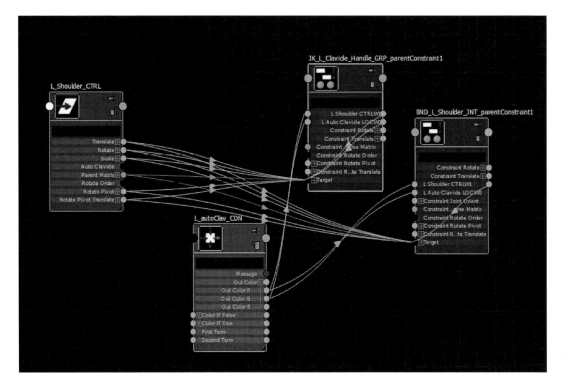

FIGURE 7.30 Connection of the automatic clavicle switch

At this stage the shoulder control—with the *autoClavicle* attribute set to *Off*—allows for the manipulation of the shoulder. We'll now set up the driven keys for the automation.

1. Open the Set Driven Key editor (**Animation > Animate > Set Driven Key > Set. . .**).

2. Load the **IK_L_arm_CTRL** into the Driver section.

3. Load the **L_autoClavicle_LOC** into the Driven section.

4. Select the **Translate Y** channel for the **IK_L_arm_CTRL**.

5. Select the **Translate X**, **Translate Y** and **Rotate Z** channels for the **L_ autoClavicle_LOC**.

6. Key them at their zeroed out values.

7. Translate the **IK_L_arm_CTRL** to **50** on the Y-axis.
8. Rotate the **L_autoClavicle_LOC** to **45** on the Z-axis, translate -**0.4** on the X-axis and **0.6** on the Y-axis.
9. Set a key in the Set Driven Key menu. This takes care of the upward movement of the arm.
10. Select the **Translate Z** channel for the **IK_L_arm_CTRL**.
11. Select the **Rotate Y** channels for the **L_autoClavicle_LOC**.
12. Key them again at their zeroed out values.
13. Translate the **IK_L_arm_CTRL** to **55** on the Z-axis.
14. Rotate **L_autoClavicle_LOC** to -**35** on the Y-axis.
15. Key the driven keys.
16. Translate the **IK_L_arm_CTRL** to -**15** on the Z-axis.
17. Rotate **L_autoClavicle_LOC** to **35** on the Y-axis.
18. Key the driven keys. Forward and back movements are now taken care of!

Driven Keys

The Maya command used to set the driven keys is setDrivenKeyframe. Here's the same process we did above, this time for the **R_autoClavicle_LOC** and using a few lines of code:

```
drvr="IK_R_arm_CTRL"
drvn="R_autoClavicle_LOC"

# Set the default zeroed-out values
mc.setDrivenKeyframe(drvn+".rz",cd=drvr+".ty",dv=0,v=0)
mc.setDrivenKeyframe(drvn+".tx",cd=drvr+".ty",dv=0,v=0)
mc.setDrivenKeyframe(drvn+".ty",cd=drvr+".ty",dv=0,v=0)
mc.setDrivenKeyframe(drvn+".ry",cd=drvr+".tz",dv=0,v=0)

# Key the driven values
mc.setDrivenKeyframe(drvn+".rz",cd=drvr+".ty",dv=50,v=-45)
mc.setDrivenKeyframe(drvn+".tx",cd=drvr+".ty",dv=50,v=0.4)
mc.setDrivenKeyframe(drvn+".ty",cd=drvr+".ty",dv=50,v=0.6)

mc.setDrivenKeyframe(drvn+".ry",cd=drvr+".tz",dv=55,v=35)
mc.setDrivenKeyframe(drvn+".ry",cd=drvr+".tz",dv=-15,v=-35)
```

In this case, I'm using named variables, but this can be easily modified to fit selected objects within a larger script.

The ***driverValue*** (***dv***) is what we set on the driver, while the ***value*** (***v***) is the keyed value of the driven.

Once the values are known, it's a pretty straightforward process to setup. An advantage of the driven keys is the ability to go into the Graph Editor and modify the curves for finer control over the motions.

The rest of the arms and hands follow a similar process. The fingers are based on FK rotations, and can have additional functionality using either the driven keys or, as we've done earlier, using a *remapValue* node.

After You! No, After You—Polite Space Switching

A useful feature of a good rig is the ability to change the default hierarchies on the controls and allow switching between different rig parts. For example, the way Leaf is currently setup, moving the **COG_CTRL** will move the body and head, but the hand controls will remain behind. An obvious way to fix that would be to simply parent the arm controls to the COG, and voila! But then. . .what if the animator wishes to keep the hands behind for a certain animation, and then have them follow the hips, and then maybe place one of the hands on top of the head and, while animating the head, the hand will follow along?

This is where the space switching term comes into play. In basic terms, it's the ability to create a set of multiple override nodes that allow one controller to switch between them.

Straight parenting, in this case, will not work. The way parenting hierarchies are currently setup, a child can only have one parent at a time (except if it's an instance, but that is not applicable to our purposes).

Space Switching Using Parent Constraints

The most common way to approach space switching is using a parent constrain. By its nature, the parent constraint will override both the translation and rotation of the "child" (constrained) object, but will offer the option of having multiple "parent" (constraining) nodes, all affecting the "child" node via the weight value.

To create the switch between them is simply a matter of using driven keys and setting a condition on the weights.

For this example, we will use *Monopod*—a super basic rig setup which will help us understand the space switching concepts. Load up **06_monopod_switchSpace_start.ma** from the Chapter 7 files folder.

For space switching to work, we have to plan ahead and identify which components of the rig will be the "parent" nodes. Take a look at the scene and you'll see a few light blue shapes on the monopod rig. These will act as our "follow" nodes to our controllers (see figure 7.31). If you look under the **CTRLS** group in the Outliner, you'll notice that the arm controls are *children of an arm_follow_grp group*. This group is important since it will be what we will use to connect the controllers to the follow nodes. In addition, it will provide the actual controllers freedom to be positioned wherever they need to be. The arm control itself will have the switch attribute that will direct to which "follow" node to switch to.

1. Select the **L_Arm_CTRL** and add an *enum* attribute called *Follow*, with these enum values: *World*, *Hips*, *Head* (see figure 7.32).
2. Select the following in this order: **world_Follow, cog_Follow, head_Follow** and **L_arm_follow_GRP**.
3. Do a parent constraint on the selected objects, using the default settings (see figure 7.33).

The **L_arm_follow_GRP** is now connected to three separate switch spaces. To apply the functionality to the switch itself, we'll use driven keys, as mentioned earlier.

1. Open the Set Driven Key menu and load the **L_Arm_CTRL** as the driver and the **L_arm_follow_GRP_parentConstraint1** as the driven.
2. Make sure that the **L_Arm_CTRL** *Follow* attribute is selected and set to *World*.
3. In the Set Driven Key window, highlight **World Follow W0, Cog Follow W1**, and **Head Follow W2** (see figure 7.34).
4. Set **World Follow W0** to **1, Cog Follow W1** to **0** and **Head Follow W2** to **0**.
5. Press the Key button.
6. Repeat by going down the list of the *Follow* attribute of the **L_Arm_CTRL** and keying the appropriate parent constraint value, setting it to **1** and the remaining ones to **0**.

When the *Follow* attribute of the **L_Arm_CTRL** is set to *World*, the positioning of any other controller will not affect the overall position of the arm control. You can check that by selecting the **COG_CTRL** and moving it around. The **L_Arm_CTRL** stays in place and will be affected only by moving the **char_CTRL**—but that's due to the parenting hierarchy.

If you change the *Follow* attribute to *Cog* and move the **COG_CTRL** about, the **L_Arm_CTRL** is now moving in tandem with it. Similarly, setting the *Follow* attribute to *Head* will constrain the movement of the arm control to the rotation of the head.

As you can see, simply by setting "parent" nodes and connecting to them a pivot (in this case, the follow groups), we can set a variety of space switches on our rig and have specific control over what part of the rig overrides which control.

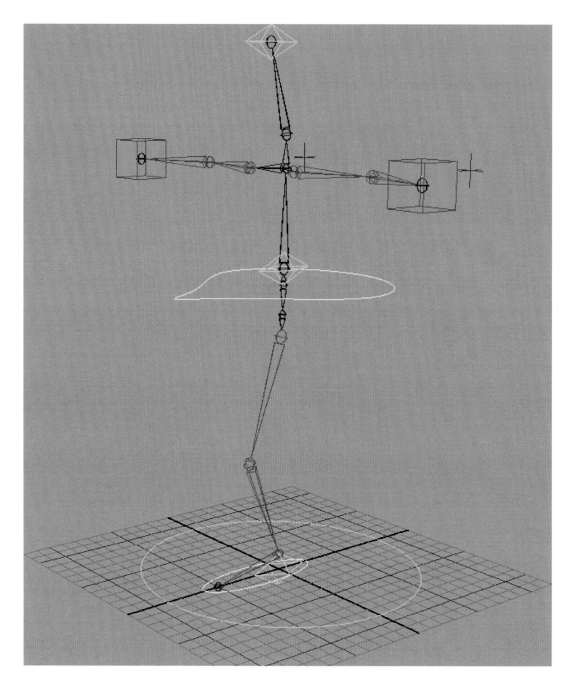

FIGURE 7.31 The amazing Monopod rig

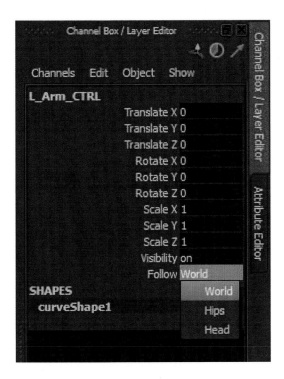

FIGURE 7.32 Add the various space switch positions

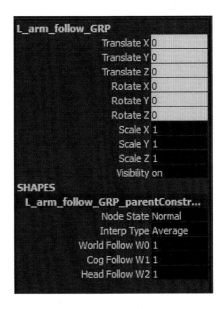

FIGURE 7.33 Parent constraints on the L_arm_follow_GRP

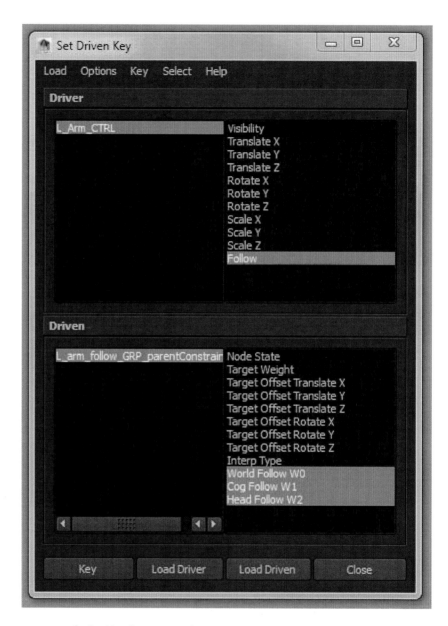

FIGURE 7.34 Setting driven keys on constraints

IK/FK Redux

When we rigged Meep's legs back in Chapter 5, we covered the basics of an
IK/FK switch. One of the most common issues with creating the switch is
actually the matching of either the IK system to the FK one, or vice versa. If it's

simply to offer the option to use one system over the other, then what we've built earlier works fine. On the other hand, if you wish to blend between them seamlessly, oftentimes the common setups you probably are familiar with will cause mismatches in position and rotation and will take a lot of time to tweak to the animator's satisfaction.

We will go over the basic logic of setting up a system that will allow us to snap one system onto the other, and then see how this can be achieved through code. This can then be applied to your own rigging scripts and offer that option to the animators.

Snappy Logic Part 1—FK to IK

There are two aspects to this snapping system. Let's start with the simpler one—FK to IK. Simply put, we want to get all of the rotation values of the relevant IK joints and transfer them over to the FK system, be it on the FK joints themselves, or the controllers that manipulate them.

From the Chapter 7 folder, load **07_FK_IK_snap.ma**. We have a very basic scene with two joint chains representing a generic limb. One has FK controllers and the other an IK control including a pole vector (see figure 7.35).

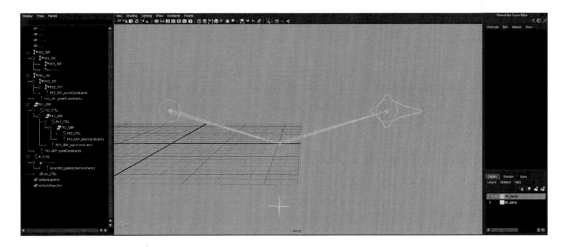

FIGURE 7.35 FK and IK switch setup

To see this in action, select the **IK_CTRL** and move it around the viewport to a different position while leaving the FK controls at their default. Feel free to move the **pv_CTRL** as well. With the **IK_CTRL** selected, run the bit of code below.

```
# FK to IK snapping
import maya.cmds as mc

# select IK_CTRL
sel=mc.ls(sl=1,fl=1,type="transform")

# find attached IK handle
selHandle=mc.listRelatives(sel,type="ikHandle")

# query the IK handle for the joints it solves
jntList=mc.ikHandle(selHandle,q=1,jointList=1)

# Get the last joint of the chain (not returned by the jointList flag)
endJnt=mc.listRelatives(jntList[(len(jntList)-1)],children=1,type="joint")

# append the last joint to jntList
jntList.append(endJnt[0])

#create an empty list to hold rotation values
ikRot=[]
for i in range(len(jntList)):
    selRot=mc.xform(jntList[i], ws=0,q=1,ro=1) #use local space

    ikRot.append(selRot) #use append instead of extend to keep separate lists

# apply the x,y,z rotation values to the FK controls
for x in range(len(ikRot)):
    rVal=list(ikRot[x]) # extract the values from each list using list()
    x+=1 #our FK controls start at 1, so we needed to "cheat" the numbering
    updRot=mc.rotate(rVal [0], rVal [1], rVal [2],"FK{0}_CTRL".format(x))
```

Here's a breakdown of what the code is doing: After the **IK_CTRL** is selected, we query it and find the IK handle that's connected to it. This in turn allows us to find the joints that are affected by the IK handle solver. Unfortunately, this doesn't include the last joint in the chain. Not a problem, we use the **listRelatives** command on the last queried joint, with the **children** flag set to true. This gets added to the jntList list and we are back in business.

In the next phase, we create a new list called ikRot that will hold the X, Y and Z rotation values of each joint. We are using the **xform** command to do so. Note that we are not using the world space, since it will throw the calculations off-kilter. Instead we will set the **worldSpace (ws)** flag to False (remember...1 and 0, True and False). We then append each set of values to the ikRot list. If we had used the **extend()** command instead, it would have created one big, long list. Instead, we are now getting individual lists with the rotation values of each joint within our main list.

In the final part of the code, we begin to loop through each one of the lists in ikRot. We use the Python **list()** command to extract the values of each of our lists and assign them to the rVal variable. Since our FK controls start with 1, while our lists are index-0 based, we cheat the counter and add a 1 to it for assigning them to the proper FK control. The rotation values are then applied using Maya's **rotate** command.

A few things to keep in mind: a basic version of this could simply have been done with using Maya's **getAttr** and **setAttr** commands. This would have entailed creating a variable for each of the rotation values of each IK joint and then applying them to each of the FK controls, channel by channel. It's doable, but a messy method in my opinion. By using loops and lists, you keep the code cleaner and more dynamic. The one potential pitfall in our code is that the last line includes hardcoding the names of the FK controls. For this example it's fine, but keep that in mind as you create more automated setups for your rigs. Sometimes there is no escaping hardcoding values and object names into your scripts, but try to keep that to a minimum if you can.

Snappy Logic Part 2—IK to FK (with a dash of pole vector magic)

The biggest issue with manipulating the IK control is the positioning of the "bend" joint (can be the elbow, knee, or an equivalent), especially if there's a pole vector constraint attached to it. The initial part, which is to position the **IK_CTRL** on top of the FK wrist joint or control follows the same procedure as we did above where we get the position of the FK control and apply it to the IK one. To match the bend, we will use the OpenMaya **MVector** command once again to calculate the proper angle and position.

I know, I know. . .math. You might say we should leave that to the brainiacs out there, and focus on the fun stuff and make gooey aliens with tentacles, riding on giant mecha-robots. But math is fun too, especially if it helps us rig those gooey tentacley aliens.

One thing that I'd like to explore before going over the IK snapping is the actual positioning of the pole vector control. We are going to go off on a tangent for a bit, but hopefully this will make things clearer as to the logic behind this process. Yes, there is a method to the madness.

You will very often find that the pole vector is positioned in a relatively haphazard way, typically by creating a locator, snapping it to the knee (or elbow) and then translating it along whichever axis is roughly perpendicular to the IK handle. And yes, I'm guilty of that too, when we created Meep. To everyone's defense, it works *for the most part*, especially when the bend angle obtuse and the joints are drawn on a flat, orthogonal plane. Issues begin to arise when the bend angle is acute, and when the joints are off the orthogonal planes. Think of the T-pose as the flat orthogonal, versus the A-pose as the off orthogonal. We will look into a more "scientific" way of positioning the pole vector, which we will achieve with some basic math and coding.

First, let's do a quick recap: for IK systems to work properly, especially with pole vectors, the engaged joints have to be properly oriented, aligned and on a flat plane. If they're not, it's an opening to a lot of frustration and misbehaving controls. Open **08_PV_setup.ma** from the Chapter 7 file folder (see figure 7.36).

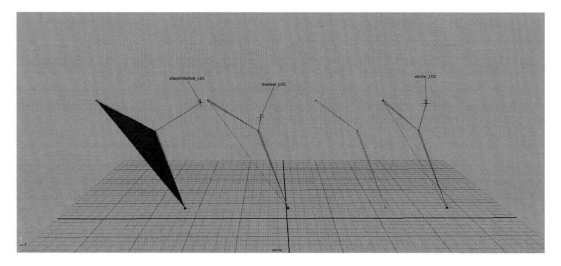

FIGURE 7.36 **Different ways of setting a pole vector**

The three joint chains are identical to each other. Their joint template was used to position the original chain and then redraw the joints so they are properly aligned to each other.

The leftmost chain (**planeOriented_JNT**) has a polygon plane within it that visually shows the flat plane we just discussed above. To position the **planeOriented_LOC**, I selected the vertex of the plane on the bend joint and translated along its normal to an arbitrary position beyond it, where the locator was then placed.

The **manual_LOC** was simply snapped to the bend joint and translated in the Z-axis. The **vector_LOC** was placed via a script which we will discuss shortly. You'll see that there's also a curve that shows the connection between the bend joint to the relevant locator. These curves are there just as visual guides for the next part. If you select the joints in the chains, you'll also see that their rotations are zeroed out, which is how we wish to keep them.

Let's test this out and see how the position of the pole vector can affect our IK chains. For the time being, we'll use only **the orientPlane_LOC** and **manual_LOC**. Select them, then select their respective IK handles and constrain the pole vectors.

You'll immediately notice that the joints connected to the **manual_LOC** jumped out of place, in comparison to where the guide curve was. If you select the top joint of the chain, you'll see also that there are rotation values on it. Basically, the IK system tried to solve toward the pole vector, but because it was placed in the wrong plane it had to compensate by rotating the joints. Not good.

On the other hand, the plane-oriented locator worked like a charm. Open **09_PV_enabled.ma** to see the end result (see figure 7.37).

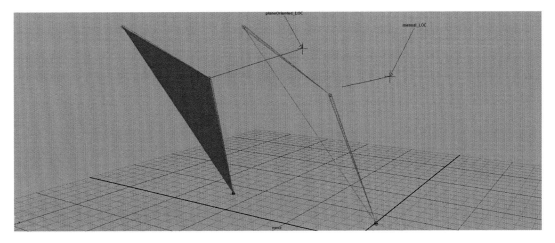

FIGURE 7.37 Enabling the pole vector and the "jump"

One quick-and-dirty way to accomplish this is by using a couple of constraints to get the proper pole vector aimed towards the right position. Open the **10_PV_example.ma** file to start (see figure 7.38).

1. Create a locator and name it **pv_CTRL**.
2. Group it to itself and name the group **pv_GRP**.
3. Select **start_JNT**, **end_JNT** and **pv_GRP** in this order and point constraint. You'll see the locator halfway between the joints, along the IK curve.
4. We'll add an additional layer of control to our pole vector. Select the **pv_CTRL** and group it again to itself. A new group will appear above it. Rename this group to **pvRot_GRP**.
5. Select **bend_JNT** and **pv_GRP**, and open the aim constraint options (see figure 7.39).

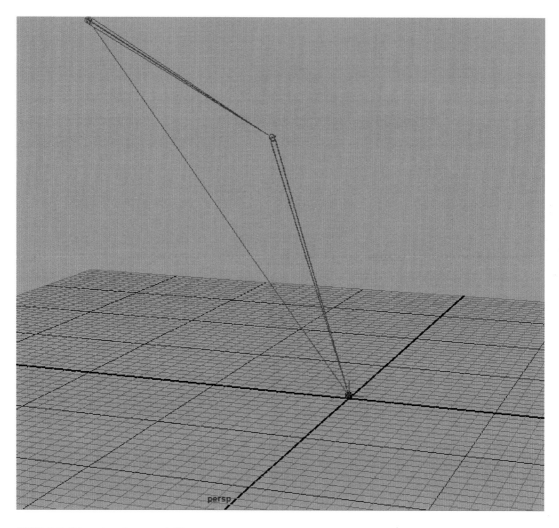

FIGURE 7.38 Pole vector setup example file

6. Change *World up Type* to: ***Object Rotation Up***. Enter **bend_JNT** in the *World up object* field.
7. Make sure you are in Local translate space and select the **bend_JNT**. You'll see which way the joints are aiming (this is based on the default XYX orientation). We are trying to match this as closely as possible (see figure 7.40).
8. ***IMPORTANT!*** Delete the aim constraint on the **pv_GRP**!
9. Select the **pv_CTRL** and translate it on the X-axis. You'll see that it intersects the **bend_JNT** as you move it in front of the joint chain.
10. Freeze translation on the **pv_CTRL**.

11. With the **pc_CTRL** selected, shift select the **pv_IK** handle and constraint pole vector.

Voila! No jumping joints, with zeroed out rotations. You can now either control the **pv_CTRL** directly by translating it or rotate the **pvRot_GRP** on the Z-axis (see figure 7.41). Open **11_PV_example_done.ma** to see the final result.

Since we're all about automation, let's see how we can do this with code. First, here are a few useful terms to know when dealing with vectors:

- **Vector**—a mathematical object that has a length (magnitude) and a direction; it is defined also by a tail and a head (the start and end of the vector); the length is always a positive value
- **Unit vector**—a vector with a length of 1
- **Normalize**—divide the length of a vector by itself with a resulting value between -1 and 1, where 1 is parallel to the vector's direction, 0 is perpendicular and -1 is parallel but facing the opposite direction

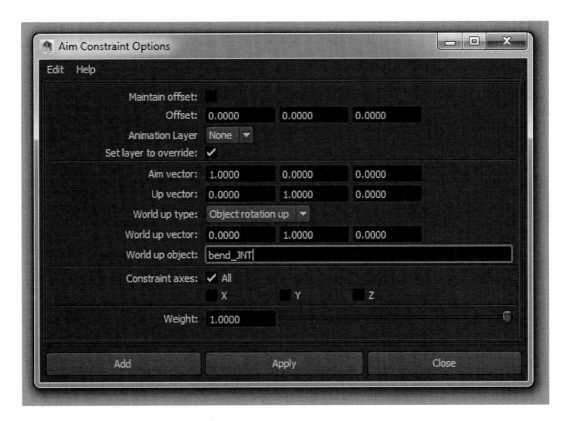

FIGURE 7.39 Aim constraint options for pole vector

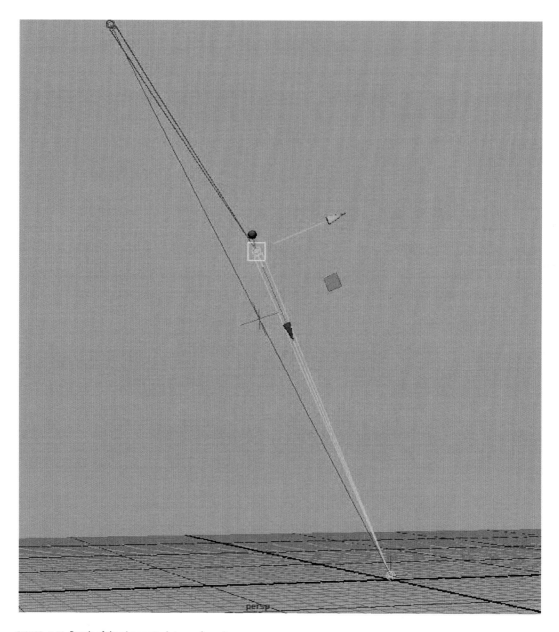

FIGURE 7.40 Result of the aim constraint on pole vector

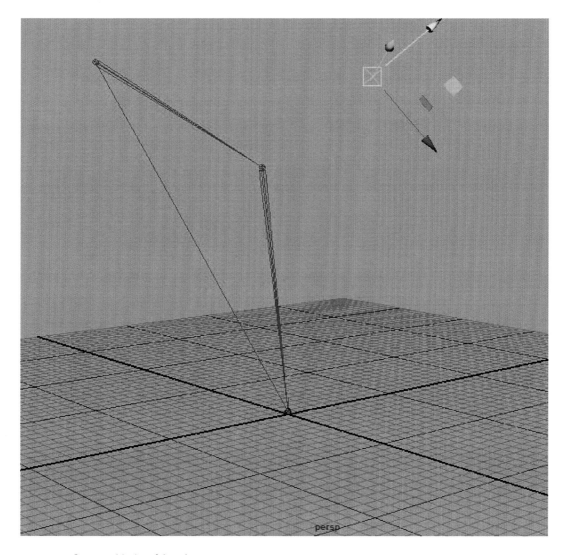

FIGURE 7.41 **Proper positioning of the pole vector**

- **Scalar**—a numerical quantity that is defined by its magnitude (i.e., length, mass, speed) but has no direction
- **Dot product**—the multiplication of two vectors, returning a scalar value
- **Cross product**—the return of a third vector that is perpendicular to the plane created by the two original vectors

NOTE: A couple of great resources for math-related stuff, including vector math, are www.khanacademy.org and www.mathisfun.com. These sites manage to make math digestible and enjoyable, which is a wonderful thing. You will find a lot of in-depth information on the concepts mentioned above, on those sites, as well as dusting off your old calculus and physics books from high school.

We are going to calculate the vectors between the start and bend joint (see figure 7.42), and between the bend and the end joint (see figure 7.43). One thing about vectors, it doesn't matter where they are located in space. They are simply a direction and a length. By default, the tail of the vector starts at the origin.

Once we have those values, we will add the two vectors together, which will give us the direction we should be aiming our pole vector at (see figure 7.44). We will then normalize our aim vector (see figure 7.45). Remember, this will give us the proper direction, but with a magnitude of 1. If we don't normalize, we will get a random number based on the above calculations, which will make it a pain to attach our control (trust me on this—or try on your own and experiment around with the code and see what you get). By normalizing, we know we are dealing with a set value, which will then multiply with a number of our choosing in order to extend the length of our aim vector to something more manageable. Finally, we will move it in 3D space and align it to the bend vector. Our aim vector will extend towards where we should place our pole vector control (see figure 7.46).

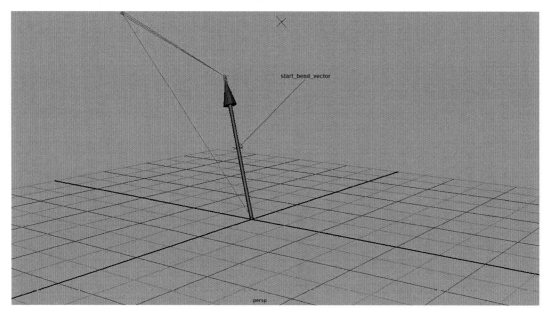

FIGURE 7.42 Direction of start bend vector

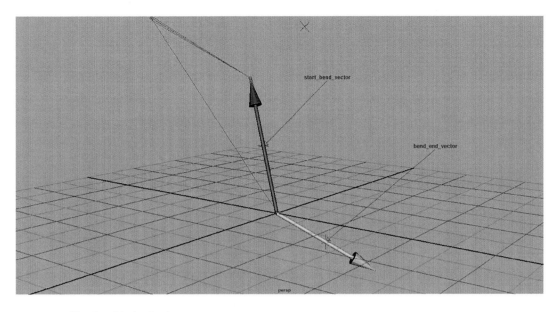

FIGURE 7.43 Direction of the bend end vector

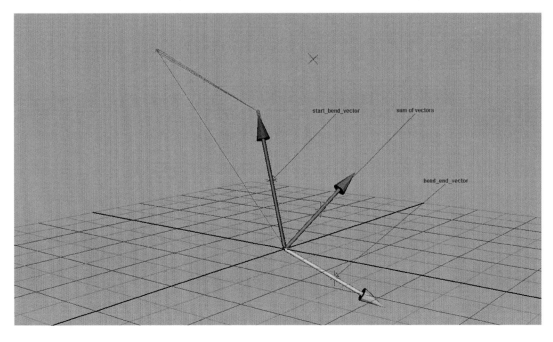

FIGURE 7.44 Sum of total vectors

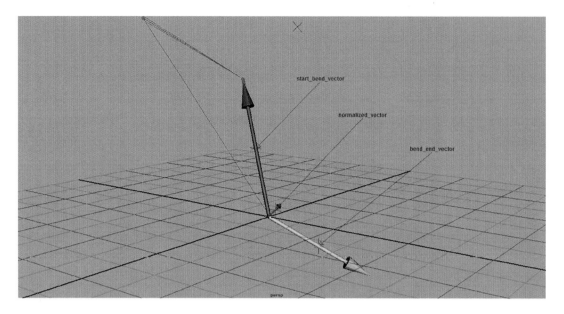

FIGURE 7.45 Normalized total vector

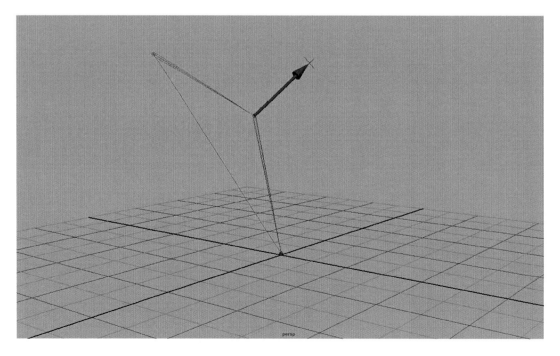

FIGURE 7.46 Proper positioning of pole vector along bent joint

```
import maya.cmds as mc
import maya.api.OpenMaya as om #for api 2.0

# vector method
def getVector(selJNT):
    vc=om.MVector(mc.xform(selJNT,q=1, translation=1, ws=1))
    return vc

# select the three joints in order (start, bend, end)
sel = mc.ls(sl = 1)

# get the vectors for the selected joints
startVc=getVector(sel[0])
bendVc=getVector(sel[1])
endVc=getVector(sel[2])

# calculate the two "arms" of the chain
startBend= bendVc-startVc
endBend = bendVc-endVc

# get the sum of the vectors
aimVc = endBend+startBend

# normalize the aim vector
aimVc=aimVc.normal()

# add a multiplier to the aim vector(can be any number you choose)
aimVc*=10

# position the aim vector
poleVc= bendVc+aimVc

# create the pole vector
loc = mc.spaceLocator(n="pv_CTRL")[0]
mc.xform(loc, translation = poleVc, ws=1)
```

By the way, this setup can also be accomplished through the utility nodes, in case you're curious.

And back to our regular programming. . .now that we see how vector math can help us align our pole vector, we will use that same logic and use it to properly snap our IK system to the FK one.

Reload **07_FK_IK_snap.ma**, and this time rotate the FK controls to a new position. In this example, select all 3 FK controls (**FK1_CTRL**, **FK2_CTRL**, **FK3_CTRL**), the **IK_CTRL** and the **pv_CTRL** last. Run the script, and this time the IK system will snap into position on top of the FK one.

```
# IK to FK
import maya.cmds as mc
import maya.api.OpenMaya as om #for api 2.0

# vector method
def getVector(selJNT):
    vc=om.MVector(mc.xform(selJNT,q=1, translation=1, ws=1))
    return vc

# select the three FK controllers in order,
# the ik_CTRL and lastly the pole vector control
sel = mc.ls(sl = 1)

# get the vectors for the selected controls
startVc=getVector(sel[0]) #FK1_CTRL
bendVc=getVector(sel[1]) #FK2_CTRL
endVc=getVector(sel[2]) #FK3_CTRL
ikVc=getVector(sel[3]) #ik_CTRL
pvCtl=sel[4]

# move IK_ctrl to FK "wrist"
mc.move(endVc.x, endVc.y,endVc.z,sel[3],rpr=1)

# calculate the vectors of the chain
startBend= bendVc-startVc
endBend = bendVc-endVc

# get the sum of the vectors
aimVc = (endBend+startBend)

# normalize the aim vector
aimVc=aimVc.normal()

# add a multiplier to the aim vector (any number)
aimVc*=5

# position the aim vector
poleVc= bendVc+aimVc
```

```
# position pole vector in place
mc.move(poleVc.x,poleVc.y,poleVc.z, pvCtl, rpr=1)
```

The script is very similar to the pole vector script we initially wrote, with a few minor changes. Hopefully now things are much clearer in terms of workflow and you'll be able to incorporate this into your own scripts that involve switching between IK and FK systems.

NOTE: Depending on your setup, you might not need to normalize the vector. Remember to test every step of your scripts along the way.

Finalizing the Rig

Getting back to Leaf, the last part of our rig is to connect all of the various rig components together and clean up any of the unattached elements in the Outliner.

The important thing at this stage is to make sure that all of the BND joints are connected to their control counterparts. The arms, legs and spine are taken care of. Make sure that the ones from the neck up are linked as well. Do that as well with the **BND_Root_JNT** and link its Transform attributes to the **ctrlRoot_JNT**.

Adding Global Scale to the Rig

As with Meep, we'll create a **char_CTRL** that will act as the top controller of our rig. This controller will reside at the origin. Add a *globalScale* attribute to the **char_CTRL**, with a minimum value of **0.1** and a default value of **1**.

Create another controller and call it the **COG_CTRL**. Snap it to the **ctrlRoot_JNT**, and freeze transformations. Make it a child of the **char_CTRL** (see figure 7.47).

Parent constrain the **ctrlRoot_JNT** to the **COG_CTRL**. Once that's set, select the **hip_CTRL** and **torso_CTRL** and make them children of the **COG_CTRL**.

Finally, select the **IK_L_Leg_CTRL**, **IK_R_Leg_CTRL**, **lookAtFollow_GRP**, **IK_L_Arm_CTRL**, **IK_R_Arm_CTRL** and make them children of the **char_CTRL**. Make sure your Outliner looks like figure 7.48.

The global scale setup will follow a similar overall workflow as we did with Meep, but we will have to take into consideration the spline IK we used for the spine.

343

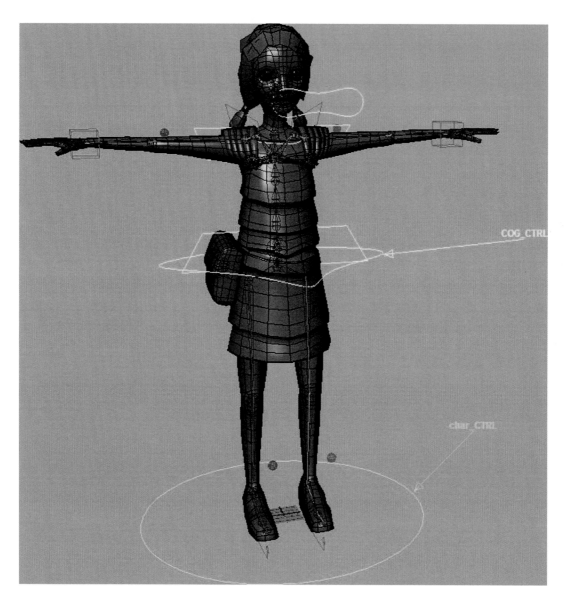

FIGURE 7.47 Main and COG controls

First, to prevent the double-transformations on the mesh, select the **GEO** group and in the Attribute Editor, uncheck ***Inherits Transform***. That will keep the mesh properly scaling with the joints.

Next, open the Node Editor and load the **char_CTRL** and **GLOBAL_SCALE** group. Connect **char_CTRL > Global Scale** to the three scale channels of **GLOBAL_SCALE** (see figure 7.49).

344

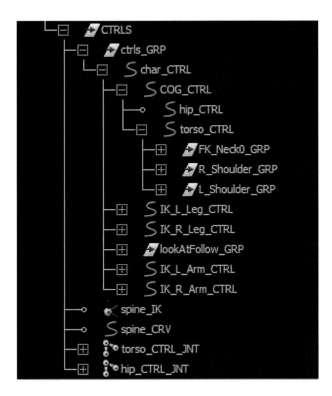

FIGURE 7.48 Hierarchy of Leaf's controls

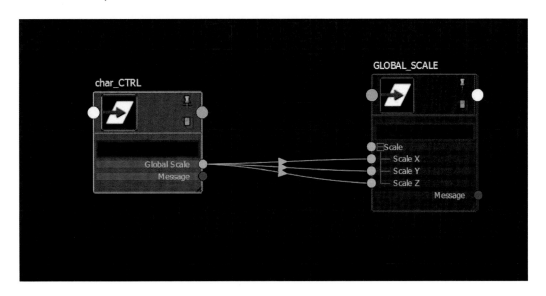

FIGURE 7.49 Connection of global scale attributes

If you try this out, you'll notice that everything works pretty much as expected, other than one very noticeable glitch (see figure 7.50)! The culprit causing the double-transform in this case is the **spine_CRV**. Select it and uncheck its ***Inherits Transform*** from the Attribute Editor. Problem solved.

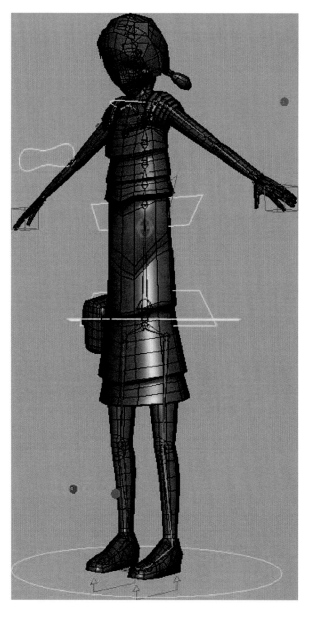

FIGURE 7.50 Global scale glitch

To ensure also that the stretchy function of the spine works as it should, we're going to slightly rearrange some of the connection nodes and prevent further unpleasant surprises.

Create a *multiplyDivide* node called **spine_globalScale_MDN**, and set its operation to *Divide*. Load the input and output connections of the **torso_CTRL** into the Node Editor and look for the **spineStretch_MDN**. Disconnect it from the **spineStretch_CDN** we created earlier on (see figure 7.51).

1. Connect **spineStretch_MDN > OutputX** to **spine_globalScale_MDN > Input 1X**.
2. Connect **char_CTRL > Global Scale** to **spine_globalScale_MDN > Input 2X**.
3. Connect **spine_globalScale_MDN > OutputX** to **spineStretch_CDN > ColorIfFalse R**.

The scaling of the stretchy joints works properly now, and keeps its relative ratio and doesn't break our rig.

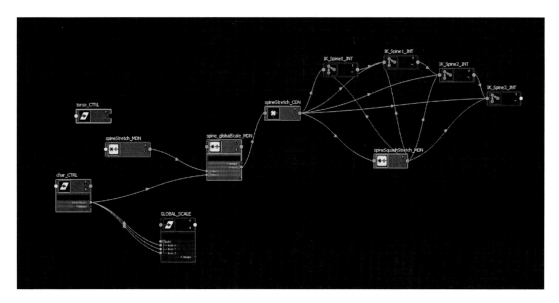

FIGURE 7.51 Global scale node connections

Cleaning Up the Channels

Now that all of the main elements of the rig are connected between the bind joints and the various control joints, it's important to ensure that any unnecessary channels, joints and other objects in the control rig are not visible and/or accessible to the animators. The goal is to have a rig that is as streamlined and animator friendly as possible. This typically prevents mistakes such as selecting the wrong control or keying a channel that should not be keyed.

NOTE: Pressing the "S" key in Maya is the fastest way to set keys on an object, but as we all know, it also adds keys on all visible channels in the Channel Box. Hiding (and locking) any unnecessary channel in the Channel Box typically makes for a happy production overall. Also, cleaning up the Graph Editor using **Edit > Delete by Type > Static Channels** helps get rid of any unused, keyed channels.

A common issue is having elements visible in the scene that we would like to hide in order to keep the focus on the control rig. Simply hiding these elements by turning off their visibility attribute won't work, since selecting **Display > Show > All** will turn the visibility back on.

A useful trick is to enable the *Drawing Overrides* options in the Attribute Editor and turn off the *Visible* checkbox for the selected object. This will keep the objects hidden, even if the option to display hidden objects is enabled as above. Here's a quick script that will do it for us. You can put that button on your shelf for quick access:

```
sel = mc.ls(sl=True)
for i in range(len(sel)):
    # use 1 for On, 0 for Off to reverse the order
    mc.setAttr(sel[i]+".visibility", 0)
    mc.setAttr(sel[i]+".overrideEnabled", 1)
    mc.setAttr(sel[i]+".overrideVisibility", 0)
```

You can reverse the order and create another shelf button to turn the visibility back on. Now if being invisible could be that simple in real life...

Another very useful feature in Maya is the use of Sets. In a nutshell, think of Sets as a basket filled with objects, components and anything else in Maya you can think of, which can then be quickly selected and manipulated without affecting the scene's hierarchy. You can use them to organize various rig components such as joints, controls and other elements.

You can access them via the **Create > Sets** menu option, or by typing the following command:

```
mc.sets(name="nameOfSet")
```

Read up about them in Maya's documentations. There are a few flags that provide additional features, as well as combining them with the use of partitions for further precise control.

Sets are very useful also during the shading, lighting and rendering part of the pipeline when creating linking relationships between various scene elements. For example, instead of light linking 20 different objects to two lights, creating 40 individual links, you could place the objects in one set and link the set to the two lights, creating only 2 links instead. This helps keep the file size small and makes the overall scene much lighter.

You can find the completed version of Leaf's rig in the Chapter 7 folder under **12_Leaf_rig.ma**.

And . . . ?

So the question that begs to be asked now is "Are we done with the rigging process?" The honest answer is simply: no. Rigging is like painting a picture. Ask any artist, and he or she will tell you there is always one more thing to add to the painting, and then one more, and then one more. It's never completely done. We can keep on working on these rigs and constantly improve on them, and add additional functionality. Sometimes you will have to go back and revisit what you've worked on depending on the changing requirements of the project. But such is the nature of digital production.

At times, deadlines, delivery dates, program limitations and a myriad more causes will force you to stop working on the rig and move on to the next thing. Automating as much as possible and keeping the rigs modular will hopefully help take care of all of the basics, allowing more time to refine the custom bits that every rig has that makes it unique from the other ones.

Keeping up with the changes of the current 3D and gaming technologies also offer new and interesting ways of approaching rigging. What is a "standard" and accepted practice in rigging today can easily be considered passé in the next version of the software. Limitations that force the 3D artists to work one way in order to adapt and meet the requirements of a game engine can easily be changed with the next current engine update or by using the brand new game engine with the snazzy bells and whistle features that just came out.

At the end of the day, understanding the production pipeline, automating repetitive tasks and having a solid grasp of scripting logic, along with a good creative sense will provide the right foundation to succeed as a technical artist in the world of digital entertainment. The most important aspect of what we've covered in these last few chapters can be summed up as the knowledge you've gained by going through the scripting and rigging process. Create a new mesh, and start making your own tools to facilitate your own rigging workflow.

Chapter 8
Game On!

Exporting to Unity

We are finally ready to export out our rig in the game engine. This process can be applied to most modern game engines currently available at the time of writing this book. As mentioned earlier, I will be using Unity since it's the engine of choice for the *Tin* game. I initially debated which game engine to use while conceptualizing the development of the game, and Unity offered the greatest amount of flexibility and necessary tools to answer the requirements of the game.

Animating for Games

The animation process for video games characters, as you've probably guessed, is very different than it is for cinematics. With cinematics, the animator keys the character motions to act for the camera. It's a passive process in the sense that the character is being *viewed* by the audience, and the sequence of the animation is predetermined by the animator according to an established narrative. Each shot is planned ahead of time, and the various actions and expressions are animated accordingly. The amount of poses the animated character can make is effectively infinite, limited only by the rig controls.

Animating for games, on the other hand, is a dynamic, albeit limited process. In contrast to the cinematic animation, game animation acts as an interactive gateway between the game and the player, allowing for an immersive experience through gameplay. You, as the player, define where and when and how the character will act at any given moment in the game. This control, obviously, greatly limits the range of motions and actions as compared to what is available for a cinematic animation, since they are defined by the game design and game mechanics. For example, a game character in a platformer-style game will usually have the following cycles in the animation library:

- Idle
- Walk
- Run
- Jump (and possibly double-jump)
- Climb

- Crawl
- Push/pull
- Fight action (shoot, hack and slash)
- Interact with objects/environment

These are some of the common actions found in most platformer games. Depending on the game itself, more (or less) cycles will be created, depending on the game animation requirements and style.

Once the cycles are animated, they are imported into the game engine, to be called via code during gameplay. This code connects the animation to the interactive game controls (keyboard, joystick, mouse, etc.) which load the correct sequence depending on the player's actions and what is shown on the screen.

Prepping the Rig in Maya

In order to export the rig properly out of Maya and into Unity, there are a few steps we need to follow in order to ensure that everything works out as it should. As we mentioned in Chapter 2 in the file referencing section, the scene needs to be clean of all unnecessary components before sending it to Unity. Make sure to go over your rig scene with the proverbial fine-tooth comb and clean up any rogue elements. This includes:

- **Freezing transformations**—all controllers, relevant group nodes and geometry should be zeroed out. Pay attention especially to the scale channels.
- **Delete history**—nodes that don't require active history connections to function, such as the mesh should be free of history. If there is a case where a deformer is implicitly connected to it, you can use delete non-deformer history.
- **Proper naming conventions**—self-explanatory, and critical not only for scene organization but also for potential scripts that require naming standards.
- **Solid, watertight geometry**—the exported mesh gets triangulated in Unity. If it isn't properly modeled prior to that, you'll encounter visual glitches during gameplay.
- **Polygons meshes only**—Unity (and most other modern game engines) can accept only polygon meshes, so no NURBS or any other geometry type (looking at you, subdivision surfaces).
- **Remove any unnecessary textures and shaders**—use only what is relevant to the object. Any other textures or shaders used for testing purposes, or remnants from imported files, should be deleted.

- **No animation keyed on mesh**—the meshes should be clean of any keyframes. Save the animation on the controllers, which in turn animate the joints via baking.
- **Mesh bound to single joint hierarchy**—when exporting to Unity, the mesh should be bound to the bind joints, and completely separated from the control rig. As a matter of fact, the control rig and all its related features should be removed from the scene. The only objects you should have in your game objects file are the mesh and the bind joints.

These tips will ensure that your game mesh is ready for export to Unity as smoothly as possible.

Methods of Exporting Animation from Maya to Unity

There are two acceptable methods of bringing animations from Maya (or your choice of 3D software) to Unity. Both work equally well, but have their own pros and cons. Consider which method will work best for your project, or combine them for different characters.

The first method is to have all of the animation of your character animated in one single file, exported to Unity, and then "splitting" the animation within Unity.

For example, animate the "idle" cycle from frames 1–24, "walk" from frames 25–37, "run" from frames 38–48, etc.

The advantage in this method is that you're dealing with one single file, which can save overall space when importing assets into the game engine. The main—and major—disadvantage with this method is that in case of a change in the timing of the animation of one of the cycles, all of the cycles along the timeline will have to be adjusted accordingly to reflect that change.

The second method, which in my opinion offers more flexibility, is to have a base character model exported as an FBX file and imported into Unity consisting of the base, non-animated geometry and joints. The animations are then baked and saved as separate scenes. Only the joints are then exported and brought to Unity individually. For example, if we were to use Leaf as our base character:

1. Export Leaf's mesh and joints as described above as **_Leaf.fbx_**.
2. Animate the various cycles, and save them as separate files.
3. Within each cycle file, select only the joints and export selection as **_Leaf@ cycleName.fbx_**.

NOTE: It's extremely important to maintain this naming convention when exporting the animation with this method. The name of the character followed by the "@" symbol tells Unity to properly attach the animation cycle. Otherwise, it will not work.

This method will allow you then to make changes to any one of the cycles without affecting the other ones present. As well, if you wish to later add additional cycles to your character, connecting them to the existing ones will be straightforward without having to reshuffle frames around. Once they are loaded into Unity, the animation cycles can then be blended with one another.

The major disadvantage is file sizes. Each animation cycle is one more file to add to your Unity project, and that can add up quickly and go over the overall size budget of your game. This is especially true if the game you're developing is on a mobile platform.

NOTE: It is possible to combine the best of both worlds and animate separately, and then combine the cycle files into one main file. You'll need to write a custom script in Unity to parse and extract the animation as well as help with the splitting. There are lots of useful resources that cover Unity scripting in-depth, both online and in print.

As an aside, Unity *can* read native Maya files directly, but it is not recommended to do so. For one, Maya has to be installed alongside Unity. Someone without Maya would not be able to open your project files. Maya files also save many additional nodes that are not relevant to your game project, thus inflating the overall file size. The FBX format is a good overall option that is compatible with many additional industry tools and works well with Unity.

Baking the Animation Keys

Once you decide on the animation cycles you'll need for your game and animated them using the control rig, it's time to transfer that animation to the bind joints using the **Bake Simulation** function in Maya. Baking a simulation doesn't prepare you to be the next great pastry baker—although it would be nice if it could. Rather, it applies any animation from controllers and other elements directly onto the selected joint by placing a key on every frame. Once the baking is done, you can safely delete any animated controllers, knowing that the animation will be preserved directly on the joint.

NOTE: Make sure to save your file with *prebake* and *postbake* versions. You will need to go back, either if it's to tweak the animation or add a completely different set of keys. Remember to always save your work multiple times. Back it up on hard drives, USB keys and the Cloud.

Here are the steps to bake out the bind joints:

1. Once your character is animated, select all of the bind joints (use the **set** command as discussed in the previous chapter for easy selection).
2. Go to **Edit > Keys > Bake Simulation > □**.
3. Make sure that the time frame matches the length of your animation, either by using the time slider, or setting a start/end point (see figure 8.1).
4. Press the Bake button, and presto! Instant keys on all of the joints at every frame.

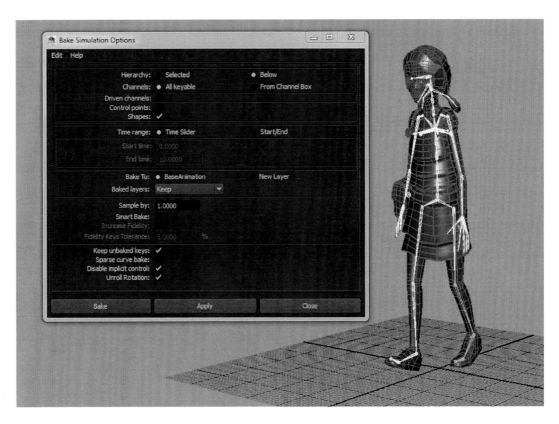

FIGURE 8.1 Baking animation simulation keys options

You can now safely delete your controllers and additional connections, since they are no longer necessary. This also includes the *utility nodes used for the rigging process*! A quick way of removing all of these elements is by selecting **Hypershade > Edit > Delete Unused Nodes**.

Just make sure that when you do it, you do so in a methodical manner. Sometimes, simply deleting control objects or groups can affect the bind skeleton—depending on how they are connected. Playback your animation; it should be the same as you had with the controllers.

Another useful tip is to remove any static channels in your animations. By default, all channels in the Channel Box will be keyed. When baking out the animation, the affected channels will usually be the rotation channels. By deleting the static channels, you ensure a lighter scene file without any unnecessary keyed elements. You can apply that to all of the relevant animation keys by selecting **Edit > Delete All by Type > Static Channels**.

One thing to keep in mind before exporting to Unity: Maya has a feature called **Segment Scale Compensate** that is accessible under the joint Attribute Editor option (see figure 8.2). This option allows the joints to compensate when a parent joint is scaled non-uniformly, to prevent the mesh from squashing and stretching strangely. It is on by default. Some game engines do not like that feature at all and will mess up the mesh import. If you've left that option on, a quick way of disabling it is by selecting the bind joints to export out and run the following code bit:

```
# disable segment scale compensate option
sel = mc.ls(sl=True)
for i in range(len(sel)):
    mc.setAttr(sel[i]+".segmentScaleCompensate", 0)
```

That should take care of that potential gotcha.

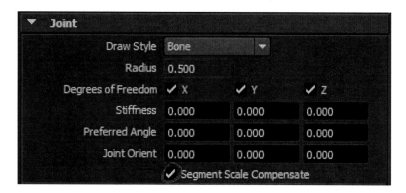

FIGURE 8.2 Turn off segment scale compensate checkbox

Exporting to the FBX Format

Using the second method of exporting animation to Unity as discussed above, we will first export the base mesh as an FBX. You should aim to have the bare

FIGURE 8.3 Organizing joints under their own group

minimum in your scene—mainly the mesh and the bind joints, without any unnecessary nodes or objects. Consider restructuring your Outliner with an identifying name group on top, with the mesh and the joints underneath as children nodes. The joints can be as a single hierarchy or under their own group (see figure 8.3).

1. Navigate to **File > Export All. . .** > □.
2. Select **FBX Export** from the dropdown menu.
3. Under **File Type Specific Options**, click on the **Edit presets. . .** button.
4. For the most part, the default settings work. You might want to test out a few variants to ensure that the exported FBX mesh behaves as you expect. Below are some options you might want to look at, found in the **Include** section of the FBX plugin UI:

- **Smoothing groups**—you might want to turn that off. Check how the mesh looks like in engine.
- **Animation**—if you're importing an object with animation, obviously you'll want that on. If it's a static object, to be either animated in engine or act as a background asset, turn that off.
- **Bake animations**—if you've baked the animations as we did previously, you can turn that off. It's the same function, except that with the method we discussed you have a few more options to control.
- **Disable lights and cameras**—you'll be using the ones provided in the game engine.
- **Constraints**—turn that off since we won't be using them.
- **Units**—by default, when you bring in an FBX object to Unity from Maya, the scale of the object is tiny, and you'll have to set it up to 1 manually. You could do it from the FBX exporter or automate that process through code at the engine level.
- **Axis conversion**—Y-axis is up.
- **FBX file format**—Unity usually keeps the FBX importers up to date on their end, but glitches have been known to happen. If your exported model comes out weird, you might want to revert to a stable version (typically, an older version of FBX). Again, the word of the day is test, test, test!

5. Export file as FBX.

For the animation cycles, follow the same procedure as described above, making sure that to export *only the joints*, and using the proper naming convention.

> **NOTE:** The FBX format is currently a very popular way of importing and exporting 3D files between different applications. It's owned and maintained by Autodesk, and you can find more information on it on their website.

Importing Animation Files in Unity

Over to you, Unity! We'll now test out how the animations came through and go through the process of importing them to our game engine. Fire up Unity and start with a new, blank project.

NOTE: You can download a free, fully functional version of Unity from their website at unity3d.com/unity/download. The *Learn* section on their website has many excellent tutorials to get you familiarized with the engine.

First, we will do a basic scene setup. We'll start by creating a cube and turn it into a floor surface to have our character walk on.

1. Create the cube by going to **GameObject > 3D Object > Cube**. Rename it **Floor**.
2. Position it on the Y-axis at **-0.5**.
3. Scale X-axis 10, Z-axis **100**.
4. Make sure that **Box Collider** is enabled.

I've also added a directional light for some basic lighting to make the scene a bit less drab.

Now import our default model into the scene. RMB-click in the Assets window and select **Import New Asset. . .** (see figure 8.4). I've changed the camera rotation and position in order to frame Leaf better in the scene. Place the mesh in the viewport, making sure that Position and Rotation are set to zero.

> **NOTE:** Scale might have a value of 0.01 to balance the Scale Factor. Ignore it for now. Scaling objects in the scene can have adverse effects on the mesh, especially with rigged characters.

Select the Leaf object, and in the Inspector window, change the **Scale Factor** to **1** (see figure 8.5) and click on the *Apply* button. Repeat the above steps, this time importing the **leaf@ leaf_idle_anim.fbx** and **leaf@leaf_walk_anim.fbx** (see figure 8.6) (*and remember to set the Scale to 1*).

FIGURE 8.4 Importing model into Unity

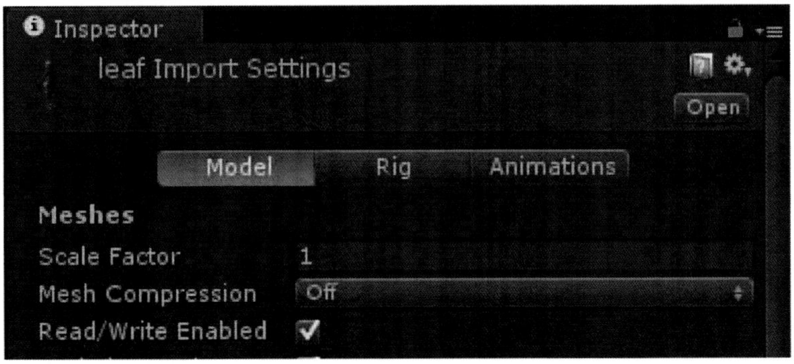

FIGURE 8.5 Change Scale Factor to 1 in Inspector window

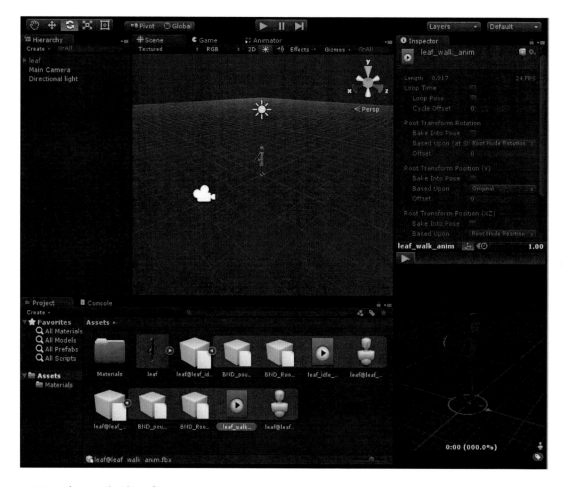

FIGURE 8.6 Import animation cycles

You can see the animation cycles by selecting the play icon in the Inspector. Follow this workflow to import all of your character's animation into the Unity scene.

Blending the Animation Cycles

The next step (intended pun?) is to connect the animations to one another. Using our example, we'll blend the idle cycle to the walk cycle.

As of version 4.0, Unity has introduced the Mecanim animation system. It has significantly improved the way imported animations work in the engine, and offers a lot of functionality over the older legacy animation system. It allows the user to blend smoothly between various animation types (i.e., walk to run) using blend trees and offers an out-of-the box logic (a state machine) that enables the user to set various animation conditions depending on the player's actions.

We'll start by creating a controller for our animation.

1. Go to **Assets > Create > Animator Controller**.
2. Rename the controller to **Leaf_Anim_CTRL**.
3. Select **Window > Animator** to see the default setup (see figure 8.7).
4. Drag the idle and walk cycles into the Animator window. If you dragged the idle one first, it will turn an orange color. This establishes it as the default animation state. You can change the default state by RMB-clicking on any other cycle and selecting **Set As Default**. Leave it on idle for this example.
5. To connect the controller to the mesh, select the mesh and take a look at the Inspector. You'll notice that the **_controller_** field in the default **Animator** component is set to **None** (see figure 8.8).
6. Drag the **Leaf_Anim_CTRL** to that field to connect the animation cycles to the mesh (see figure 8.9).
7. To see the animations, open the Animation window (**Window > Animation** or use the Ctrl+6 shortcut).
8. At the top, right under the play button, there's a dropdown where you can switch between the two animation cycles and see their respective keys in the dopesheet/ curve editor. Because we've imported the animation, they are read-only.

FIGURE 8.7 Default Animator window in Unity

FIGURE 8.8 Animator controller set to None

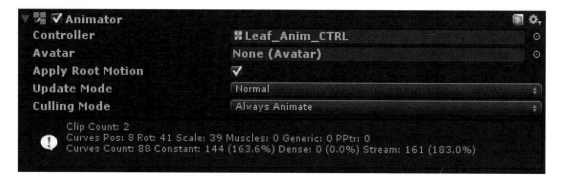

FIGURE 8.9 Drag Leaf_Anim_CTRL to controller

We need now to tell Unity to apply the cycles. We'll do that by setting parameters in the Animator window. These parameters will allow us to switch between cycles via code.

1. Click on the + besides the word parameters and select **Bool**.
2. Rename New Bool to **_Walking_**.
3. RMB-click the **Any State** button and make a transition to the walk cycle. Repeat to the idle cycle as well.
4. The arrows connecting the nodes are essentially the conditions. Click on the arrow between **Any State** and the walk cycle. Under **_Conditions_**, change it to **Walking** and make sure it's set to **True**.
5. Do the same for the idle cycle, but this time, set the condition to **False** (see figure 8.10).

To connect everything together, we will first create an empty **_GameObject_**. Think of it as an empty group in Maya, which we will use to manipulate the mesh itself. Go to **GameObject > Create Empty**. Rename it **Leaf_GO**. In the Hierarchy window, drag and drop the Leaf mesh on top of it (see figure 8.11). Make sure that the values of your character are zeroed-out inside the game object to prevent any off transform.

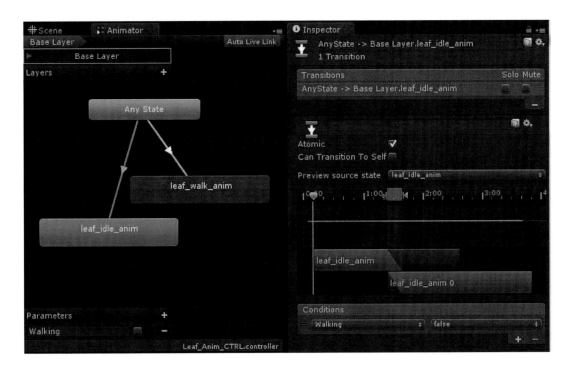

FIGURE 8.10 Set Animator conditions

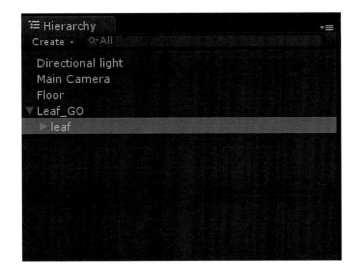

FIGURE 8.11 Create empty GameObject and rename Leaf_GO

On to the coding bits! RMB-click in the Assets area and select **Create > C# Script**. Rename it **walkingScript**. Double-click to open it in the default script editor and enter the following:

```
// Script courtesy of Ryan Miller
public class walkingScript : MonoBehaviour {
    public Animator animator;
    public float speed = 1f;

    // Use this for initialization
    void Start () {
    }
    // Update is called once per frame
    void Update () {

        if (Input.GetAxis("Horizontal") != 0)
        {
                animator.SetBool("Walking", true);
                transform.Translate(transform.forward * Time.deltaTime * speed, Space.
                  World);
                if (Input.GetAxis("Horizontal") < 0)
                {
                        transform.rotation = Quaternion.Euler(0, 180, 0);
                }
                if (Input.GetAxis("Horizontal") > 0)
                {
                        transform.rotation = Quaternion.Euler(0, 0, 0);
                }
        }
        else
        {
                animator.SetBool("Walking", false);
        }
    }
}
```

NOTE: This is a C# script. If you have MEL experience, you'll notice the similarities with the syntax. You'll also notice that, as with Python, it is an object-oriented language. Unity provides its own version of Python, called Boo. Unfortunately, out of the three languages Unity supports,

Boo is the least popular and plans are to drop documentation support as of version 5.0 of Unity. It should still work, but considering the lack of potential support, C# seems to be the language of choice for this program.

What the script does is query the movement of the game controller (keyboard, joystick, mouse, etc.) and engage the animation parameter. Since our parameter is set to Boolean, the script checks to see if there's any change in the condition. If it's not equal to zero—in other words, the condition is True—then enable the "Walking" animation we set earlier, and move it forward in relation to the game world. Otherwise, the "Walking" parameter is set to False.

The next condition checks to see if the controller is less than zero or greater than. If less than zero, then rotate the object the script will be attached to 180 degrees in the Y-axis. Otherwise, leave the rotations as is.

Make sure to end every relevant line with a semi-colon, and check the curly brackets!

Back in Unity, select the **Leaf_GO** game object, and drag and drop **walkingScript** in the Inspector window to connect them (see figure 8.12). You'll notice there are a couple of fields that match the classes we created earlier with our script.

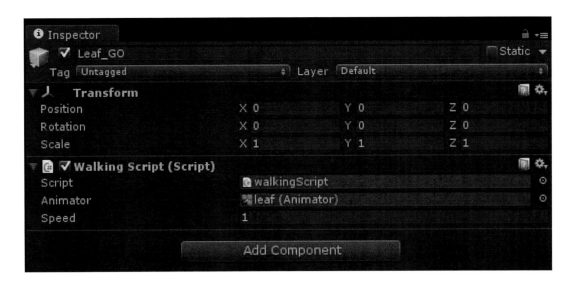

FIGURE 8.12 Connect walkingScript to Leaf_GO

Finally, drag and drop the Leaf mesh object onto the **Animator** field. The script can now reference the animation states we established earlier and provide control of the game object via the input controllers.

If you press the play button at the top of the screen, you'll now be able to move Leaf along one axis using either the A or D keys—or a joystick, if you have one plugged in to your system. Mission accomplished.

As mentioned earlier, the use of Unity as a game engine is way beyond the scope of this book. I would urge you to look further into it as an excellent option to develop your games, and explore the possibilities it offers.

Epilogue

So here we are! We've completed together the first stage of a long and exciting journey into the challenging, puzzling, sometimes frustrating but invariably fun world of rigging. In this book, we've covered some of the basic (and not so basic) concepts of rigging a game character, while discussing how these rigs can also be applied to the cinematic world. The learning curve never ends, but that's what makes this aspect of the production so much fun. There is no limit to what can be achieved with rigging. There will always be a better and more efficient way to build the proverbial (and oft misquoted) mousetrap, and figuring out how to do it is what makes this particular aspect of the 3D pipeline so exciting.

Learning the scripting languages is but a small aspect of it. Who knows, Python might be dethroned one day and be replaced by another faster, more powerful, more efficient language. What will always remain is that healthy sense of curiosity, logic and—in our case—virtual tinkering with the tools provided. Hopefully, now that some of the questions you might have had way back when you started reading this book have been answered, you can shed some light into new ways of approaching the rigging pipeline. Keep exploring new and innovative ways of going about creating animation-ready characters, and—most important—don't be afraid to try new things and go off the beaten track. That's where innovation exists.

Thank you again, Dear Reader, for embarking on this journey with me. It was a humbling experience for me, but I hope that some of the knowledge shared throughout this book will help you in your rigging endeavors.

—Eyal Assaf, March 2015

Appendix
Description of Scripts

The files and scripts used in this book can be found at **www.thetingirl.com**. As mentioned earlier, formatting code in print, especially a language like Python, which is space sensitive, can be a bit cumbersome and not come across properly in the editing. Downloading the actual scripts and reviewing them in your favorite script editor will ensure the correct formatting and proper execution of the code. You will find further comments throughout the scripts, providing additional details and relevant information.

> **NOTE:** Code is like a living organism. It changes and evolves, often times for the better. There is a possibility that some of the scripts that you find on the website might be updated versions of what we've covered in this book. Should that be the case, additional comments and explanations will be provided on the header of each script.

Below is a list of the scripts we covered in the preceding chapters, with a short explanation of their function:

tgpGears—Our first introduction to Python. This script will be used to create various types of gears, while presenting some basic Maya commands. Especially useful if you're coming from a MEL background.

tgpBaseTabUI—This script introduces us to classes in Python. We will create a UI framework using custom tabs to separate the layout.

tgpBaseUI—A lighter version of the above UI class, with only one layout.

tgpMechanix—A class to create rig-ready springs and pistons to be used in your mechanical creations. The UI is called from the classes we created earlier.

tgpControlOrient—A very useful script used to create FK controls for your characters. It takes away all of the tedium of doing the same repetitive actions over and over.

tgpBlendColors—Allows you to blend two attributes to a target object via the *blendColors* utility node. Useful to create switches such as IK/FK.

tgpFKStretch—A combination of the features from the **tgpMechanix** and **tpgControlOrient** scripts that allow for stretchy FK controls. Experimental fun.

tgpLimb—The class that builds the IK/FK arms and legs of a character. Part of the **tgpRigger** script.

snapAB—A simple utility script that snaps an object to another. There are various flags that provide additional options.

Index

AE *see* Attribute Editor (AE)
animation 22–3; baking keys 354–6;
    baking simulation keys options
    355; exporting 353–4; first
    playable prototype 20; for
    games 351–2; importing;
    principles 187–8; production
    22–3; wings 213
animation cycles 360–6; controller
    361; default Animator window
    in Unity 361; drag Leaf_Anim_
    CTRL to controller 362; empty
    GameObject and rename
    Leaf_GO 363; set animator
    conditions 3632; walkingScript
    to Leaf_GO 365
arms: driven keys 323–4; setting
    up clavicles 319–23; space
    switching using parent
    constraints 326–8
Attribute Editor (AE) 64

base man default mesh 71–2; finger
    joints 72, 74; finished symmetry
    on joints 72, 74; symmetrical
    joints 72, 74; symmetry options,
    joint tool menu 72–3
basic leg joint setup 280
bind skeleton, analyzing 255–60;
    A- and T-pose comparison
    257; base HiK binding skeleton
    260; default HiK skeleton
    259; details of HiK menu 259;
    human IK overview; loading
    HiK menu 258; T-pose 256–8
bind skeleton, creating: binding
    mesh to skeleton 271–3;
    completed bind skeleton 266;
    corrective blendshapes 267;
    default rotate order hierarchy
    268; deleting HiK nodes
    263; deleting the skeleton's
    right side 263; HiK Skeleton
    Generator 261–2; influence
    objects 267; initial joint
    placement 262; smooth bound
    skeleton 277; *ngSkinTools*

276; orienting joints properly
    264; paint skin weights tool
    277; rotate order 267–8;
    scripting tgpRotateOrder
    268; setting arms in a T-pose
    261; smooth bind overview
    273–6; tgpRotateOrderscript
    268; verifying arm position
    265; weight assignment and
    painting 276–7; 02_Leaf_
    skelPrebind.ma 273
body 237–45; BND groups to body_
    CTRL 239, 241; BND_root_JNT
    position 238; body_CTRL 238;
    char_CTRL 245; char_CTRL
    to CDN node 242–3; creating
    L_legVis_CDN connection 242,
    244; double transformation on
    BND joints 239, 242; double
    transformations issue 242–3;
    double-transform problem,
    connections for 242, 244;
    leg and wing setups 237;
    legHold_LOC in outliner 238,
    240; legHold_LOC, position of
    238–9; structure 237
button functionality 137–8, 149–51

channels, cleaning up 347–9
character sheets, concept art:
    character scale sheet 38; facial
    expressions of leaf 35; leaf
    body sketch 36–7
clavicles 319–23; automatic clavicle
    switch 322; setup 321; shoulder
    control, positioning 321
COG and main 165–6, 168
color scripts 15–17
concept art: character sheets 35–8;
    final concept of leaf 27; first
    concept of leaf 26; image
    of USS Texas battleship 33;
    references 31–4; sketches
    and thumbnails of leaf 27–30;
    sketches of trees 31–2
condition node 203–12; If-Else
    statement 203, 205; IK stretch

condition 205, 207; stretch
    IK node 207–8; stretch
    multiplyDivide 206–7; switch
    multiplyDivide 205–6
connectors 143–5
constraints: attaching meshes to
    joints 88; channel selection
    62; dedicated transform nodes
    62; effectiveness 63; menu
    62–3; multiple constrainers
    and influences 62; offsets
    62–3; rotate (Orient constrain)
    61; scale (Scale constrain) 61;
    selection process 63; standard
    translate (Point constrain) 61
Construct 2 23
control rig: basic leg joint setup 280;
    building the IK Leg 282–93;
    remapValue utility node 279;
    reverse foot control setup 281;
    snapAB script 281
creative cycle 3–6; dictionary 5;
    focused observation 20;
    literature 3; music 3; page
    to screen 1–2; personal
    life experiences 3; popular
    media 3; post-production
    23; pre-production (*see*
    pre-production, creative
    cycle); production 6–7, 20–3;
    randomly picked words 5;
    "tangible" creative expression
    1; 3D design 24; travel 4; word-
    association technique 6
CryEngine 23

DAG *see* directed acyclic graph (DAG)
    nodes
deformers 67–9; bend/squash
    deformer 68; blendshapes
    69; cluster 69; deformation
    order stack 68; lattice 69;
    nonlinear 69; troubleshooting
    68; twist and flare tool 67;
    wire tool 69
dependency graph (DG) nodes 54–6
DG *see* dependency graph (DG) nodes